Volume I

The Reminiscences

of

Admiral Edwin J. Roland
U. S. Coast Guard (Retired)

Interview No. 1 with Admiral Edwin John Roland, U.S. Coast Guard
(Retired)

Place: His residence in Old Lyme, Connecticut

Date: Monday morning, 19 January 1976

Subject: Biography

By: John T. Mason, Jr.

Q: Admiral, it's been a delight to meet you. I've been looking forward to this series of interviews with you.

As I wrote you, the proper way to begin a talking biography is to tell me where you were born, the date, and something about your family background.

Adm. R.: I was born in Buffalo, New York, and the date was the 11th of February 1905. My father was in the Fire Department in Buffalo and the family wasn't very well off financially. We had a few hungry days now and then! I went to schools in Buffalo. My father died when I was fourteen years old and I went to work at that time for a milkman in the neighborhood. I became a milkman and I continued to do that for several years. I did that through high school and through two years of college.

Q: You certainly worked your way through then?

Adm. R.: Yes. Then I dropped out of college.

Roland #1 - 2

Q: Where were you attending?

Adm. R.: I went to Canisius College in Buffalo and went also to Canisius prep school before that, each time on a scholarship. The one at the college was an athletic scholarship, and I left the college because I wasn't able to take the courses that I wanted to take. I wanted to become a civil engineer and the courses required time on classes and laboratories that were also required at football practice! I would have lost my scholarship if I had insisted on those courses, so I left the school, hoping that I could hook up somewhere else.

Q: I take it you were very active athletically?

Adm. R.: Yes. Well, I only played football at Canisius College.

Q: Had you played it in high school?

Adm. R.: I had played in high school and I played baseball in high school. I was a pretty good athlete. After I left Canisius I had an offer from Fordham, but Fordham's requirement was about the same as Canisius.

Q: Was it a scholarship from Fordham?

Adm. R.: It was a scholarship. The offer was for a scholarship at Fordham and I wouldn't have been able to take the courses I wanted there either. So I left Canisius and went to work for an uncle of my father who was a contractor in Buffalo. I worked for him for a year.

Then I went to see my congressman who was a man named James Meade.

Q: Oh, Jim Meade of the Post Office Committee?

Adm. R.: That's right, he's the fellow, from Buffalo. I wanted to get an appointment to West Point or Annapolis. I talked to him and he offered me an appointment to West Point but it was an alternate. He also told me about the Coast Guard Academy. I had never heard of the Coast Guard before that time, but he recommended it and suggested that I take the examination, at least, and so I did take the examination.

Q: Did you also take the alternate?

Adm. R.: I took the alternate examination, too, for West Point, but my principal passed also, so I couldn't get that. But I did pass the examination for the Academy and chose to go there because I was at the age limit then, you see. I was twenty-one years old and the limit is twenty-one. You can go in under twenty-one - or, you could at that time, go in while you were twenty-one but not after. I was twenty-one in February of 1926, the year I went to the Coast Guard Academy.

Q: What did your mother think of this direction for your career?

Adm. R.: She was pleased that I was going to get something. She wanted me to be a civil engineer because I wanted to be a civil engineer.

Q: Were there others in the family?

Adm. R.: I had a sister. There were just the three of us. She was perfectly willing for me to do this because I think it was obvious that we weren't going to be able to pay for my education in college.

So I chose the Academy and it was a blind shot. Now, if I had it to do over, I would do it the same way. I would choose the Coast Guard now. I think it's a different service now and perhaps I would have known about the Coast Guard if I were interested at this time. But at that time I found out after I had taken the examination that there was a lifeboat station in Buffalo and that that was part of the Coast Guard, but that was about all there was there.

I took the examination for the Academy in the office of an old fellow who had been in the Lifesaving Service and ran that district, those lifeboat stations that were nearby there. The man's name was Rasmussen. He was a well-known politician around Buffalo and in the neighboring country. He was a very outgoing fellow and his name was in the newspaper a good bit. I got to meet him when I took my examination.

Q: How were the appointments actually made to the Academy?

Adm. R.: As they are now, entirely competitive throughout the country. We had about twenty-five or thirty people who took the examination in Buffalo, and they came from places as far away as Rochester, so it was an area gathered together there. Then, there were examinations in other places.

Q: Were these under the aegis of Civil Service?

Adm. R.: No, it was not Civil Service. Our examination was held by the Coast Guard in the person of this man and the examinations were held at Coast Guard units throughout the country. I don't think they were held in any other places. They may have had some of them in Civil Service offices, but they were under the jurisdiction of Coast Guard personnel.

I arrived in New London on September the 6th 1926, which was the day we were ordered to report, with two other young fellows who had taken the examination with me. They were both from Rochester. As my train went through Rochester, these two people came aboard and I had met them at the examination so we came in together. I found that the Coast Guard Academy wasn't much better known in New London than it was in Buffalo because we went to a cabdriver and asked him to take us to the Coast Guard Academy and he had to go to another cabdriver to find out where it was!

At that time the Coast Guard Academy was not where it is now. It was at Fort Trumbull, farther down the river in New London. That was an old revolutionary-time fort and it still stands. It's now on the Navy site of the Underwater Sound Lab.

I arrived in all my glory and there were some upper classmen waiting for us and we had a pretty rough time. There were no restrictions on how you could treat third classmen.

Q: You mean the hazing began right then?

Adm. R.: It began right then, yes. These people were supposed to be on leave and they stayed back so they could greet us. They were waiting and they gave us a good going-over.

The only athletics at the Academy at that time was basketball. Al Richmond was an ensign and a classmate of his named Richards was also assigned at the Academy. There was no gymnasium at the Academy, so we did our basketball practice at the YMCA down town.

Q: What was the student body, how large?

Adm. R.: My class came in with fifty-six, and the class ahead of us had about fifteen. They graduated ten. I don't know how many they had when they came in. The class ahead of them had twenty-two and those twenty-two were to graduate in January. There was an early graduation, so that twenty-two were graduated in January of 1927. Twenty-two is how many they had and the class after them had fifteen, and then our class came in with fifty-six.

Q: Was there a quota and was it being enlarged every year?

Adm. R.: It was being enlarged and the reason was that the rum patrol was drawing people in.

The Coast Guard at that time was also taking in officers from other categories, too, people who had seagoing service they were bringing in and making them temporary officers to serve aboard the ships in order to fill them up.

About that time the Coast Guard took on twenty-five Navy destroyers that were in mothballs.

Q: Old four-stackers?

Adm. R.: Yes, the old four-stackers, the broken-deck ships, from World War I. Admiral Hamlet was in charge of getting those destroyers in commission and he became commander of the destroyer force in New London.

Q: Where were these ships largely? On the West Coast?

Adm. R.: When we operated them?

Q: No, when they were in mothballs.

Adm. R.: No, mostly in Philadelphia. That's where Hamlet's headquarters were, Philadelphia. There were some in other places but I don't know just where. Anyway, I got a little off the track of my entering the Academy!

My class, of course, was considerably larger than the others and we got together immediately and had a class meeting, when we could get away from the upper classmen, and talked over our affairs and what we would like. We decided that we would like to have a football team.

Roland #1 - 8

Q: I can hear your voice entering into that discussion!

Adm. R.: I was involved in that quite a bit, yes. I had played football from the time I was about four feet high.

So Al Richmond's classmate, Richards, we talked to him and he decided that he would take on the coaching job and do what he could. He did a very good job. He got us a schedule of five games that year. We didn't even have a jock strap! We didn't have anything. I wrote home to my mother and she sent me the football equipment that I had around, an old pair of football shoes and an old pair of pants, and a jersey. I had an old helmet, you know.

Q: This was entirely student organization?

Adm. R.: Yes, and everybody in the class did the same thing, so we got together enough stuff that we could use in practice. Richards, somehow or other, did get hold of some money, so he got some equipment. I think we probably had about two footballs for the whole season! We used the same one for this game and the next game, too.

Q: How did the administration of the Academy look at this?

Adm. R.: Well, of course, we didn't have much direct contact with them. They, however, must have thought it was a pretty good idea because they came to the games. The people who were on the staff came to the games. There weren't very many people on the staff. There couldn't have been more than fifteen, a dozen or fifteen officers. At that time there was one civilian on the staff, whose name you may have heard. His name was Dimmick, who was a famous man in the Coast Guard. All the rest were regular officers and people like Richards and Richmond. They had graduated in 1924 and here it was the fall of 1926 and they were teaching at the Academy. Admiral Hall, who now lives here in Old Lyme - he's in Florida right now, but he lives in Old Lyme - he was on the staff. He was a lieutenant commander.

One of the people who became famous in the Coast Guard because he pushed a helicopter deal later on was named Kossler. You may have heard his name. He was an electrical engineer and he was on the staff at that time. The staff was made up of regular Coast Guard officers who came into the Coast Guard to be sailors and engineers aboard ships, but not to be teachers. They were doing their best to teach.

I had a physics instructor named McElligott and he was a very sincere man. He was a fine officer. He became a flag officer later and died just a year or so ago. He was a very able officer in the Coast Guard and he taught us physics. We had some cadets who knew more physics than he did, but his wife was pretty good at it! He would go home at night and he and his wife would go over the lesson and she would explain things to him! He got so that he could handle his job all right because he worked so hard at it and was so sincere about it. But he was not trained as a teacher and he was not trained in physics! Anyway, we got through it.

Q: How did you take to the regimen? What was the routine there at the Academy?

Adm. R.: We had been there about a week when we began classes. Before that, it was all drawing uniforms and drilling. We had a sailing ship at the time, not the present sailing ship, of course, but one that was named the Alexander Hamilton. It was a barkentine, a three-masted ship. It was square-rigged on the foremast and fore and aft on the other two. In the course of that week we were all required to climb the rigging and put our hats on the truck of the mast and come down the rigging on the other side. That was our indoctrination.

Q: To see that you had courage enough to do that sort of thing?

Adm. R.: I think everybody did it. There may have been some who got out of it in some way or another, but nearly everybody did it. If I could do it, being as scared as I was, everybody else had as good a chance!

Then we began classes and, when classes began, the routine was classes from eight o'clock in the morning until three-thirty in the afternoon. There were no study hours. We had one hour off classes during the day and during that hour we sat in our rooms and we put a pair of earphones on and they sent us dots and dashes.

Q: So you were learning even then?

Adm. R.: That was part of our communications course, as a matter of fact, taking these dots and dashes. So we started right off with it, yes. During the week, of course, we were told that a dot and a dash is an A and a dash and three dots is a B. We had about a week to learn this, then we just did the best we could. They would send this up to us and there was no way of questioning them. If you didn't get it you had a blank and you had to turn your paper in, so you got marked on this.

The rest of the time we were in classes all day long.

Q: When did you take time for drilling and that sort of thing?

Adm. R.: That was part of it, too. We had three hours a week for drill, the last hour of the day on three days was taken for military drill. Then, of course, in the barracks, those upper classmen kept after us about the drill, too. We were marching up and down the corridors through half the night sometimes!

Q: That was the nature of the hazing, was it?

Adm. R.: That was part of it, yes. That and push-ups and all sorts of things. Emptying their wastepaper baskets and all that kind of business.

Q: Just little annoyances!

Adm. R.: Yes, little annoyances, and some of them were pretty irritating. Some of them were probably a little dangerous.

You had to sit on a bayonet. Turn the bayonet up and then sit on the point of the bayonet. Of course, that meant that your muscles were holding you up. A few people got cut. That is one of the forms of hazing that was early done away with. They did away with that before I ceased being subject to hazing, and it was never done again that I know of.

Q: Was it the result of some accident, that they did away with it?

Adm. R.: It probably was, because there were several accidents. I think the upper classmen, even being the beasts they were, understood that, so I think they might have quit it themselves but they may have been told to quit it. The doctors knew about it because they had some repairing to do.

Q: How did you have time for football practice and these athletic events?

Adm. R.: We didn't have much time for it but we got up early in the morning. Reveille was at six o'clock and before we began the football practice we would go out and run in the morning or else row. We'd alternate. We'd either go down to the dock and get in boats and row across the river and back or we would go out on the road and run. We would get back into the barracks at a quarter to seven in the morning, and breakfast was at seven o'clock. So we didn't have much time in between. And during that time we shaved, too. The rush was tremendous in the time we got back. They always got us back in time all right and sometimes they got us back a few minutes early. We had fifteen minutes then to get ready for the day, because we went to breakfast and then we went back up to our rooms, gathered up our books - our bunks were supposed to be made by them but they usually weren't so we made them in that time. Then there was formation at eight o'clock and we went to classes. And there was always an inspection of the rooms during the day.

It was a pretty rough deal but you can get used to anything, you know. We really got so we could do the things that we had to do in the amount of time that we had. Then we would steal a minute here or there, too.

Q: Did any of the boys find this too difficult?

Adm. R.: Yes. It wasn't long before our class was down to about - well, I think we wound up the January examinations with about thirty left in the class.

Q: That's a large attrition.

Adm. R.: Yes, we lost a lot of people right in the beginning.

To illustrate that things were done differently in those days than they are now. We had one fellow in our class who I don't think had ever finished grammar school. He didn't know what a fraction is. His name was Jerry Buchanan. I met him years later down in Jacksonville, Florida, and he was a bartender down there. His father had been in the Coast Guard. He had one of the lifeboat stations down around there. Jerry said that he had somebody else take the examination for him.

Q: The entrance exam?

Adm. R.: The extrance examination to get into the Academy. Such a thing couldn't happen now - well, maybe it could, but I don't think it could happen now. But it did happen and he came in and of course never had a chance. He was there for about a month, I think, and then he was gone. Others just gave up because of the kind of life they were leading.

I would say that after Thanksgiving, the upper class began to ease off, and they promised us that if we behaved ourselves after January they wouldn't bother us at all. We never got to that point. They kept bothering us, all right, but they did let up after January.

As a result of attrition during those first few months and the examinations in January, I would say we were down to about thirty - maybe one or two more, but about that figure.

Q: Was that the average kind of attrition?

Adm. R.: I think that our attrition after that wasn't very much. You see, that class that was behind us still had fifteen when we came in and they lost five from that time on. I think the attrition had been spread out a little more before, and ours was not spread out.

Q: The culling process took place all at once?

Adm. R.: Yes, it seemed to be all in that first term that we lost people, and we didn't lose very many after that.

Q: I wonder, we might speculate on it, whether the formation of the football had some bearing on the fact that they maintained interest?

Adm. R.: I think it might have. The cadets were staunch backers of the football team. The football team wasn't very good either. We had people playing with us who had never played football before. When you have that many people to build a team out of - we won a couple of games that year and the next year we had a 50-50 season, but we had a fuller schedule. I think we had seven games the second year and we won four. Then the third year we won five games. We were getting better. We got a few more in each year, you see, to build up. At the end, just as I graduated, they got a professional in to coach, Johnny Merriman. He came in to coach everything. He was alone in the physical ed department for a long time.

Q: So you really witnessed the beginning of organized athletics at the Academy?

Adm. R.: Yes. In 1922 a group of cadets got together and formed a football team which they called The Shamrocks. It wasn't called Coast Guard Academy, it was called The Shamrocks. I guess probably the administration didn't go along with it. In the history of football at the Academy, they say that it started

Roland #1 - 16

then. They played local teams and I think that they managed to get a game with a freshman team somewhere, too. Maybe Brown or somebody like that. Then it died out. There wasn't any team in 1925 and there wasn't any in 24 either. 1922 and 1923 I guess were the ones.

Q: Then it jumped to 1926?

Adm. R.: Yes. They had it even worse than we did, I guess, because there was one class that graduated in there that had one fellow in it. That was the class of 1923.

Q: Tell me about the courses.

Adm. R.: The courses were very difficult and the instructors were very demanding, and we did not have very many good teachers. They didn't know how to teach. In most cases, they knew their subject, in some cases they didn't, but they worked hard at them. The getting of passing marks was a pretty difficult thing, and we got a mark about every week. They were distributed but they were posted about every week, and at the end of the month marks were distributed to the cadets and also sent to their parents. If you got a failing mark for the week, you were "on the tree" for a week, and that meant you had to take time out of your liberty time and spend it in your room studying, and, of course, liberty time didn't amount to very much. We got out at one o'clock on Saturdays on liberty and we had to be back in at midnight.

On Sundays we could leave at eight o'clock and we had to go to church. We always had to sign a church book, and people would check the churches to see if you were there! Then regular liberty started at one o'clock. If you were excused from going to church, you couldn't go ashore until one o'clock, and then liberty was up at seven o'clock in the evening.

Q: Saturday and Sunday, that was liberty for the week, was it?

Adm. R.: Well, later on they put in a Wednesday afternoon liberty that ran from about 3:30 to about six o'clock, and you needed it to get haircuts because there wasn't any barber on the base. We had to get our hair cut on our liberty time. If you didn't rate liberty - if you got a certain number of demerits, you didn't get liberty - but if you had to have your hair cut you could go and get permission to get your hair cut. They'd give you just time to go and get your hair cut and come back.

This business of getting ashore was an awfully important thing for us. It meant an awful lot to us and we got doggone little of it.

Q: Then if you didn't keep your studies up there was further encroachment on it?

Adm. R.: Yes, you had to study during liberty time, if you got failing marks.

This business about the tree continued throughout the time that I was a cadet and I suppose it continued for sometime afterwards.

You asked about the courses. The books we used were standard textbooks, I think carefully selected, and the instructors generally taught us strictly from the book. They didn't hit much that wasn't in the book.

Q: Was it learning by rote? Did you have to memorize lots of things?

Adm. R.: We didn't have to memorize, I wouldn't say. Of course, most of our stuff was along the engineering line. We did courses in English, there were no languages, I guess we didn't have any history. A lot of what we had to do was problem work and we got so we could work the problems. It seemed to us and I think it seemed to the instructors that that was the test of whether you knew the subject or no - if you could work the problems!

Q: That was the application of what you learned?

Adm. R.: Yes. The man that I mentioned before, McElligott, did insist on our being able to discuss the theory of the things that we had in physics. He insisted on a problem or two but he wanted us to understand the business about gravity and all that, more or less to be able to talk about it besides working the problems.

We had an instructor on a course that was called Boilers, and this fellow came in with a notebook every day - almost every day, he didn't do it every day but I would say three days out of four - he would get up and he'd start writing on the blackboard and we had to copy his notes. He would copy out of his notebook onto the blackboard and he would sometimes not say anything except good morning and goodbye. He'd write and write and write up there and he'd fill up the blackboard, and then he would come back and he'd rub it off, then fill that blackboard again until the time that he'd leave us, and there it was.

Q: What about the application of this?

Adm. R.: Well, of course, we got examinations. He gave us examinations and if you knew what was in his notes you got a good mark in the subject.

The difference between the Academy then and now is tremendous. It's just great. The kids now know what they're studying. They know what they're doing and they will question their instructors. We didn't question. If the instructor said something, we didn't question him, you know. We might ask him why or something like that, but you hesitated to do that even.

Q: But that was a different time, and youngsters in that time were not in the habit of quizzing their superiors, I suppose?

Adm. R.: That was a different time and I think that it showed, too, in the people that came out of the Academy. When we came out of the Academy we came out thinking that we were educated to be sailors. We knew we were intended to run ships and maritime things, and this is all we thought of. Things like ecology and publishing or something, we hadn't heard the words. We were interested in navigation and we were interested in the engines that ran the ships and the auxiliaries aboard the ship. We were still interested somewhat in sail, and things like that. Now, of course, kids come out and they have such a good knowledge of their environment that they're thinking men, about furthering this knowledge, about postgraduate work. And, as a matter of fact, I guess they make their choices when they graduate as to what they're going to go into. They have to make decisions while they're at the Academy, too, about their courses. When I was a cadet everybody got exactly the same thing. There were no choices, none at all. Now, after one year, they choose the direction in which their education is going to go. This is a tremendous thing.

Q: Back in the 20s was it an accredited school? Did it belong to an association?

Adm. R.: Yes, it had accreditation from the Engineers Council for Professional Development, ECPD. But ECPD, I think, caught up with the Academy in the middle thirties. While I was there as an instructor they caught up and they removed their accreditation, but then we did get accreditation by the Northeast Council or whatever it is. Now we're back to ECPD, too. That's because it's different than it was then. I don't know how we happened under ECPD when we did, but it was a pretty prestigious thing then, and it was a thing that the Academy and the Coast Guard was very proud of, the fact that we had ECPD accreditation.

Q: What sort of courses did you have in navigation and that type of thing? Here, you were going out to man these destroyers.

Adm. R.: We had Dutton and a book that was put out by the Navy - no, Dutton was the name of that. The other one I'm thinking of is Bowditch. Dutton was the book that was published by the Navy and used by the Navy also at the Naval Academy. Then, of course, pamphlets like tide tables, nautical almanacs, and things of that nature.

The most modern system of celestial navigation then was Marc Saint-Hilaire. It was a purely mathematical formula, you know. You take an altitude of the sun and take the time, and from there fill in the form. You assumed a position and you came out with an altitude of, say, the sun, if the sun was out, was what the altitude of the sun would be if you were in that position. And you compared that altitude with the one you actually got, and the difference gave you a thing called an intercept. You got a line of position that you put on the chart.

Then we learned piloting, a system of navigating by soundings, things of that nature, taking bearings and putting them on the chart. We did so much of that that we really knew what we were doing in navigation, I think. Then seamanship was another that we put a lot of time on.

Q: Did your two years at the college in Buffalo help you, aiming toward engineering?

Adm. R.: Yes, it helped me. When I was in college I took a course in physics. I never attended the laboratories because the laboratories came during athletic practice, but I went to the classes and I took the examinations and passed them. I got a passing mark in the physics course and, of course, I learned something about physics all right. I didn't do the lab work but I did that. I also took a course in chemistry and I had a course in calculus and descriptive geometry. Those courses particularly helped me.

But before I went to the Academy the only physics I'd had was that one year I didn't follow up. We took physics for just one year at the Academy. This is what McElligott had had when he came and taught physics. He had had the physics that he got in the Academy and then he came and taught. The same thing happened to me in 1934. I went back there principally as a coach. Johnny Merriman was coaching everything, you know, and he didn't have any assistants so he wrote me and asked if I would like to come and help coach, and I said yes. So I got transferred to the Academy. I was assistant coach in football, basketball, and baseball. We were the athletic department, except for an enlisted man or two to take care of equipment.

Roland #1 - 23

Q: Going back to the 1926 period, 1927, you were going to be trained and going out to deal with smugglers. So did you have a course in international law or anything of that sort?

Adm. R.: Yes, we did, we had a course in international law. Then we had a course in navigation law. I think we got both of those courses in our last year, and they were courses we were taking when graduation came upon us.

Q: Was yours a shortened period similar to the class - ?

Adm. R.: No, we went three full years. The 15th of May was always graduation time at that time. It was changed later on, you know, because our people graduated on the 15th of May and the Naval Academy people graduated in June, so what when they came together and were engaged in operations, our people who had graduated in the same year were senior to them. This resulted in changes. We changed ours later on so that we would not graduate ahead of them. We have since graduated on the same day, and so do the other services now. Before, they didn't care much about the Army, when they graduated. Then the Army got involved and there were joint commands and so on, so now everybody graduates on the same day, so the President can only go to one graduation now!

Q: He has to rotate!

Adm. R.: Yes.

Q: Tell me about your summer activities when you were there.

Adm. R.: In the summer we went on the cruise, and the cruise left immediately after graduation, the next day. I made two cruises.

Q: Where did you go?

Adm. R.: The first time, in 1927, we sailed in the <u>Hamilton</u> and we got to sea. We didn't have much wind so we weren't sailing, we were under power, and the tail shaft broke. We lost our propeller. It dropped off. So they came out and got us and towed us in. Then we made the rest of that cruise aboard one of the regular Coast Guard cutters. We went to the Azores.

Q: The entire class was on board?

Adm. R.: Everybody, our class and the class ahead of us.

We went to the Azores and to Oslo, some place in France, I'm not sure just where, and Coruna, Spain, Gibraltar, Casablanca, the Canary Islands, Maderia, Bermuda, and that was it and we came home.

Q: How were you occupied that first cruise?

Adm. R.: We were occupied in seamanship courses that they gave us and navigation. We had to take a lot of sights. Everybody came up on deck and took sights two or three times a day. Then we stood watches and we did the work about the ship. We did painting, cleaning, scrubbing.

Q: Who were the sailor boys on board?

Adm. R.: On the Hamilton there were only about three sailors. On this other ship they kept their engineers aboard and there were a couple of bo's'uns' mates probably, but the rest of them they put ashore and we filled in. Of course, they had people like radiomen and technicians of various kinds. But we did the work of enlisted men and we stood watches with the officers, not in place of the officers but with the officers. There was a cadet officer of the deck and a commissioned officer of the deck, and the same with the other billets.

Q: But you also had studies?

Adm. R.: No, we didn't have studies, except seamanship and navigation. We didn't have the other things. We didn't take physics and calculus and all that sort of thing.

Q: Did you have any instructors on board from the Academy?

Adm. R.: Oh, yes. A detail from the Academy would go along and usually they would take off some of the ship's officers to make room for these people. They would instruct and at the same time they would do the ship's duties, too.

Q: How much money did you have to spend when you went on shore leave in these various exotic places?

Adm. R.: They gave us a cruising allowance, but I forget what it was now. It wasn't very much. They gave us maybe about ten dollars at each place. Some cadets beat the system by getting from home, but we were specifically warned about it. We weren't supposed to get it. A couple of people who bought things that cost more than their money were questioned and they admitted that they had the money from home. They weren't thrown out but they were given a whole batch of demerits. They didn't get liberty in the next port! There wasn't much money, I'll tell you that.

Q: The cruises were in a way, I suppose, an application of what you'd been learning during the school year?

Adm. R.: Oh, yes.

Q: Application of theory?

Adm. R.: That's right, and then, of course, we ran into things like the details of watchstanding and things like that that we were learning for the first time.

The cruises were good practical experiences, there's no question about it. We were becoming what we thought we were to become, sailors, and this was more training, really, than education, I think.

Q: What was the second cruise like? Where did you go?

Adm. R.: On the second, we went on the Hamilton and an additional ship, one of the destroyers, went along. By that time, you see, we had another class in and the new class came in with I think about forty or forty-five or something like that, so we had more people going on the cruise and needed another ship. So we took a destroyer which happened to be the <u>Shaw</u>, the one that I was first assigned to, actually, after I graduated. It was arranged on that cruise so that the football squad got the last tour on the <u>Shaw</u> and we got back in about a week early for early football practice. Well, we didn;t actually get the early football practice, we went on leave then and came back a week early for football practice.

The second cruise was about the same. We went to London again and we went to Hamburg. We didn't go to Coruna that time. Maybe we went to San Sebastian that time in Spain - we went somewhere in Spain. One ship went to Lisbon and the other one went to Gibraltar, and then we went to Maderia and the Canary Islands again.

The system was supposed to be a northern European cruise, then a southern European cruise, then a South American cruise, but it didn't work out for us. We didn't get the southern European cruise, which would have gone into the Mediterranean, but we got two really of the northern. They all wound up coming back by the same route. The <u>Hamilton</u> stopped at Horta in the Azores on the way over because that was a coaling station and she burned coal. So we coaled ship in Horta in the Azores.

Q: So you had that experience!

Adm. R.: Oh, we did all right and it was really an experience, too, because we closed up everything tight on the ship that we could, including our lockers, because that coal dust got into everything. It was in the lockers and it was all over the place. It took us several days to get down through the coal dust. There was more scrubbing done and that white ship was an awful-looking thing when they got done. They carried this stuff from the barges up over the side of the ship and dumped it down into the bunkers. The cadets joined in, too, but they had workmen with the contractor who was doing it so they would get it done in a hurry.

I think that during the three years that I was there there was a discernible improvement in instruction and certainly there was an increase in the staff. I think the people they brought in were probably more carefully selected than they had been in the past. And, of course, there was an increase in the size of the cadet corps. I think one of the things that impressed me about the improvement was the fact that, as I graduated, they brought in a professional to handle the athletic part of the business. From then on, he was sort of on his own. He did his own typing and all that. He didn't have any help except for occasional help from some member of the staff who might come out to help him on a given day. But nobody was assigned to athletics, except this one man.

Q: This was giving athletics a certain status it never had before?

Adm. R.: Oh, it did give us a status, yes. Before he came, when somebody talked about making a schedule, nobody knew how to go about making a schedule and didn't know anybody at any of the schools who could help him to make a schedule. But when Johnny Merriman came in, he had been a coach at Trinity. He was a Springfield graduate and he had coached at Trinity for some years, maybe three or four years, and then we got him at the Academy, and we got him by making him an ensign. We made him an ensign in the Coast Guard.

Q: So that he had a salary?

Adm. R.: That was the way he got his salary, of course. Probably some other ensign was deleted from some other place in order to get that billet!

Q: How was the athletic program financed in that time? You told me about having to rent suits and that sort of thing.

Adm. R.: The only appropriated money that went into anything like that was the money that went in for physical education, and that is a thing that was built up about the end of the time I was there. I don't think there was any money for physical education before but during my last year there was, and the cadets had an association called the Academy Athletic Association and then the cadets had to belong to it and the cadets had to pay dues. Officers could belong to it, and they were charged dues, too. But the cadets took the brunt of this business and the money that ran the athletic business at the Academy, the intercollegiate athletics part of it, came from the cadets and from the people who belonged to the Athletic Association. There was no appropriated money.

Q: Were there any admission fees from games and that sort of thing?

Adm. R.: No. There was money that was given to us by institutions where we traveled to play. They would pay us a guarantee which was intended to pay our expenses going and coming. This was a thing that we fudged on as much as we could. In my last year at the Academy, my last football season, I talked to Richards about getting a game with Canisius, the team I had played with in Buffalo. I wrote out there and he rode out there and we did, we arranged a game. We got a game with them, and they gave us a decent guarantee. We went out there with a football squad of fifteen players. We played the game. Some of us limped through the most part of it, I think, but we played and we lost. They gave us a pretty good beating, but really not bad because Canisius had a good football team. They were playing Boston College and Holy Cross in those years, and they beat us 28 to 0. We put up a pretty good game.

We made money on that trip because they gave us a guarantee. They figured that we would have a squad of twenty-five men, you know.

Q: Commensurate with what they had?

Adm. R.: Yes. They paid us and that paid off some of our other expenses, I guess.

Q: Tell me about the teaching facilities and that sort of thing in that period when you were a student.

Adm. R.: Nothing. Our classroom building was a World War I wooden building and so was our barracks that had been taken over by the Coast Guard after World War I for the Academy. The physics laboratory had a pendulum in it, I guess, and a couple of mercury barometers and a few things like that, but other things that were dreamed up for experiments were largely homemade by the engineers at the Academy. The material was homemade.

We had a chemistry course which started while I was there. It wasn't there in my first year. They had equipment. They had test tubes and chemicals and things and we made all sorts of smells around the place. We did simple experiments in chemistry and had a standard textbook that we studied in class. We had an instructor in chemistry who wasn't very good at the subject but, like others, worked hard.

Q: But the physical accommodations?

Adm. R.: The physical set-up was extremely poor. We had an electrical laboratory that I think might have been pretty good. It was well taken care of and I think the equipment wasn't old, and that was improved while I was there. The man Kossler whom I mentioned a while ago had that laboratory. He was sort of an eager beaver and I think he got some things that were required. I think that that was a pretty good thing for the times. I'm not acquainted with what other schools had at that time. I'm sure they were far ahead but this was a pretty neat arrangement and well handled by him.

Otherwise, as far as space was concerned, we had no more space. At the time that I graduated, they began building a gymnasium, a small building - well, it had a basketball court in it, so it wasn't too small, and it was a decent basketball court, too. But that didn't go in for about a year after I left.

Q: Did you have a library?

Adm. R.: We had a library which was a single room in the building where all of the faculty offices were, a building which had probably a dozen offices in it and then one bigger room, I would say it might have been 20 feet by 15 and it had a library, yes. It was lined with books! I don't know much about what they were worth! I didn't feel required to inhabit the library very much so I didn't.

Q: You say you took the course in surveying?

Adm. R.: Yes, well, surveying was in the curriculum. There was a course in surveying and our part in that was to survey the site that had been determined for a new academy. It was then a woods and cliffs and rocks, terrible-looking place. When you look at it now it's a beautiful place, but it was nothing like that at the time. There were no buildings on the land. There was a bridle path across there and the girls from Connecticut College rode through there. As a matter of fact, my wife was one of those who rode through while we were working there.

That was the beginning of the present academy.

Q: And you say the surveying job was not completed when you graduated?

Adm. R.: It wasn't completed when we graduated but they kept six of us there as ensigns to finish it up. We did the whole thing. We did the actual surveying and we made the drawings and all. We had a fellow in my class named di Martino who was an exceptionally good artist and very good at such things as making these drawings. He did most of that work. We would go up and work and get figures and deliver them to that part of the detail which was working in the drawing room at the Academy, and they would put it on paper. That was the original survey. I don't know whether they did any more than that later. I think they might have. I don't think they trusted us that much. They probably did do more later, but it was the first survey and I'm sure that it was of use. I don't think they'd have kept the six of us to finish it up if it hadn't been.

Q: The piece of property was then owned by the Coast Guard?

Adm. R.: Yes. It was given to the Coast Guard. Whether the actual transaction had taken place, I'm not sure, but I think it had.

Q: Who had owned it prior to that?

Adm. R.: The City of New London presented the property. There's a park up there called Riverside Park and I think this was part of the park that hadn't been developed. The rest of it had.

Q: What acreage is there now?

Adm. R.: I think we must have had about fifteen acres. It has been enlarged since then. We have encroached some on the park. There's a building up there called Roland Hall. I tell everybody that in case they don't know it. It's the gymnasium. We got twelve acres out of the part of the park that the city had developed, we put that on, and then we had grown up in the other direction and bought property that had belonged to Connecticut College. There were some private homes in there but there was also college property. We go up now quite a way. I'd say that where we probably had maybe ten acres in the beginning, we may have (eighteen) acres now.

Q: A personal note. You said that your wife had ridden through that park while you were on the surveying job. Did you meet her at that time?

Adm. R.: That's where I met her.

Q: That's rather romantic.

Adm. R.: She had been to cadet dances and I had seen her but I had never met her. She hadn't been to any cadet dances while I was a first classman, I guess, but she had been to dances with a fellow in the class ahead of me. She went to Abbott Academy in Andover which is now combined with Andover. She went there to school and then she went to Connecticut College. She finished three years at Connecticut College and then we got married and they wouldn't let her come back in. They wouldn't let married women in then! Now, it doesn't make any difference whether they're married or not.

Q: After you finished your surveying stint you had some leave and then you were assigned to a destroyer?

Adm. R.: Except that I played football for three years afterwards. The Coast Guard had a team. It had been a destroyer force team and then the Coast Guard took it over as representing the Coast Guard, and it was based in New London. We started practice in August and we played into December. We trained on an island out in Long Island Sound, Plum Island. I played with that team, so when I finished with that surveying thing I reported to the ship that I was ordered to, but there were orders then for me to leave the ship immediately. So I reported in and then left on temporary duty with the football team. We played our last game in December that year and then I came back to the ship.

I was the gunnery officer on the ship, so I got back in December and then we went down to St. Petersburg, Florida, where all the destroyers came down, a division at a time, for target practice. They had a target-towing detail and there was also a rifle range on Egmont Key, in Tampa Bay, where we went on the rifle range. I went down there for that exercise.

We won the gunnery trophy and I got credit for it, but I had had little to do with preparing for it because I was playing football while someone else was doing most of the work. I stepped into the shoes of the gunnery officer, so I got a letter of commendation.

Q: It went in the records!

Adm. R.: This football team, I think I should say a little more about now. The reason for this was that there was a thing called The President's Cup, and the Army and the Navy and the Marines played for that each year. Each team played a regular schedule and, in the course of the schedule, they played one another. Then they played one game at the end, in December, two teams were selected from the three, to play for The President's Cup.

Q: Where was this game played?

Adm. R.: It was played in Washington. That first year we were one of the two teams that played, and we played the Marines in Washington on the 7th or 8th of December.

Q: The Coast Guard had been added to this original three?

Adm. R.: Yes. I thought I had said that but I guess I didn't.

The Coast Guard decided they wanted to join the competition for this thing, so we did, and we played about a ten-game schedule, I guess. We played a couple of Army teams and one Navy team, and we didn't meet any Marine team until the final one. The rest of our schedule was a college schedule. We played, among others, Canisius again. I played against Canisius that year and again the next year.

Q: How did you qualify as a graduate already of the Academy?

Adm. R.: In the President's Cup competition one officer was allowed to play on each team in that competition. Of course, the Navy and the Army had several people playing with them, but not in the President's Cup competition. Those people had to sit on the sidelines, except one at a time. I was the only one on our team, so I managed to play. One officer could play in that competition, the rest of the team was enlisted.

We played the Marines and we lost to them that year 12 to 0. Then the next year, 1930, we again played the Marines and it was again in December, and that time we lost to them 7 to 0. Then the next year we won it. We beat them 13 to 7, I think, or something like that. So we won the competition, and that was the end of our football team because the Depression was on and they couldn't afford it any more. We had all these men who were just playing football.

Q: For that period of time.

Adm. R.: Yes. We must have had sixty men on that detail. We went out to this island, it was an Army fort, and they didn't have anybody there but one caretaker, so when we went out there we took over a barracks, so we had to maintain the barracks and we had to keep the field where we practiced in reasonable shape. Then there had to be cooks and there had to be medical people. There were fifty or sixty people.

Q: Yes, it cost money.

Adm. R.: It was an expensive thing, all right, but it was a marvelous thing. People still talk about it, you know. In my career I have been pretty lucky because I got into things like that and I met more people in the Coast Guard during that time who all loved this football team because it was the first team the Coast Guard had really had. It stood out and represented us. We lost two games in one year, the second year we lost two games, the first year we only lost one game, and the last year we didn't lose any games. So we had a good football team.

Q: Who was coaching the team? Merriman still?

Adm. R.: No. Irving Baker. Old Merriman was still at the Academy. Irving Baker, who is retired now and lives out on the West Coast, and he had an assistant named Chet Anderson. They both started out as JGs, I guess - maybe they were lieutenants, but anyway they were lieutenants when the thing wound up.

I was lucky in that and then in this target business down in

St. Petersburg. But the last year, right after our team finished that last year in 1931, they always picked the target-repair detail from the football squad. We had a bunch of good healthy people and this was an active job. So I went down in charge of that thing that year and I was there for the whole business - twenty-five destroyers, they all came down and I knew them all, met them all, and I got to help them make out their reports and all that, ran the target practices for them. Then when that was over, instead of sending me back to my ship from there, they sent me to Norfolk with my target-repair party to another target and we did the same thing for the cutters. I met a lot of people then.

So I got to know all these people. Then, later on, I came back to the Academy in 1934 and met all of those people who were in the Academy in '34 and who came in during the next three years - the next four years - then I left and I came back again in 1950 and I was there for four years that time as commandant of cadets. So I had a close contact with all those people.

When I left in 1938 there were people in the Academy who didn't graduate until 1941 and I had met all of them. I missed the people who came in from then on, through the war, but then I picked up again in 1950, so I was hitting people who came in then, who graduated that year, who came in in 1947. I missed the ones who came in in 1946 because they had graduated when I got there. So you see I had a real good view of all these people. My experience with personnel in the Coast Guard was very, very extensive. I know many people quite well. When you're commandant of cadets, you get to know those cadets very well. Even though there are a lot of them, you get to see and know all the details, especially the ones that get in trouble!

Q: Tell me about this President's Cup. Did it just disappear with the advent of the Depression?

Adm. R.: We got the President's Cup. It was to rest with the team that won it until the next time it was played for. Well, it has never been played for again, but I don't know where it is. We have tried to find it. I have lost track. It went to Headquarters, then I didn't know anything about what happened to it, but when I was commandant of cadets there was a fellow named Lee Baker, brother of the guy who coached the football team, who spent quite a bit of time at the Academy, he was a Coast Guard officer, he's dead now, but he came to me and wanted to know about the Cup because he wanted to do something about it. He was interested in athletics and all. We tried and tried and tried but we never have been able to find out. It's probably on somebody's shelf at home. It has never turned up again.

Q: And the competition stopped?

Adm. R.: The competition stopped at that time. There is no President's Cup now. The whole deal is off. I don't think the other teams ceased playing, but I think they ceased having a team that represented the whole service. Quantico was usually the team that played for the Marines. They were the Quantico Marines during the year, but when they played us they were all the Marines.

Q: Admiral, when you were assigned to the Shaw part of her duty and the duty of all the other destroyers in the Coast Guard was to combat smuggling, was it not?

Adm. R.: Yes.

Q: You were not involved directly in these operations, were you?

Adm. R.: Well, I was involved as a person in the ship's crew. We made patrols. We went out for ten days - no, we went out for a week and were in for two weeks, and while we were out -

Q: And your home port was in Florida?

Adm. R.: Our home port was in New London. There were destroyers in Boston and destroyers in New York and two divisions in New London. There was one division in New York, one in Boston, and two in New London, and the destroyer force headquarters was in New London.

We would go out and patrol for a week and there would be three or four destroyers out at a time, and we were patrolling the area where the offshore rummies would come to unload into the speed boats. We would heckle them as much as we could -

Roland #1 - 42

Q: This was beyond the 12-mile limit?

Adm. R.: Beyond the 12-mile limit, yes. We would go out and circle them, trail them, and try to prevent contact with the speed boats, to the extent that we could. Of course, we didn't have enough destroyers to cover all of them and there was plenty of contact, there's no question about it. Then we would lose these things, too, in fog and things of that sort.

One night when I was the officer of the deck on the Shaw, we were trailing one of these fellows and he was behaving himself, going straight ahead at probably 5 or 6 knots, and we were trailing along right behind him, keeping an eye on him.

Q: Was he a regular merchantman?

Adm. R.: It was a sailing vessel, probably a 65-footer or something like that. They had sails up but they were under power, too. We were faithfully trailing along behind them, about 100 yards behind them. The skipper came up on the bridge and we were standing there watching the process. We had a 1-pounder on each side, just below the bridge, on the forecastle, and there was a man standing by each one of these guns. That was part of the routine, you know, we kept a man up there when we were trailing. This fellow suddenly picked up speed. He went up ahead a little bit, then he turned around and came back. I gave an order to turn, too - of course, we couldn't turn like he could, but I wanted to be heading in the same general direction. The skipper said,

Roland #1 - 43

"Fire a blank." So the guy got down, he was almost alongside of us, and we fired a blank and the smoke came up in our face like this and we never saw the rummy again! By the time the smoke cleared away he was gone. He just disappeared in the darkness and we could never find him.

Q: It frightened him away! What was your legal prerogative?

Adm. R.: In firing at him?

Q: Yes.

Adm. R.: We didn't have any, but we did all sorts of things. They would come alongside sometimes, as we were going along, and they'd shout insults at the skipper. The skipper would stand up on the bridge, and the skipper of the Shaw didn't hesitate to tell them a thing or two once in a while, too. He enjoyed it.

One day we were out there and a rummy came up alongside about midships. I was up on the bridge at the time and the skipper was up there. He was exchanging words with these people on the ship and a couple of extra people came up on deck on the rummy and they said some insulting things, and they directed them toward midships where some of the crew were standing. Right back of where our people and crew were standing there was a locker that had potatoes in it, a spud locker. They must have had a signal or something because, all of a sudden, they all turned and they all loaded up with potatoes and they turned around and bombarded that thing. They really lambasted them! They must

Roland #1 - 44

have thrown about three bushels of potatoes.

There were quite a few exchanges between us while we were out there, talk back and forth.

Q: Who were these rummies?

Adm. R.: They were Canadians. All that I ever saw were Canadians.

Q: And where did they get the rum? In the West Indies?

Adm. R.: No. I think the islands of St. Pierre and Miquelon. That's where most all of them operated out of. Some of them came from other places, I suppose.

Q: What kind of liquor did they have?

Adm. R.: Golden Wedding was a very common one. One of the things that happened to me while I was on board the Shaw was that we were in port and they had brought in a rummy named the Flor del Mar. It was an offshore rummy and it had liquor aboard, and somehow it was inside of Long Island. They must have had a rendezvous in there, and our patrol boats picked them up and pursued them and fired at them and ran them up on the beach. So our people descended on them and they towed her back into New London and she was tied up down at the destroyer force base. They wanted to unload this thing because it was leaking and they wanted to get it unloaded and in the warehouse. So they called for working parties from the ships that were in. We sent a working party down and I had the duty on this day. We sent about half a dozen people. There were all kinds of people who wanted to do it, and that should have made me suspicious but it didn't! And other ships sent people, and there were half a dozen ships in there. They all sent working parties. So they unloaded in a short time, I guess, because they were really going to town.

During the evening an officer came in and said to me: "You know, an enlisted man just asked me if I wanted a bottle of whiskey." And I said, "What did you tell him." He said "I told him no." and I said, "What did you tell him that for?" He said, "Well, I was on my way and I didn't pay any more attention to it."

Then somebody smelled a rat and before the boat had been unloaded an awful lot of that whiskey was missing. So we restricted everybody to the ships, so a lot of whiskey went overboard on to the bottom from the ships.

In the course of this thing, our skipper was notified and he came down and we searched the ship and we found an awful lot of liquor. We had a stateroom and they must have had twenty-five cases of liquor in there.

Then we went to sea the next day. Our patrol started the next day, so we went to sea, and when we got out to sea we continued to search. We were out a couple of weeks and we searched the ship and we kept finding it. Almost every day we'd find some more. It was stuck in the ventilators, plates were taken off of things, you know, and it was stuck in, in boilers. Those guys would go to great lengths to hide a bottle of whiskey. That was really something.

Of course, the Coast Guard was always getting a black eye for our rummy business and they wrote about that for a long time, made up all kinds of stories about it. Just the bare facts were bad enough. It was negligence. It was negligence on my part, you know, sending those guys out there to get into that liquor like that and not take any precautions. I never should have let any one of them back aboard without going over them from top to bottom, but I didn't. And neither did anybody else.

Q: What was the penalty if they were caught?

Adm. R.: I suppose they would have gotten a court-martial of some kind. The penalty wouldn't have been too bad.

Q: On your own destroyer when she went back out on patrol duty, did you catch any of them?

Adm. R.: We didn't catch anybody. We just found the liquor.

Q: The evidence but not the people.

Adm. R.: No. Of course, none of them knew anything about it. Must have been somebody from the next ship who put that down there!

Q: What actually was the disposition of liquor that was taken in this fashion?

Adm. R.: We turned it over to Customs, and Customs either destroyed it or sold it for medical use. That liquor was all Golden Wedding. That ship was just loaded with Golden Wedding.

I had another experience. One time there was a rummy named the Yvette June and she was a speed boat. Our people picked it up after they had made contact one time and chased them into the Sakonnet River and they were firing at them with their 1-pounders and with machine guns. The patrol boat rammed her. They couldn't help it, you know, she cut across the bow and they ran into her and sunk her. These people had been chucking the stuff overboard as they came in. Anyway, the thing sank.

I was in New London at the time. It was after the football season and I was at loose ends in New London. They had a station ship down there that they called the Argus and I was living aboard it, waiting for the ships to come in. So they put me aboard the boat with a couple of divers and a crew, and they put me in charge of it. I was still an ensign, and they said to go up to this place and locate this boat, anchor, and send the divers down and unload it.

We went up there and we found it. We could see where it was because there were boats all over, dragging grapnels, picking up these things that they'd thrown overboard. We knew where it would be, but anyway we did locate the boat.

Q: What was the depth?

Adm. R.: Forty feet of water. It was in the Sakonnet River, just inside it. We waited till the next morning to send the divers down. One of them was a warrant gunner and the other one was an enlisted man. The enlisted man went down first and he started unloading, then he was relieved by the gunner and he worked on it for a while. The enlisted man hurt his arm, he injured his arm, so he couldn't dive any more, and the gunner came up and said that he was sick and he didn't want to dive any more. He suggested we get some other divers.

So I called the base and told them the situation and they said, "Well, just hang on for a while and we'll give you some instructions."

When I was a cadet I got a little instruction in diving. They had AD equipment and they took us down to the end of the pier, those of us who wanted to, and we'd get into the thing and go down and explore on the bottom, pick up star fish and search around. So I put the stuff on myself and went down, and I unloaded the thing. They had done nearly half, I guess, and I did the rest. I unloaded the forward compartment, emptied that, and then went back to the after compartment and went through that. There were 550 cases of liquor aboard that thing.

Q: How big was this speed boat?

Adm. R.: Oh, she was probably 50 feet, a good-sized boat. I had a line, you know, and I would tie the line under the sack and they would pull it back up and take it aboard the diving boat, ar then they would send the line back down to me and I would hook it onto the next one and they would take that up.

When they got these things up near the top, they would hook them with a grapnel in them and pull them in. Most every time, I guess, they broke a bottle because I could smell the liquor coming through the air hose to me. It wasn't enough to bother me but I wondered what was going on!

Anyway, we finished the job and there were altogether 550 cases of liquor and that was all Golden Wedding, too. We loaded that on our diving boat. Our diving boat didn't have any power, we had to tow it, and we towed it in to Providence and turned it over to the Customs in Providence. They destroyed that liquor. In the course of doing this, we pulled up a couple of cases that had 1-pounder projectile in them. They fired into the hold and the projectile had stopped in the middle of the case and came up with the liquor.

Q: How numerous were these rummies?

Adm. R.: There were a lot of them and they were well known. This particular boat, the Yvette June, after we had done this and had gotten rid of the liquor, taken it in, we came back out and located the boat again and it seemed to me that, unloaded, she might come to the surface or something, and so we hooked onto the bow of this boat and gave it a couple of yanks, you know, and got underway and it did come up. It came up to the surface. So we made a turn and headed out to sea. I was going to take it into Providence too. We had to come down the Sakonnet River and go over to Narragansett Bay in order to get to Providence. I called New London and told them that the boat had come up and that we had it in tow, and if we stopped it would probably sink again. So they said, "Take it out offshore till you get a couple of hundred feet, then cut the line."

Q: Sink her?

Adm. R.: Yes. So we took it out there a way until on our sounding we had probably 125 feet or something like that, then we cut the line and let it go. Do you know that several months later the Yvette June was again operating.

Q: You'd been observed apparently?

Adm. R.: Oh, I guess so, yes. They had gotten the thing up and taken it in somewhere and repaired it. How could they do that, with a boat as big as that, bring it in somewhere, they had to stick it up on a dry dock somewhere and work on it.

Q: It was a very difficult assignment for the Coast Guard. It was a well-nigh impossible assignment?

Adm. R.: It was an impossible assignment, yes. If we had had the equipment to run an effective patrol and to stop the flow of liquor, it would have cost ten times as much as it was costing. You couldn't do it with one-sized ship. We had these destroyers and destroyers were fine for patrolling offshore but when you get into the Sakonnet River you might as well not have anything as have the destroyers. They're just in the way, a hindrance. You had to have big ones and little ones. We did operate a lot of their boats that we had captured, you know, and had repaired, fixed up, and they were fast enough. They were useful to us. We operated some of their boats and we had some pretty good patrol boats of our own, 75-footers, that were useful to us, but you needed something that would do 40 knots so that you could stay with some of these things because they were awfully fast.

There was a fellow going up and down the Sakonnet River while we were unloading that was pointed out to us by some guy who came aboard, some local man, and he said, "Keep your eye on that fellow. He's a hijacker. If he gets a chance to get over here and take this liquor from you, he'll take it from you. He'll do whatever he has to do in order to get it." So we kept our eye on him. He didn't bother us but he did go up and down the river and he was a good-sized boat, too. But they said that he would go out and he would overtake these things that had made contact, overpower the people aboard, and take the liquor. What he did with the people, I don't know. I don't know whether he threw them overboard or whether he enlisted them as part of his crew from then on, or what he did.

Q: The whole coast was vulnerable to smugglers, wasn't it?

Adm. R.: Yes, but the area around New London was terrible. Up off the Sakonnet River there was a hotbed of it. That was a very bad place, and Narragansett Bay, and Long Island, of course.

Roland #1 - 52

Q: I would take it that the Caribbean and that area would be pretty vulnerable, too?

Adm. R.: Yes.

Q: And what about from Mexico and the Gulf? Was there a problem there?

Adm. R.: We were full of problems down there. I wasn't associated with them and I don't know just exactly what their problems were. I think, though, that if their problems had been equal to the problems here probably some of the destroyers would have been down there, because they didn't have the equipment that was used up here for patrolling. We had most of the cutters and we had all of those destroyers.

Q: Was the Coast Guard attempting anything on the West Coast or was there any smuggling there from Canada?

Adm. R.: I really don't know. There must have been. I know our effort wasn't anything like it was on the East Coast. I think that we had problems because of the fact that Pierre and Miquelon, the people in the government up there were completely out of the world. They wouldn't have anything to do with us or with cooperation, and they didn't mind that this was illegal. In their mind it wasn't illegal, I guess, but they would not cooperate with us in any way. These things used to come in up there and they would unload, shift cargoes into other vessels, and be maintained and all that. They had a perfect base up there. Maybe they

Roland #1 - 53

couldn't find a place like that in these other locations. The West Coast should have been a good place for them, I would think. But the problem wasn't there like it was here.

Q: You said earlier that the Coast Guard had to accept the criticisms and all that that came your way because of the failure, really, to enforce the prohibition law.

Adm. R.: Sure, and, of course, the thing was handled in a good honest way, I think. As far as I could see. You know, the thing about the <u>Flor del Mar</u> that was on the station, but as far as people taking bribes and things like that, I don't know of any case of anything like that ever happening, and I don't think that there ever was one of any officer - well, maybe a warrant officer - but occasionally some guy would look the other way and let them go in and get some reward for it and they found out about it. And it was the whole Coast Guard because one guy like that would do that and, of course, that's what you'd expect, especially when people are so unsympathetic to what you're trying to do. Nobody wanted us to accomplish what we were trying to do. It was a terrible job.

Q: What effect did that have, the knowledge that the populace on shore wasn't particularly anxious to have you succeed? What effect did this have on the morale of your crews?

Adm. R.: We had crews aboard our destroyers and aboard our patrol boats that probably couldn't have made a living otherwise. We had

Roland #1 - 54

pretty much dregs in our crews. WE had a bo'sun, a warrant officer, named Cornell who was just a nut about this liquor-running business. I don't know whether he drank himself or what, but anyway he just had no mercy on anybody who was running liquor if he was on the scene, and his boat shot up more rummies than anybody else's. He would come in to New London and he would have been out at sea for a couple of days in a 75-footer and it was time to rest up. He'd put the crew ashore and put a new crew aboard and Cornell would stay aboard and go out with the new crew. He would never leave that boat. He was just dedicated to that job. There were many officers and people in charge who had the same feeling, but I don't think anybody acted as he did. He just was after that job all the time, and he accomplished a good bit. But it was only a drop in the bucket, of course, all that he did. The number of his boat was the 290, a 75-footer, and I think it might have been the one that shot up the Yvette June.

Q: You said earlier that when you captured liquor in this fashion you turned it over to the Customs Service people. Was there any additional cooperation with Customs intercepting liquor that came in in legitimate ports and places like that?

Adm. R.: I don't know how the law reads now, but you know at that time and maybe still a graduate of the Coast Guard Academy is a customs officer ex officio. It has to be an officer. It's not true of enlisted personnel. So we did much consultation with them. They rode with us a good bit of the time, too. They would put people aboard, just as the Fisheries people do now. They'd go out with us. But we actually, by law, were customs officers, so we were part of the Customs Service for that purpose.

Q: What is the prevailing rule governing liquor on board Coast Guard ships?

Adm. R.: Unless there has been a recent change, we're allowed to have beer aboard and we can have beer messes aboard the ships. And, in some cases, I understand, they have even had machines that would dispense beer on some of our units.

Q: You say this came into being immediately upon repeal?

Adm. R.: Immediately upon repeal we were allowed to have beer on board. We were not allowed to have hard liquor, but allowed to have beer on board immediately upon repeal.

Q: Was that something that was true before we had prohibition?

Adm. R.: I'm not sure about that because before prohibition I was in high school! So I don't know.

Q: How does that work out in terms of foreign navy ships and so forth? I mean you can reciprocate in terms of hospitality in a way our U.S. Navy cannot?

Adm. R.: Well, yes. We always when we went to foreign ports particularly have wished that we could do something. Aboard the ships of any other navy we are always served drinks in moderation, particularly British ships, all the officers come and greet you, you know, come to call, make a wardroom call, and they would all like to have a drink with you separately. You'd have one with each one of them, but it adds to the feeling of the meeting, I'm sure. I think that if that weren't so on board their ships they wouldn't have the same kind of a greeting for you. They wouldn't all be there, I don't think. I think that it does add to the greeting, and other ships do the same thing.

In the 1930s I was aboard several German ships in Spain and they did the same thing. Of course, French ships, I guess probably they live on wine, anyway. They all have it, and during the time that I was in Spain, on one of our ships in Spain, we did have beer aboard and we served beer. Perhaps it was a good thing we only had beer at that time. I was stationed at the Academy on a cadet cruise in 1936, and we had been into a port in France and were crossing the Bay of Biscay when the revolution started in Spain. We were sent in to San Sebastian to take the Embassy out. The summer embassy was in San Sebastian, so we went in there to get the ambassador and his staff and take them out and take them to France. We had to take out refugees, too. So we did that. We went in and we picked up the embassy people and we took them over to France, and then we were ordered to pick up refugees.

We went to Bilbao and there met some U. S. Navy ships, battleships, which were also making a cruise, and we transferred our cadets to the battleships and they came back to the United States in that way. We stayed over there, taking refugees off the north coast of Spain for a couple of months. In between trips with refugees, we anchored in Bilbao Harbor, and ships of other navies did, too. The French were usually there. There were always a couple of British destroyers and the Germans had a cruiser named the Koln and they usually had besides the Koln a destroyer or so in there, too. We were the only ship in the whole group that had movies, and so they used to come to our ship to see movies every night. They all wanted to see Ginger Rogers in The Gay Divorcee, so I think I must have seen The Gay Divorcee a hundred times myself.

On the way down there we had been to Copenhagen and Hamburg also, and we had a terrific lot of beer on board. Our holds were full of beer, and after the movies everybody would come down to our wardroom and we would sit around the table and drink beer. This was a good wholesome way of entertaining them, so we enjoyed having the beer. But if we had had more I'm afraid there might have been some - if we had had other kinds of liquor, it might have been a little more difficult.

Q: How does this rule work in terms of entertaining the U.S. Navy?

Adm. R.: Well, when they came aboard, while the cadets were

moving over to the battleships –

Q: I mean just generally speaking. When the U.S. Navy comes aboard your Coast Guard ship, do you offer them the hospitality of the ship?

Adm. R.: Oh, sure, yes. All ships don't have beer messes, but those that do have them offer them a beer, yes. In the case of Bilbao when we were moving our cadets, there were Navy boats running back and forth and Navy officers came over and had a beer with us while they were loading the boat. They enjoyed it as much as we did.

Q: The Coast Guard must have been very popular!

Adm. R.: Yes, well, several people said at the time that they picked the wrong service when they came in!

Q: Well, Sir, in 1932 – in September of that year – you went out to the Great Lakes?

Adm. R.: Yes, when I'd finished with my target-towing detail, I went to Bay City, Michigan, where they were building this new ship, the Escanaba. She was a 165-foot icebreaker built for service on the lakes.

Q: Was she a new type?

Adm. R.: She was a new type, yes. She was the first of a series of five of them, three or four of which were built in Bay City and the others in Wilmington, Delaware.

Q: Perhaps we could divert our attention for a minute and talk about the design of Coast Guard ships. Who supervises this?

Adm. R.: A man named Honeywell was the architect and he was in the Coast Guard, in Coast Guard headquarters, and he was in charge of it. Whether he actually did the design, I'm not sure, but I think that he probably did, because he did it in the case of other ships that the Coast Guard had, and it was his approval on the thing that put it in motion, anyway. It was an icebreaker with a cut-away bow. It didn't have enough power really to be a good icebreaker. It was a 1,500 horsepower vessel, but it was only 165 feet long. It was intended that the ship would be able to break ice in the Straits of Mackinac. It turned out that it could break some ice in the Straits of Mackinac but it couldn't break enough to get through. It wasn't sufficient for that purpose, although the ship did travel through the straits in the wintertime on a couple of occasions, but it had to do it when the weather was right, when the wind was opening up leads and so on.

Q: Even so, wasn't it an improvement on the earlier types of icebreakers you had?

Adm. R.: Oh, I think so. There was one named the Acushnet that was reputed to be an icebreaker. It was stationed in Bangor, Maine. But she was not as good as the Escanaba. The Escanaba, considering her size and her power, was pretty good. Her design was all right, and we did a lot of icebreaking. At that time there were quite a few ships running on the lakes, passenger ships that ran all year from Milwaukee to ports on the east side of the lakes. One of the ports was Grand Haven, the other was Muskegan, just north of Grand Haven. Then there were car ferries, which ran all year out there, in several places on Lake Michigan. They, however, in themselves were pretty good icebreakers because they had a lot of power.

Q: Were there any iron ore boats that ran in the wintertime?

Adm. R.: No. No ore boats ran in the wintertime but at times it was necessary for tankers to run up there. Tankers would come up from the lower part of Lake Michigan into the Green Bay area and to the town of Escanaba, when they ran short of oil. They had a difficult time and we assisted those ships a good bit with the Escanaba and also the passenger ships that ran over to Milwaukee from where we were stationed.

The Escanaba was taken out of the lakes when the war started and used as an escort ship on the run to Greenland from the United States, and she was lost. She was torpedoed during that time.

Q: For how long a period in the winter would the lakes be frozen over and require the use of an icebreaker?

Adm. R.: I would say most of the winter. The main traffic in the lakes was through the locks at the Sioux and they used to close those locks on the 7th of December and then open them up on about the 1st of April. Traffic on the lakes could move all the year round if the locks could be operated through the winter. That was the drawback, operating the locks in the ice.

Bigger icebreakers as we had later on could break through at any time and if the ships could get through the locks they would be able to operate all the year round. The situation is still the same, I think, as far as the locks are concerned. It's very difficult to operate them, although they have improved their operation and operate for a longer period now than they did before.

The first ships usually run in the latter part of March up there, or they did at the time I was up there. Then they'd run until sometime in December. They continued to run in the lakes but not through the locks. They'll continue to run in the lower part of the lakes for a while and, in some cases, like between Toledo and Detroit, there are ships that run all year. They carry freight and, at that time, they were carrying coal between Toledo and Detroit, to factories in Detroit. Our Escanaba, however, was confined almost entirely to operations in Lake Michigan during the winter. We got down into the St. Clair River and the Detroit River on a couple of occasions, but they were not usual sorties for her to make.

Q: How did a ship command the services of the Escanaba? How was this arranged?

Adm. R.: We kept a continuous radio watch aboard and these ships all had radiotelephones so that ships in our vicinity could get us directly. If they couldn't, they could call our district office. At that time, our organization was a little different than it is now, and we had a district office in Chicago. They could call them either by ship-to-shore telephone and land line or by direct radio, tell them the story, and then our district headquarters would get us on the job.

Our duties on the Escanaba, other than the wintertime, were attending festivals mostly, I think, and, of course, we did make that trip to Chicago to guard the area where Balbo's planes were tied up, to patrol that area. We were engaged for quite a while in that because Balbo, if you remember –

Q: This was Italo Balbo?

Adm. R.: Yes. He was en route for a long time. He lost at least one airplane on the way over. I think he lost it in Ireland, but they finally arrived at Chicago quite a bit late.

Q: Was that in 1932?

Adm. R.: 1933, at the Chicago World Fair. The Chicago World Fair was going on at the time, and that was the occasion.

Q: And he was sent over as an official representative from

Mussolini, wasn't he?

Adm. R.: Yes, that's right, and he came in with five planes, I think. There were many threats as to what people were going to do with the planes and all that, but we had some speed boats that we manned and patrolled the area where they were tied. They were tied up to mooring buoys, off the Navy pier, and we patrolled in the area all the time. But there were never any real threats or efforts or attempts -

Q: But why was the Coast Guard called in on this particular operation?

Adm. R.: I think probably because we had a ship out there and because we were available.

Let's see, that was in 1933. Then it was the next year that I was transferred out of there, so I was aboard her from 1932 - we arrived at Grand Haven in December 1932, we went in commission in Bay City in September, arrived in Grand Haven in December, and then I was aboard that ship through 1933 and 1934 until about August when I came to the Academy. During that time we had quite a time with personnel in the Coast Guard because of the Depression. We were releasing, discharging people ahead of time, and we had a pay cut during that time.

Q: Were you subject to the 15 per cent pay cut?

Adm. R.: Yes, we lost 15 per cent of our pay. So we ran short-handed aboard the ship, but not being a very big ship it wasn't a real problem.

They now have a park out in Grand Haven that they call Escanaba Park. Of course, the ship is long gone. As I said, it was lost during the war, but we have another ship in there, 180-footer, and they continually try to get the big icebreaker, the Mackinaw, assigned there but they haven't succeeded yet.

Q: During the summer while you were on duty with her, were you called upon for any rescue work?

Adm. R.: Yes. We had a number of searches for small vessels. We didn't have any bigger cases. There weren't any serious accidents on the lakes at that time, at least none that we got in on. There was another Coast Guard ship up at the Sioux, which was bigger than the Escanaba - the Seminole. She wasn't an icebreaker but she was a very capable ship. At that time, when winter came around, they closed that ship off. They put shutters around her and they moved the people ashore into a barracks. They stood a watch on the ship to see that nobody came aboard and removed things, but the ship did not operate in the winter.

Q: Did this mean that her hull was not as tough as the one of the Escanaba?

Adm. R.: Yes, her plating was not heavy enough and her design was such that she would jam herself into ice. She had a very fine bow. The Escanaba, and any icebreaker really, has a sort of a rounded bow and it's cut off so that it will ride up on top of the ice, and that plating is very heavy. The plating on the Escanaba - I mean on the Mackinaw at the waterline is 1 3/8th inches. That's the other icebreaker, the big icebreaker. I don't remember what it was on the Escanaba, but it was heavy plate at the waterline, where the ice presses.

Q: Does this do anything to her speed?

Adm. R.: Oh, yes, of course. It takes more power to push the ship along and it does affect speed, yes. You need more power to push that additional weight, and it makes a good difference, too. If you double or triple the thickness of her plate, you've done a lot.

Q: In a given winter, how many operations were you called on to perform?

Adm. R.: Very many. One of the early stories of interest to me, a search and rescue story, occurred the first year we were there. We arrived early in December and between Christmas and New Year there was a party in town. At that time, everybody, of course, had to have evening dress uniforms, tails, fore and aft hats, and all that business, and we were all down at the party dressed up in our "soup and fish," and we got a call. At that time there was trouble in the airline, I forget which it was, in the mail service, so that the Army was carrying air mail for the Post Office. An airplane had left Milwaukee headed for Grand Rapids,

Michigan, in the afternoon, about four o'clock, and we got this call probably about 9:30 that night. We were all out dancing! Of course, we had to go.

We left and went down to the ship in our "soup and fish," threw off the lines, and got underway. We had no idea, of course, where this fellow was going to be. We knew that he was headed from Milwaukee to Grand Rapids, but we didn't know when he went down and we didn't know whether he had been blown off his course, so we decided that we would head right straight for Milwaukee, which was about 80 miles. We decided to run over there, then we would run down ten miles and then run back, run down ten miles, run back, and sweep the area that way.

I had the midwatch and I guess it was may be one or two o'clock in the morning and it was snowing, snowing hard –

Q: You had powerful searchlights, I take it?

Adm. R.: We had searchlights, yes. But the snow stopped and I saw a flare and I took a bearing of it, and the flare went out. So I headed for it. I had the bearing and I sent for the captain and he came up. Of course, we hadn't got anywhere near Milwaukee yet. I told him I had seen this thing and he said, "How far away was it?" I said, "I don't know, but it was just a flare and there was nothing to compare it with. I don't think it was very far because it was bright. I should think that it might have been five miles, maybe ten." So he said, "OK, we'll head down and check it out." So we headed down, went down, down, down, and about two hours and a half later it started to snow again. The snow had let up so you could see a few hundred yards and, here, out on our port beam, was an airplane sitting out in the water with two men sitting on the wing. When they landed they had knocked off a pontoon, so they had to sit out on the wing where the pontoon remained in order to keep the thing from rolling over, and they had been out there all that time.

We stopped and I was assigned to the boat. We went over to this airplane and I had the crew back in under the wing, and these guys were covered with ice, just covered with ice. I said, "Do you want us to take you in tow?" And this deep, southern drawl said, "Brother, all I want from you is to stop for one brief moment." So we got hold of the thing and got them aboard and then we sent a couple of men aboard to take the mail out. We rode back to the ship and put these fellows aboard. They were just covered with ice.

Q: What had happened to their flare? Had it burned out?

Adm. R.: Oh, yes, a flare does that, you know. You shoot them up in the air and it exploded and we just happened to have seen it. Maybe they'd been doing it before, I don't know.

Q: They both survived?

Adm. R.: They both survived. They were perfectly well next morning, but, boy, they were really pooped when we got them on board. I was still in the boat while they were getting aboard and the skipper said, "Well, can we take that thing in tow?" and I said, "I think so. We can go out and put a line on it and try it, anyway."

So they handed me a line to run out there to the thing and we started out. We got about halfway out and the thing just rolled over and went down. So we never saw it again. Of course, if they had still been aboard I guess it would have stayed up because they were balancing it. But it was real cold, you know. It was awfully cold.

And this happened to me at this stage of my career and I have never forgotten it. I have told this story hundreds and hundreds of times and I don't think that I embellish it. I try to tell it simply because that's the way the thing happened. And I'll never forget that voice. The last thing I expected was a deep southern drawl.

Q: Were there any other rescues of a dramatic nature?

Adm. R.: No, nothing like that. We had no other things as dramatic as that while I was there, anyway. Of course, in the career of a ship -

Q: Oh, yes.

What about the enforcement of safety regulations?

Adm. R.: We patrolled a good many regattas out there and enforced those things, and we boarded vessels in the summertime wherever we went. WE always put a couple of boats over and boarded everything in sight. We checked their equipment.

Q: Did you ever meet with any resistance in doing that?

Adm. R.: Not real resistance, but objections, yes. People don't want you to stop them when they're going somewhere. We did that a good many times. Usually, though, we would do it in harbors. We boarded fishermen out there a good many times. We assisted fishermen in the wintertime a good many times. They would work when the wind was right, you know, and would blow the ice offshore so that they could get out, and the Coast Guard, too. They know that when the wind shifts it's going to close in again and they can't get back in, so we would go out and get those people and that kind of ice is likely to be slush ice, so the Escanaba could break it and work her way through. Then these things following couldn't follow because they were in the slush right on our tail, so we would have to tow them through. We did quite a lot of that, getting these fishermen back in after they foolishly went out.

Q: You said there were ferry boats that ran across the lake, you had to inspect them, too, I take it?

Adm. R.: No, we didn't bother with them because Marine Inspectors did that, and we didn't have marine inspection at that time.

Q: I see.

Adm. R.: They were regularly inspected. These were pretty big ships. They carried railroad cars. They ran from a number of places on the east side to a number of places on the west side of Lake Michigan. The main line, the Grand Trunk, included a trip on the car ferry.

Q: Lake Michigan, in particular, is subject to very dangerous situations developing very quickly in the summertime, is it not? Storms and that sort of thing?

Adm. R.: I don't think as much as - I think Ontario and Erie are the worst, they're the shallower ones, you know. They kick up more quickly and are more miserable, and more dangerous, too. The western end of Lake Erie is a dangerous place for a ship of any size because there's just a channel through the west end of that lake. The rest of it is too shoal for a ship. It probably runs about 10 or 12 feet, the rest of the lake.

Then from Cleveland to the east it's deeper, but from Cleveland to the west, over to the Detroit River, you have to go through the channel, which is a dug channel, off out in the middle of the lake.

Q: That must have been very interesting duty.

Adm. R.: It was, remarkably.

Q: Quite different from rum-runners!

Adm. R.: Yes. I've had a lot of experience on the lakes. Of course, I come from Buffalo, and then I had that experience on that ship, and later I was the skipper of the Mackinaw, and I was the chief of staff to the district. So I had seven or eight years out there on the lakes.

Q: When I say quite different from rum-running and that sort of thing, was there any of that on the lakes?

Adm. R.: There was but we weren't involved in it because most of it up there was across the St. Clair River and the Detroit River, particularly the St. Clair River, and this was handled by the customs people and shore people in small boats. We weren't much involved in that. There must have been some cases where the Coast Guard was involved, but we weren't on the Escanaba when I was out there. We were on Lake Michigan most of the time and that's the United States all the way around, so we were not involved.

But up at the St. Mary's River, too, there was a lot of smuggling up there. Along the St. Mary's River they had at that time many, many lookout stations and they were for various purposes. One of them was to report any such activities as smuggling if they saw it, and also to report ship movements in the river.

Q: At that time was the Lighthouse Service - ?

Adm. R.: In 1939 the Lighthouse Service was taken over. We were ahead of that.

Q: You were on the Escanaba until?

Adm. R.: I left in August -

Q: In order to report to - ?

Adm. R.: In order to report to the Academy for duty in the athletic department.

Q: This was something you really were happy to do?

Adm. R.: Yes, I was very happy to do it. When I arrived at the Academy and reported to the superintendent he told me that I was also, besides the athletic duties, to teach physics. As a matter of fact, there was no billet for me at the Academy in the athletic department, but there was one in the physics department and I had to fill that billet.

Q: Were you equally as happy for that?

Adm. R.: Well, I wasn't because I didn't have any idea - my only knowledge of physics was the year I had at the Academy and the time that I had had at Canisius College when I didn't even go near the laboratory. So I didn't really know what it was all about, but there wasn't any way out of it.

Q: How did you prepare yourself for that?

Adm. R.: I got hold of some books and went home and started to read, and when the time came for classes, I had a hard time for the first year and for a couple of years, even, staying a couple of pages ahead of these kids, because some of them had been to college and had had pretty good instruction. It was a tough spot, but I didn't try to fool them. I let them know that I wanted them to question the things that they didn't understand. I didn't want to say to them, "If you think I don't know what I'm talking about, question me," but I told them that I wanted them to question me. I said, "I don't know all there is to know about this subject, but I'll go along and learn it with you." We worked it out, and I did it for three years, and for two years I taught the second class and the third class, two different parts of the book.

Q: That must have been a very effective way of learning?

Adm. R.: Believe me, I learned a lot about physics. I hope they learned something!

I taught in class and also I had lab - I split with the others on laboratories, and besides that I ran the cadets' store and was coaching, too. So I had my hands full in that business. The trouble with this sort of a thing is that my wife thought I was doing all my jobs all right and getting them done, but you can't do all those things and I know I wasn't doing them well.

Q: They were all so different in nature!

Adm. R.: They were all different. If I had one of those jobs, I would have done it well, I think, and I don't think I did any one of them really well the way I was doing them. Running that cadets' store, if I had to do it now, I would really complain about it, because there was quite a bit of money involved. We handled purchases for cadets. I had a storekeeper who worked for me in the store who kept the books, handled the counter, and that sort of thing.

Q: Did you look after the buying of supplies?

Adm. R.: I had to when I had the time, but he did a good bit of it. I'd come down and the papers would be ready for me. Some of them I had no idea about and he'd have to explain them to me. In some cases, I didn't agree with him about things, but I didn't have a chance to really check on what he was doing. He did many things, I know, that got by me and I probably would have stopped if I'd known about them.

The fellow was honest. I'll have to say that. If he hadn't been honest, I could have been in some very serious trouble because it would have been my fault.

Q: How big an operation in terms of money was it per year?

Adm. R.: I guess probably $25,000. We bought books. We developed the thing a little bit, too, into things for other people besides cadets. If somebody wanted to buy a refrigerator, we would order the refrigerator for them and it would be delivered to us, then we would sell it to the fellow, you see.

Q: You mean a staff person?

Adm. R.: Yes, somebody assigned to the Academy. We ran it like they run an exchange now, but we called it the Cadets Store. We sold a lot of things like ice cream and candy and things of that nature, but we made some pretty big purchases. On some occasions, we bought some of the clothing for the cadets. One year we bought all the shoes for the cadets. This amounted to quite a bit. There was a big sum of money involved in that. It would have been easy for this fellow to slip some of that into his own –

Q: Padded things?

Adm. R.: Yes, he could have padded it all right. I'm glad that things like that are taken care of by more adequate men now, but even with more adequate men it can happen and it was more likely then. I was lucky that I got away with it.

Q: Did you implement some of this when you became commandant? Did you draw on this kind of experience?

Adm. R.: By the time I became commandant, I think that matters of manning of things of that nature were better taken care of.

Q: They were systematized by that time?

Adm. R.: Yes. Even when I was back there as commandant of cadets, I handled a lot of these things that the store had handled before. As commandant of cadets, I had a staff of about half a dozen people who did all – we handled all of the finances on cadets' clothing and books and things like that. We did it all right there, rather than through the store.

Q: Tell me some more about the teaching activity.

Adm. R.: One thing that was better about the Academy at that time than it is now is that I think that our classes were smaller numbers, so that we got to know the cadets better. I didn't have more than twelve people in a section. The people that were in my classes I knew extremely well. At that time I didn't have direct contact with them unless they were involved in athletics, in which case I did, so I think that having these small classes, too, was helpful as far as my ignorance of the subject was concerned because I think that the kids were more likely to come at me because they knew me better, too. They were more likely to come at me to settle their problems with the things that we were studying.

After a year, of course, the pressure was off me, as far as staying ahead of them was concerned and I could do a little better after a year, but I don't think that I ever got so I knew more than any of the cadets. Always there were coms individuals who knew more than I did about the subject! We had some people who had come close to being finished with college by the time they got there and had had engineering courses and were pretty well qualified. Now, of course, if somebody is like that he'd be excused from some of these classes. We never would excuse anybody from anything.

Q: They simply had to go through it, anyway.

Adm. R.: Oh, yes. If they'd had calculus for two years, we gave it to them for another two years - or a year, I guess it was.

Q: In the time that you were there on the teaching staff, what was the organization? I mean were there frequent faculty meetings and that sort of thing?

Adm. R.: No, rare faculty meetings. There was an academic board which met only to consider the results of examinations, and this was only heads of departments. Other than that, there were no meetings, except within our department and within our department, physics and chemistry, we had five people. One fellow who had chemistry and the rest of us had physics.

Q: What were the standards? I mean what was the minimum a man had to do in order to stay in the Academy at that time?

Adm. R.: Well, we marked on a scale of zero to 100 and the passing mark was 65. I think that had varied at various times in the Academy between 55 and 70. But while I was there the passing mark was 65.

If somebody flunked one subject, he could take reexaminations and then, if he passed, naturally he stayed in, but if he flunked two subjects he was out. And if he flunked the reexam he was out. There is more leeway now. I think they depend more on what an instructor will say about a kid than on the exact mark. There was a big difference between 64 and 65. It was a standard that was rigidly adhered to, and we weren't that exact in our marking, I don't think. We didn't know enough about it to be that exact in the marking, but we did it anyway.

It's a tremendous improvement in the Academy that it's the way it is now. When people go to the Academy now, they don't go right away. They go to school first, and then they go to the Academy and teach. Some people go for as long as two years.

Q: To learn teaching techniques?

Adm. R.: To learn teaching techniques and to learn their subject, too.

Q: What was the role of the superintendent in that time?

Adm. R.: Administrative more than anything else. He had direct responsibility for everything, as the commanding officer of a ship does. He had a man they called an executive officer, which is what Pyne was at that time. Then there was a physics department - a science department, I guess, because chemistry and physics were together, a mathematics department, there was an electrical department, there was a marine engineering department. I don't remember what others there were, but there were several things like that.

Our facilities, of course, were pretty good at the new place, which we were in then. We had room, anyway. The Academy was built to accommodate 250 cadets, two to a room. Of course, now they have over 1,000 and there has been extension after extension on that barracks. I think that with the number they have now they probably have room. They have over 1,000. The school, the academic part, that has expanded correspondingly, as much as the barracks part and it's a really well-equipped place now. And the people are so much better qualified. A Ph.D. was unheard of when we were there, I don't think we even had a master's degree, unless it was Dimmick. I suppose he did. As a matter of fact, I think Dimmick was a Ph.D. Ninety-five percent of the people there were people who had graduated from the Academy and had no other degrees and there was little PG work then.

We sent a few people to the naval postgraduate school, which was then at Annapolis, and there were two people in the physics department with me, Tyler and Cowart, who had been there. They were teaching physics and they were marine engineers. One of the things that happened towards the end was that they began to get other people in from civilian life and put them in uniform as professors, but in uniform. One came to the general studies department - they had by then formed a general studies department - and he was head of that. His name was Al Lawrence.

Q: What kind of rank would he get?

Adm. R.: He was a two-and-a-half striper. And they brought another fellow in named Brasefield and he came in in charge of the science group. He had the same rank.

Q: Why did they bring them in as civilians?

Roland #1 - 80

Adm. R.: I think that at that time they thought that there was some good effect on cadets if they associated with people who were in uniform. I think they wanted to keep it strictly a military thing and keep away any flavor of the civilian.

We had by that time one civilian who was teaching French, Gaston Buron.

Q: They'd added language then?

Adm. R.: We added language, yes. We taught French and later on they added Spanish and he taught that, too! But they later did get another man in, a fellow named Colby, who taught Spanish. Jimmy Hirschfield once taught Spanish there.

Q: You've been out of the Academy for a few years and have had experience on various ships. When you came back, did you have any developed concept of the kind of education that a young cadet should receive?

Adm. R.: I think that I formed the opinion pretty early that we had to have a broader education with knowledge of the different departments aboard ship, and I think that it became apparent that we needed much more than that to handle our responsibilities with other agencies and just to carry on business.

Q: It had to be more than just a professional school?

Adm. R.: Yes, it had to be more than that, it had to be even more than it was when I was commandant of cadets in the 1950s.

It had broadened a good bit then. They had - I don't think they called it a humanities department, but we were getting into a number of different sorts of things. We were broadening at that time.

Q: I suppose this parallels the Naval Academy itself. It went from a professional trade school, really to a much broader education?

Adm. R.: Yes, but, you know, even when I was commandant there weren't any options at the Academy.

Q: Not any electives?

Adm. R.: No. There was only one direction to go, and the advisory committee, the group that advises the commandant and the superintendent - do you know about them?

Q: No.

Adm. R.: They're a group made up of people from the outside, some people from business, education, and other. I don't think there are any Coast Guard people in it at all. I'm sure there aren't any Coast Guard people in this. Maybe a secretary or something like that. They meet with the commandant once a year, and they came down one time to see me, probably our second meeting, and we got into a discussion about this and I told them that I would like to have them open it up a little bit. I said I'd like to see some cadets go in the direction of management and some go in the direction of engineering. Now there are nine paths. They wanted to do it, I think anyway. But they did that right away, the next year. Now a cadet chooses after one year one of nine directions in which he goes. I think probably they take a lot of common subjects. I guess there are probably some things that go with engineering that also go with oceanography and things of that nature.

Q: But you had begun to think in this larger direction when you were there on the teaching staff?

Adm. R.: Yes. Well, I think there were quite a few people who were thinking that way back then. And, of course, as soon as we got these people from outside, Al Lawrence and Brasefield and those people, there was more and more about it because they —

Q: They came from the academic world?

Adm. R.: Yes, they were teaching in other places where there were no limitations like that and, from the beginning, they were that way. Al Lawrence was sort of a rebel anyway. He didn't like to have people tied down too much to one thing.

Q: Tell me a little more about the third job you had, which was the assistant athletic coach.

Adm. R.: At the Academy?

Q: Yes, in the 1930s.

Adm. R.: By that time Johnnie Merriman had arranged a pretty good schedule. WE played a schedule of about seven games a year in football, and I think around sixteen games in basketball. The baseball schedule was always kind of a problem because the cruise always started while other schools were still playing and, of course, weather always interfered with the other end of the schedule in baseball. But we had a schedule of about a dozen games in baseball at that time.

Q: Did you have track, cross-country and that?

Adm. R.: No, we didn't have track, though we had swimming and there was some fellow who lived locally in New London who came and taught swimming and did it on his own hook. I guess maybe we had a rifle team, but we didn't have anything else. We didn't have any hockey or anything like that, but Johnnie kept adding things. We had boxing and we had a good boxing team. We had a fine coach. His name was Micky McClernan and he had been a professional boxer at one time. He lives out here in Old Lyme now. He's retired long since, of course. We stayed with boxing for a long time and did very well in it. We had some champions, a few intercollegiate champions. We boxed teams like Syracuse, Navy, and Penn State, teams that were very good in boxing. Yale was on our schedule. Any of the New England schools that had boxing teams we met and we had probably eight or ten meets a year. It was the most successful sport we had at the time.

Q: All cadets had to participate in the sports program, did they?

Adm. R.: Yes, everybody had to take part in them. Then we started an inter-class program about that time for those who couldn't compete with the others, and that later turned into an inter-company, so that the first classmen were playing the second classmen and fourth classmen and so on. That was run sort of in a haphazard way because we didn't have any faculty or any people assigned to the Academy to run it. Johnnie did all he could with it and I got in on it once in a while. I used to go down and referee inter-class basketball games almost every day during the winter. They were roughhouses, too. It was quite a thing. They didn't know what they were doing. They didn't get competent coaches or anything like that, but there were rules that we tried to explain to them. They played a good bit of football along with their basketball, but it was competition and later on they developed an inter-class soccer thing and that became an intercollegiate soccer team, and this Gaston Buron, who was the French teacher, took that on and coached it. They were successful to some extent but not very successful. Anyway, they did get up a program.

By the time I left there in 1938 I think we must have branched out, instead of the three sports, we must have had half a dozen. And, of course, it wasn't long after that that we began thinking about the war. The classes began to get bigger and we began to get more people in.

Q: I take it that by the time you left there the concept of competition in sports and so forth had become a part of the philosophy of education? This was necessary in developing a true cadet?

Adm. R.: Oh, yes. Johnnie Merriman was sitting with the academic board then, but he hadn't been before. He was off by himself in Billard Hall. If they wanted him they'd call on him, but he was included in the doings of the faculty and I think they even went so far at one time as to assign a mark to cadets in their physical education business, and Johnnie was involved very much in that because I think that there might have been some people who were let go from the Academy because of a lack of coordination and inability to handle themselves properly.

Q: Can you make any observation at this point as to the overall effect on the cadet corps, the product as turned out by the Academy? Was it a superior one because of this?

Adm. R.: I'm glad you mentioned that because this was a great help to the young officers who left the Academy. When an officer leaves the Academy and goes to a unit, the unit always has a baseball team or a basketball team or something like that and the junior officer is always the guy who runs it, unless there happens to be somebody who is adept at this particular sport, and this is not often the case.

This, as a matter of fact, was a consideration when they brought Johnnie into the faculty business, the fact that a young officer should be able to have a speaking knowledge of these activities in order to direct the activities when he goes to a unit and coordinate the athletic activities of the enlisted personnel at the unit he's going to. So this was a pretty important consideration at that time.

Q: That's very interesting. Now it does bring forth another question, and that is you said earlier, when you were a cadet there, that you were required to attend church on Sunday morning, the church of your choice. This requirement continued, did it, when you were there on the staff? And what did the authorities think this added to the development and education of a cadet? The fact that he got religious training of some sort in his own church?

Adm. R.: By the time - are we talking about the 1930s now?

Q: Yes.

Adm. R.: Maybe I can't answer that question, then. By that time, though, the faculty would occasionally bring in a minister, a priest, or a rabbi to talk to the cadets about some religious subject. Before that there had been no such thought. Now, during the war, which came shortly after I left there, we acquired a chaplain and we've had chaplains ever since. There are now two, at least, a Catholic and a Protestant. I think, though, the development - well, the idea of this being part of the development of the cadet into an officer, I don't think that that got a lot of thought. At least, it didn't get a lot of thought from me. Admiral Hamlet wasn't there at that time, of course, but he was the commandant in 1936 and he was concerned about things like that. He was so concerned about it that he insisted upon the building of a chapel at the Academy which wasn't done, but his insistence continued while he was commandant and it continued after he retired. Finally, the chapel was built.

Q: The reason I asked that is because I know that in the recent past, when the Supreme Court stepped into the picture and forced the academies to rescind this, the argument offered by the Navy, I know by Admiral Moorer, was that this was a part of the necessary training of a cadet - or midshipman - that he should understand the requirements of his men and was a part of leadership. That was the pitch they made in the courts. I wondered if this was also in the thinking of the Coast Guard, that this was a part of leadership?

Adm. R.: At that time, probably not, although it probably was in the thinking of a guy like Admiral Hamlet, but I hadn't heard it expressed myself. But, you know, during the war many officers held services. I did myself. During the war I had a division of destroyer escorts and we had services at least once a week, and the skipper or the exec or if there was another officer who liked to do it, or I would have a service. We just did it out of a book. But people asked for services, they asked us to have services, and they asked us to have them at times other than the scheduled times. They were scheduled for Sunday morning, on two occasions on Sunday morning, one of them was an early one and one of them was a late one because some people were on watch. I think that maybe during the war people thought more along those lines. They were a little more concerned about what was going to happen to them if they got hit, what happens after that. So I think that it might have developed at that time, this thought, but the thought did develop eventually in the Coast Guard, of course, and is still there.

The chapel I don't think is too well attended. When I was in New London after I retired - no before I retired? this goes back to when I was commandant of cadets, I went to church, to the Episcopal Church, in New London and there were a lot of cadets who attended the services at St. James. They started a Sunday morning breakfast which came after the eight o'clock service, between services, and college girls and cadets would come to this and there'd be as many as thirty-five kids come for doughnuts and things like that and coffee. They had a pretty good time and they formed an association and began meeting in the afternoon or in the evening.

Then when I retired and came back the cadets didn't come any more. They still offered the coffee and the girls from the college, but pretty soon the girls stopped coming, too. The girls wouldn't come if the cadets didn't come, I guess and vice versa.

Interview #2

Admiral Edwin John Roland, U. S. Coast Guard

At his Residence in Old Lyme, Connecticut

Monday morning, 23 February 1976

Interviewer: John T. Mason, Jr.

Q: It is nice to see you on this beautiful day that's emerging from winter, but not quite there yet.

Adm. R.: I'm glad to see you here on such a nice day. It's a beautiful place.

Q: It is indeed.

Adm. R.: It was during 1936 during my first tour of duty at the Academy as an instructor that I made the cruise. In the course of that cruise on the USCG CAYUGA, only one ship made the cruise. The first class was a small class so we were able to take everybody at that time. There were only about 40 in the first class and the other class wasn't large enough to need another ship. So we did it all on one ship.

We visited ports in Scotland, France, and Spain. Then as we were crossing the Bay of Biscay we were ordered to go into San Sebastian on the north coast of Spain in order to remove some of the embassy from San Sebastian which was the location of the summer embassy. We were informed before we went in there that the revolution had started just a couple of days before. But we arrived and there was a revolution on that we could see from the ship.

Q: It was centered in that part of Spain, wasn't it?

Adm. R.: Yes, they were very active around there. There were a few small Spanish ships lying off the coast right there that were firing into the countryside. They weren't firing into the city but they were firing behind the city. You could see the explosions in the hills where these things were hitting. It looked like just countryside and I don't know what the purpose of their firing was.

Q: On whose side were they?

Adm. R.: They were on the government side, the communistic side. We put a couple of officers ashore of whom I was one. Another one was a lieutenant commander named Morris Jones. We hunted up the embassy and were quite thrilled by our trip through the streets to find the place because the streets were pretty well deserted. But there were people looking out all the windows and there were guns inside all over the place. People were carrying guns.

Q: What kind of transportation did you have?

Adm. R.: We were walking. We made some inquiries. Morris Jones could speak a little Spanish and he made some inquiries. We found the embassy. They were willing to go all right, except the Ambassador was not there. He was at a place called Fuenterrabia which was farther east in Spain on the French border.

So we met up with these people and we would remove them. They arranged for a truck and put things in it. Their people came down to the ship and they unloaded the embassy and locked it up.

Q: They moved under the protection of the American flag, did they?

Adm. R.: Yes. So we got them aboard and we sent a dispatch to Washington and told them what had happened and said that we were headed farther down the coast in order to get into Fuenterrabia and find the Ambassador.

Q: How many of the staff members came on board?

Adm. R.: We had probably about 25 people, I think, altogether. They probably didn't have everybody there in the summer on the sea, but there were about 25 people.

Q: This, together with the cadets, must have crowded your ship.

Adm. R.: Oh yes, but our run to France wasn't very far. We would do it in about 12 hours or so.

So we got underway and we went to France and unloaded these

people. I'm trying to remember the name of the port now, but it's the farthest south, a resort in France where it joined Spain. We put these people ashore in our own boats. They were met by Americans there in the consulate, I suppose, and taken care of. Then we went back and some people went ashore and went down to this place which was not on the coast but farther down. I was not one of those. But these people saw the Ambassador and he said he was not going to leave. He said, "This thing is going to be over in a couple of days. These people haven't got a chance against the government. This thing won't last more than a day or two." He said Franco didn't have a chance.

So we went back - these people came back to the ship and we reported that to Washington. They said to insist to the Ambassador that he must leave and if you need to, take him out of there.

Q: Take him by force. And the Ambassador was whom?

Adm. R.: Claude G. Bowers. So our people went back again and saw him and explained the situation. It wasn't necessary to carry him out. He said, "Well, if they feel that way, all right, I'll go with you."

So he came with us and he then stayed with us for over a month.

Q: He stayed on board.

Adm. R.: He stayed on board and reported to Washington that he was going to for the purpose of going to the various ports that we would go to to pick up refugees and see what the situation was.

We then headed to Bilbao, which was the first place that we had any business at, and our business there was to meet up with a couple of American battleships that were also making midshipman cruise in Europe. They had come in there to meet us in order to get our cadets and take them back to the United States. They didn't need two battleships to do it but two battleships came in any way. I guess they were curious, too.

We had a pretty interesting time. We went into the inner harbor and the battleships had to stay outside the breakwater. This, of course, made it easier for us to unload our cadets and their gear because the weather was bad. It took a couple of days really to accomplish this but we did eventually get our cadets aboard. In the meantime, we were visited by many volunteers from the battleships who wanted to have a bottle of beer with us, since we had the beer and they didn't.

But this was accomplished and the battleships left immediately. All our cadets went on one battleship and the other battleship went down to Gibraltar. That one that had our cadets aboard went back to the United States.

Q: Your cadets must have had quite a thrill at this whole episode.

Adm. R.: Oh, the cadets were having the time of their lives. They liked that ervolution, I think.

But while we were in Bilbao, we could see groups of people ashore and these were people who were on the government side. They were drilling. They were young people in their teens, you know, and all carrying guns of various kinds. I suppose some of them might have been wooden guns, but anyway, they were marching up and down on the docks and in the streets.

The Consul in Bilbao invited the captain and a couple of officers to come up and see him in this consulate and have lunch with him. I was one of those officers. We went in in our own boat to the dock and we were met by a car which was an armored car. We got into the armored car and drove through the streets. There were people all over with guns. We didn't see any shooting at the time but there were people all around who were carrying guns. Hardly any did not have guns.

We got to the consulate and went in and had our lunch. The trip was uneventful for us except for seeing the sights that we saw along the way.

Q: Was the Consul General apprehensive? Was he to be evacuated too?

Adm. R.: No. He intended to stay. There wasn't any actual fighting in Bilbao at that time, but they were preparing for it.

So we finished our lunch and talked about taking refugees and arranged. He was already gathering refugees.

Q: American citizens?

Adm. R.: American citizens, yes. Later we cooperated with others, particularly the British, but we took out some French, too. We took out their people. But the first load we took out from Bilbao was made up entirely of Americans as I remember. We took a boatload aboard the next day. We took them back and unloaded them in France in the same place where we had taken the embassy. The place is St. Jean de Luz.

Then we returned and went farther out. There were a few more ports out along that north coast. One of them was Vigo. The others were small ports, I don't remember the names, but there was a Consul in each one. They were gathering these refugees in the meantime and we picked them up when we got there. In the meantime, of course, we still had the Ambassador aboard. He was taking part in all these things except he didn't go to lunch with us at the consulate. I don't know why that was but he didn't.

Then we continued doing this, running back and forth between all these ports from the French border out to the place where the coast turns south. It runs west along the Bay of Biscay and then it turns south.

Q: That's where you get to Coruna.

Adm. R.: Coruna is around the corner. We did get there later on but we didn't go there for I think it must have been two or three weeks before we finally did get to Coruna. We had been to Coruna, as a matter of fact, as part of our cruise beforehand.

Q: And then the Spanish naval base is just up a bit from Coruna.

Adm. R.: We continued to do this for probably a month and a half or two months. We spent a lot of time in Bilbao and of course we carried a lot of them in the beginning. From then on it was in dribbles and we never had more than 15 or 20 aboard in the last part of our operation there.

Q: As a total approximately how many?

Adm. R.: About 580.

Q: 580 people you rescued. Now this is a Coast Guard Rescue Service with a twist, isn't it?

Adm. R.: Yes, but the Navy was doing the same thing on the south coast, you know. They had a couple of destroyers down there. They may have run into Coruna before we did, too. But anyway, we did eventually get around to Coruna and took some from there. But in the last part of our stay we were in the port of Bilbao most of the time. There were ships of other nations there -- British, German, French, and Italian. We saw a lot of them because we were the only one with movies. I think

I never said this before. They all visited us every night so we saw a lot of them.

On one occasion there was a German cruiser named the KOLN, and she was there all the time that we were there. I think, as a matter of fact, she might have been there when we came in. She never got her anchor up; she stayed right there. But there were a couple of German destroyers also operating and they were running back and forth. They were probably doing what we were doing. So we saw them.

One day an airplane flew over. One day we went in to the docks to fuel. We went in in the morning and we took on a load of fuel and then we came back out to our anchorage. That afternoon an airplane came over and dropped half a dozen bombs in the vicinity of the oil dock. This was the first actual shooting that we had seen.

The German cruiser, the KOLN, went to general quarters and fired at this airplane. I think it was identified as an Italian plane. It probably was the type of plane. There may have been Spaniards flying it, of course. That, aside from the shooting that we saw from the patrol vessels that were running up and down the coast, was the actual fighting that we saw.

I understand that there was some, that Bilbao was a pretty hot spot.

Q: Bilbao was under siege, I think, for a long time. Bilbao is in the Basque country.

Adm. R.: Yes, it's in the Basque country. They're against government. They have been opposing Franco I guess ever since.

Then finally, a Navy destroyer came up and relieved us. We then went down to Gibraltar under orders and we stayed in Gibraltar for about ten days, I think, and then came back to the United States. Those of us who were from the Academy were then put ashore and back to our teaching jobs.

Q: Let me ask you. In the history of the Coast Guard, has this sort of a rescue operation been undertaken very frequently?

Adm. R.: No. I am not aware of anything of that nature except of course in Central America and South America and Cuba.

Q: In the Caribbean area.

Adm. R.: Yes, in the Caribbean area. But I don't know of any case of where Coast Guard ships have gone into a foreign country and taken refugees out like that. I suppose the Navy has probably done it on some occasions.

During this period we were operating in the Navy. The ship was transferred to Navy jurisdiction.

Q: Oh, it was. For that particular mission?

Adm. R.: Yes.

Q: What's the reason for that?

Adm. R.: Because I guess the Navy had undertaken the job of getting the refugees out, and apparently didn't have the facilities at the time to take these people out on the north coast. They probably removed many more on the south coast because they did have facilities. They had destroyers and they were using them on the south coast. But they didn't have anything they could spare on the north coast so we were the only ones for a month and a half or so.

Q: When that happened -- when you operate under the aegis of the Navy, are there any technicalities entered into?

Adm. R.: We, from our point of view, there was no difference except that we got dispatches from the Navy instead of from the Coast Guard Headquaters. We didn't get anything from the Coast Guard.

Q: You were just under operational orders of the Navy.

Adm. R.: Yes, we made our reports of fuel consumed, personnel changes, and things like that, to the Coast Guard.

Q: And the Coast Guard paid for them, didn't they?

Adm. R.: And the Coast Guard was paying, yes. We were paid -- there was some kind of a mess about the gold standard at that time and if we were in France, we got $1.69 for every dollar of pay that was due to us, you see. So we usually found it convenient to be in France on pay day. You see, it was where we were when we were actually paid and the money was given to us. We would get a load of refugees and keep them aboard for a while and then take them in on pay day, into that French port. We'd go in and anchor and we'd get $1.69.

That didn't happen in Spain. I suppose because of the upset in their government nobody knew what the money was worth there. At least it wasn't worth $1.69, I know. The same thing continued but it wasn't $1.69, it was maybe $1.19 or something like that.

Q: That was in the British ports.

Adm. R.: Yes. But in the French ports that was a gold mine. We really enjoyed that.

So that episode wound up when we returned to the United States. When we left on the cruise there were about five or six Academy officers aboard the ship who were there as instructors and to stand watches and so on. There were ship's officers who stayed aboard, too. But in order not to crowd officers' quarters, they took some of their officers off. Of those officers from the Academy, we kept two, I guess. I was one and a fellow by the name of Alexander was the other and I think that was all. Just two of us were kept aboard. I was the communications officer on the ship. They didn't want to change the communications officer, I guess. The others went back with the cadets on the battleships.

Q: Your duties must have been augmented, being communications officer. You must have had quite a job then.

Adm. R.: Oh yes, communications was a pretty big job when this started. We were really going at it. We had a very good communications group aboard and we had very good equipment aboard. And we were able to reach the United States at times when the Navy couldn't reach them from their ships. We relayed a good bit of traffic.

We got traffic from Gibraltar that was relayed to us on the north coast so that we could relay it to the United States on a good many occasions. So it kept our communications outfits going.

Q: What codes did you use? The Navy codes?

Adm. R.: We had some common codes. We had some Coast Guard codes but we carried a set of codes that were common to both services. We always did on our ships have codes that were common to the Navy and us. So that's what we used. Codes and ciphers.

In those days, of course, you did it all manually. You sat down with a book. There were no machines to do it for you.

Q: That's why I say you must have been really busy.

Adm. R.: Oh yes, we were. Everybody was involved some in

communications. I mean, the engineers when they were off watch were decoding too. It was an interesting job and I think we did it pretty well. I was awfully proud of our equipment that we were able to get out as well as we could.

There was a good bit of time during the day when we weren't able to make it direct to the United States. But at night we were always right in there.

Q: How did it happen that the Coast Guard equipment was far in advance of that of the Navy?

Adm. R.: I don't know that it was. Maybe it was our location; maybe it was something about our particular antenna system or something of that kind. But our equipment was modern equipment. It wasn't something that had been aboard the ship for a long time. It was modern equipment and good equipment. But I'm sure the Navy had equipment that was as good. On the battleships they must have had stuff that was much better. But they were cluttered up. Communications was a different thing then than it is now. They were cluttered up with a lot of gear, you know, that probably interfered with their communications and we were relatively free of a lot of that stuff. Our armament was a 5-inch gun and a 3-inch gun and a couple of machine guns, and they were well out of the way. We didn't let them interfere with anything.

In '37 and '38 I didn't make the cruise. We had a couple of schooners at the Academy which had formerly been fishing schooners. The Coast Guard had acquired them through the rum business at one time or another and used them for various purposes but finally they ended up at the Academy as training ships. In '37 or '38 we left some of the cadets behind on the cruise and they went to classes during the summer, during part of the week.

On Thursday we would take them aboard the schooners and sail until Sunday and then we went back in and then they would start classes again on Monday. We did that each week. I was assigned to one of those schooners, the CHASE was the name of it, during that time.

Q: Were they speeding up the course or what?

Adm. R.: Yes. There had been additions to the curriculum at that time. I don't recall what they were but there had been additions to the curriculum. There was difficulty in completing the course just in the regular academic part of the year.

Q: So they had to augment it in that way.

Adm. R.: We needed the extra time.

Q: What was the nature of the additions to the curriculum?

Adm. R.: I don't remember what they were but I'm sure that they were additions in the humanities line -- history and things like that. This is when they got in these new instructors whom I mentioned.

Q: The civilians.

Adm. R.: Yes, Al Lawrence came in for that purpose. This is when that happened.

Q: This is the beginning of the broadening of the scope of education.

Adm. R.: Right. It was about at that time that besides history we added economics to the curriculum. We had never had subjects of this kind before then. So we needed the time all right.

And there was another difficulty too. Money was a little scarce at that time and if we had taken everybody, we would have required another ship. And the operation of a ship entered into the budget part of this too. So there was a combination of things. But principally it was the curriculum that caused us to have classes during the summer.

Q: How was that resolved, because that practice didn't continue, did it? To have classes in the summer time?

Adm. R.: No. One of the things that happened, of course, was that eventually the curriculum was handled in such a way that everybody wouldn't study every subject. This -- some things were not required.

Q: They were electives.

Adm. R.: Yes. This happened some time later. But the way it was handled at that time -- it wasn't settled when I left the Academy and it still wasn't settled when the war started. They were still doing this when the war started. By the time the war ended then there were electives and there had been many changes in the curriculum at that time. There wasn't very much in the way of electives but there were some and I think that, too, by that time, they may have given credit to some cadets for studies they had completed outside the Academy. Before, it didn't make any difference if you had studied the subject or not, you still had to take it. This is one factor that contributed -- I'm afraid I don't know all the details of the settling of the thing. But I think that ever since the war, there have always been some cadets who stayed behind and did various things. Some of them as part of their schedule, have visited District offices, bases, air stations, and other activities of the Coast Guard to get practical experience and see . . .

Q: While still enrolled at the Academy.

Adm. R.: While still cadets, yes. They would do this during the summer and make a cruise for part of the summer, you see.

Q: When was the four year term inaugurated?

Adm. R.: The first four year class was the Class of 1934. That class was made up of only about one-half a dozen cadets who had been in the Class of '33 and had been on the verge of flunking out. But instead, the Board made a new class out of them and they graduated in 1934. There were six of them who graduated. From there on, the classes have all been four years except during the war when they shortened it.

Q: Even the four year term in the '30s proved to be not sufficient.

Adm. R.: Yes, it was a four year course when we were holding classes during the summer. I think people were taking a pretty close look at the curriculum at the Academy and I think there may have been some difficulty with accrediting. So they had to add some things. I think the general attitude toward the Coast Guard Academy before all this happened, before the new Academy and the four year course and all. We are in the business of training people to become officers. We are not interested in making them highly educated people. We want them to be officers and we don't think much of their activities and responsibilities outside of carrying out their Coast Guard duties.

Then there began to be a change in this and this caused people to say, we need to speak better English, we need to know more about what has happened in the past in this country in order for them to understand what to do now and to look ahead to the future.

Q: You need to have good, educated men.

Adm. R.: Yes, right. This was going on in all this time. There have been many looks at the mission of the Coast Guard Academy. It was never written up until Admiral Hamlet wrote it up when he was Superintendent of the Academy. Have you ever seen the mission of the Coast Guard Academy?

Q: No.

Adm. R.: Well, it remains unchanged. It's now in a brass plaque in the floor of the cadet barracks. I think it's a very broad look. Before, I think the mission had been thought of in terms of getting the number of people each year we need in order to run our ships and other activities.

Q: That was the mission, and then Admiral Hamlet in the early '30s when he was Superintendent at the Academy stated it in these words: "The mission of the U. S. Coast Guard Academy is to graduate young men with sound bodies, stout hearts, and alert minds with a liking for the sea and its lore and with that high sense of honor, loyalty, and obedience which goes with trained initiative and leadership, well grounded in seamanship, the sciences, and the amenities, and strong in the resolve to be worthy of the traditions of commissioned officers in the United States Coast Guard in the service of their country and humanity."

Adm. R.: Since that time, there have been many occasions when the Academic Board and other groups have studied the mission and thought about what they could do about it in order to make it more definitive. But after each of these groups had finished, and had written a longer mission and a more specific one, they always decided that this original one included these things, perhaps not specifically, but the thing was written so well that it is impressive and it has continued to impress the people at the Academy and it still is the mission of the Academy. And that little framed statement that I handed you now hangs in every cadet's room.

I served on the group, when I was Commandant of Cadets, that specifically studied this matter and we worked for a couple of months. There were a half-dozen of us who did all sorts of things and we finally wound up with another thing which was in completely different words and a much more specific thing. We recommended that the new one become the model of the mission of the Academy. But it never did become because I don't think the Superintendent agreed with this and our work went into a waste paper basket somewhere, I believe.

I do believe that that is a very well written thing. It was written by a man who was himself a well-educated man, and a very broadly educated man, and a man who took careful consideration of the thing. I think he was behind a lot of the changes in curriculum at the Academy. Of course, he left in

1932 and became Commandant. So a new Superintendent came in at that time. But I know that he kept his finger on the Academy all the time.

One of his great ambitions was to have a chapel built at the Academy. This was finally accomplished, much to his like -- it wasn't until 1952 that it was accomplished but he had been pushing for a chapel at the Academy all during that time.

Q: Admiral, if I may be permitted a comment. I might say that I knew Admiral Hamlet well and liked him very much and this is indeed a reflection of the man himself, very simply a reflection of him and the way he lived and the way he thought.

Well, Sir, in 1938 you left the Academy and you decided to go to Florida and take up an assignment.

Adm. R.: Yes, I became the skipper of a 165-foot patrol boat, the NEMESIS, stationed at St. Petersburg. Our purpose was, of course, the standard purpose of the Coast Guard, search and rescue, but we did a lot of law enforcement. There was a lot of alien smuggling going on down there. There were a lot of Chinese being brought in.

The coast of Florida is an ideal place for activities like that because of all the indentations. The west coast of Florida down beyond Ft. Meyers, down in there. There's a little place just north of Tampa Bay where St. Petersburg is called Tarpon Springs. That was a sponge fishing port and there were many, many sponge fisherman going and coming and they were quite a motley group, I guess you might say. There were hardly any real Americans among them. They didn't speak English and you couldn't tell whether they were really sponge fishermen or whether they were being smuggled in.

So this was a good place and it was a place where we had a lot of activity. We were frustrated a good bit by some of the things that happened because we would seize a boat and bring it in because we were convinced that these people had been loaded aboard this sponge boat from a Cuban boat. Then they would let these people go.

Q: Were they mostly Orientals?

Adm. R.: More than half were. There were a lot of Greeks among the sponge fishermen but quite a mixture of nationalities.

On one occasion when we were on patrol, we observed the sponge fleet which usually operated in a group. They would go to one place and they would be operating there. And we observed a number of Cuban fishing vessels among them. So we made inquiries and we knew that there had been contact between the vessels because we had seen them. We boarded all of the boats -- the Cubans and the sponge fishermen -- and we came to the conclusion that -- and we found people aboard the Cuban boats that we were quite certain were not legitimately there. They were there for the purpose of being brought to the United States from Cuba.

So we seized all of the Cuban boats and we seized 32 of them, and notified the District Commander that we had done so and asked for instructions.

So they sent out a group of immigration officers who boarded all these boats and interviewed all the people. It wound up with our keeping six of the boats and letting the others go. They took them in and four of the boats, I think, were forfeited and the people were convicted of smuggling. The foreigners, I guess, were deported -- the people that were brought in. But the people who ran the boats were convicted of smuggling.

Q: Were there any repercussions with the Cuban government as a result of this?

Adm. R.: Not as far as we were concerned.

Q: That was something the Coast Guard didn't have to handle.

Adm. R.: No, it was an immigration matter. We were acting for the immigration people, of course.

On another occasion, we were notified that there was a Cuban vessel hovering a couple of miles off the coast, south of Ft. Meyers. We were on patrol at the time, not far off, and so we headed for the place. When we got there, we identified the boat. It was a sloop, a sailing vessel. It didn't have any power in it. It was probably 40 feet long, not a big vessel. As we approached it, it got underway -- it was at anchor but they got up their anchor and got underway and headed in toward the beach and they sailed it right up on the beach. We couldn't get in there because of the shoaled water. We had notified our District Commander what we were doing, you know, what the situation was. So the immigration people were there when they got there.

The crew of the boat was three Cubans, it turned out, and they never caught them. They had anchored the boat and got in a boat and went ashore. It turned out later that they had had a rendezvous with somebody ashore who was to pick these people up and they landed. The guy didn't show up so they went in to look this fellow up and that's when we came along. The people who were still aboard who were the people that were being smuggled and were not the crew of the vessel and probably didn't know anything about sailing a boat. They didn't want to get caught out there in this boat so they got the thing underway and sailed in into the beach. They scrambled ashore, but the immigration people were in the vicinity and they caught all of them, I guess. There were about a dozen of them. I think they sent them back to Cuba.

The vessel by that time was carried up by the tide and the seas and the wind and so on and was high and dry. So we were ordered to pull it off. So we did. It was an old beat up vessel. It wasn't worth considering but anyway we finally got it off. It took about a week to get it off. We practically had to dig a ditch to get it out. We had a big, long tow line, you know, on the

NEMESIS. We had an anchor down to the NEMESIS and we'd haul on this thing, you know. When the tide would get in, we'd haul on it and we finally got the thing off and towed it into Tampa where there was an immigration office and turned it over to them. The vessel was forfeited but probably the wood wouldn't burn, it was so waterlogged. It was rotten.

But there was a great deal of smuggling out there in the gulf. We knew it and our schedule was a five day patrol and then ten days in port. Then when we were in port somebody else was on our station patrolling. There were three vessels. One of them came from Key West and one from Pascagoula I think, or some place like that.

Q: Was this smuggling operation of human beings at that point of time only? Or was it something that had been going on?

Adm. R.: I think it had been going on for a long time.

Q: Now it was centering around the sponge fishing industry. Let me ask about that. I understand that in the Bahamas the sponge fishing was practically wiped out in the early '30s or the middle '30s by some sort of disease which destroyed the sponges, but this had not reached over this far?

Adm. R.: No, there was a lot of sponge fishing off Tarpon Springs and there was a lot of sponge fishing further down between where Naples is now and Key West in a bay in there. That's a good sponge fishing area right now, I think. It was just a few years ago. They had sponge wars down there. People from other areas were coming in there taking sponges and the people who lived there didn't want them in there. They were shooting at one another and everything.

There was a lot of such activity maybe about 15 years ago.

My tour of duty was ended in December of 1940. In the last part, almost the last year -- you see, I went there in '38. I went to that ship not as commanding officer but executive officer and then a few months later the skipper left and I then became commanding officer.

In 1939 we were ordered into the shipyard in Jacksonville along with other vessels of this same kind and we were armed for antisubmarine warfare. They put depth charges aboard. While I was still aboard the ship they were engaged in putting sonar aboard, too, which we had not had before.

Q: This was after the outbreak of war in Europe.

Adm. R.: Yes. The opening had been made in the hull for this sonar gear but it had been plated over. When my tour of duty ended, we were involved in neutrality patrol. Our schedule had changed by then. We were out most of the time and involved in patroling in the straits of Florida mostly, checking vessels coming and going, identifying them, and reporting them. We were involved in that and waiting for the sonar to arrive at the shipyard because these things were pretty scarce about that time. They were waiting to get these things and then they would put them in. But we had added some guns. These ships, of course, weren't very big and they had nothing aboard them before but 30 caliber machine guns and these were changed to 20mm guns, and depth charges and all the gear that goes with them, and were just waiting for the sonar gear.

Q: Did you have to augment your crews?

Adm. R.: We didn't at the time but we did later. The crew of that ship was 32 men.

Q: What was her capability as a ship? Her speed and so forth?

Adm. R.: Her top speed was about 15 knots and she would cruise at about 12 and her range was probably 1500 miles. So she was not much; she was a coastal vessel. We had a lot of those -- I say a lot of them -- we probably had about 20 of them. We acquired them in the '30s during the depression. This was probably part of the government spending program, making jobs in the shipyards.

We had those ships and we got our Secretary class ships then too -- the 327-footers, the Campbell-class, if you have heard of them. This all came in the '30s and was a big boost in the morale of the Coast Guard because the depression had hit us so hard, you see. We had lost personnel. Our ships were pretty well beat up by that time. When prohibition was repealed, we turned back the destroyers we were manning. We had 25 of those and those went back into mothballs.

Q: Were they the four-stackers?

Adm. R.: They were four-stackers, most of them. Some of them were broken deck four-stackers from the first World War and the others, about half of them I guess, were flush deck but four-stackers and they were built after the first World War. They were built in the '20s. They were good ships and we could get 30 knots out of them on our full speed trials. They were good vessels but they were pretty short-legged. They didn't have much range.

Anyway, we lost those with the repeal. And our other ships were getting old so this build-up with these 165-footers and with the Secretary class ships which were indeed good ships, very good, was a big thing for the Coast Guard and a big boost to the morale. We had lost a lot of personnel by then. By the end of the '30s we probably had about 9,000 people left in the Coast Guard. During prohibition we had built up quite a bit.

Q: When you began to take over new stations on the neutrality patrol, were you operating under the aegis of the Navy again?

Adm. R.: Yes, the Coast Guard went into the Navy during that year, during the year that we began that, which was probably '40.

Lock, stock, and barrel we went into the Navy, all of our ships. I guess they considered the Coast Guard Commandant as a sort of corps commander and he still was directing our operations but we were under the Navy.

This was Admiral Russell R. Waesche and he spent a good bit of his time in the Navy office at that time. He was consulted a good bit on things having to do with port security and he was directly involved. He was responsible to the Chief of Naval Operations.

Q: What happened to the smuggling patrols and that sort of thing when you went under the Navy?

Adm. R.: There were still some small vessels that continued to do this. We had a number of 125-foot patrol boats that were built for the prohibition business that were still in operation that continued that sort of thing. As far as our patrols down off Florida -- as far as they were concerned, we didn't do any of that. We had no time for it. We still were involved in some search and rescue operations but that was mainly because of the humanitarian attitude of the people who were running things. We were allowed to do this. We would leave a neutrality patrol for a search and rescue deal.

But the neutrality patrol was our primary responsibility. When somebody was in distress, of course, we went to them.

Q: What kind of ships were you observing on your neutrality patrols? Was it tankers and that sort of thing?

Adm. R.: There were lots of tankers and there were lots of ordinary freighters.

Q: Coming out of the Gulf of Mexico?

Adm. R.: Coming out of the Gulf of Mexico and also coming out from the Caribbean and rounding that way, coming from Mexico and places like that.

Q: Did you observe any submarines?

Adm. R.: No. We didn't observe any. During that time, the Navy assigned some submarines to Key West. Before that, I think I said in our last interview, the yard was built up at Key West but there was one officer there and he had a group of radiomen who operated his radio station and the rest of them were just civilians who kept house around the Navy yard.

But they did actually assign submarines down there at that time and other vessels, too. And of course, more men were assigned for other duties down there then too. So Key West built up fairly rapidly when this neutrality patrol began.

Q: Were your men sent somewhere to sonar school or special schools to learn how to operate some of the new ordnance?

Adm. R.: Well, as a matter of fact, one of those schools was started at Key West. We sent people to school. When I left that ship, we didn't have any sonarmen in that ship and the Coast Guard didn't have that many either. We had a lot of them in School but, of course, we didn't have the sonar gear when I left so we had no particular need for them.

But we had men from our crew who were in the school who would return to the ship when they had had whatever training they got. We were at a loss for a lot of things at that time. We had one gunner's mate aboard that ship and no sonarmen at all. We didn't have a signalman. Our quartermasters as part of their qualifications it was required that they be able to signal with flags and they had to be able to do some blinking, too. But they didn't have to be that good at it.

So we were involved in an awful lot of training at that time. We were always signaling. And many times when we were trying to identify a ship at night, we would be doing it by blinker. They would come back at us -- they would get their radioman up there, you know, and he would come. Nobody knew what was going on at all so we would send for one of our radiomen to pick them up and receive this thing. We were really in a pretty tough position.

Q: Did any of these ships you were reporting on resent this activity?

Adm. R.: Yes, there were lots of complaints. There were lots of complaints made - not to us but to other people - that their operations were being interfered with by these challenges.

We never stopped one at all. All we did was identify them.

Q: Were you under orders to stop under certain circumstances?

Adm. R.: No. We had no such orders. I suppose if there had been circumstances that we thought would require our boarding the ship to determine what it was about, I suppose we would have done it. And we wouldn't have hesitated to do it with an American ship. But many of these ships were foreign ships and actually we were in international waters. If they had thumbed their noses at us, I suppose we couldn't have done anything but throw a big bluff.

Most of the ships were put into the United States. Most of the ships we identified were coming out of - probably the tankers, and there were a lot of tankers - a lot of tankers were coming out of Beaumont and Houston and other places along there and were heading for ports on the East Coast.

There were foreign ships. I don't recall any foreign tankers, but there might have been some foreign tankers. If they were foreign, they would have been heading for their home ports which might have been anywhere.

Q: Well, you were getting nearer to the conflict, weren't you?

Adm. R.: We were and at least it was putting us on the job. You know it was a pretty free and easy life before. The five days in port and ten days at sea was really a pretty soft deal. At times we thought that was pretty hard but later on it looked like it was a pretty soft deal and actually it was. It was a pretty pleasant life in the service. We had our activities and we would get called out some time during in port periods for search and rescue jobs or other things. But we didn't live a hard life in the service.

Q: Where was your family?

Adm. R.: They were in St. Petersburg. These pictures here were all done in St. Petersburg.

I left there then in December and went to New Orleans as the communications officer for the District, the 8th District. When I arrived there, I found that my orders also made me assistant communications officer to the naval district. So I had two bosses down there: my own district commander and the Naval District Commandant.

Q: Tell me about the communications set-up because that became a very strategic one, didn't it?

Adm. R.: The Coast Guard communications set-up?

Q: Yes.

Adm. R.: We had a main traffic station in Galveston and another one on Lake Ponchartrain. We had a communications center in our district office which was by that time pretty well supplied with teletypes and we were getting come coding machines and things like that. We set up, a little after I got there, a room which was taken from somebody else and we kept track of ship movements in the Gulf.

Whenever a ship was reported by the neutrality patrol or by any other means, it was reported to us and we would plot it on our board. The whole side of the wall was a big chart. We had them all plotted on there, showing in what direction they were going and what speed they were making, where from and where bound. This was put under the communications officer. It got to be a bigger job than the communications officer job pretty soon, of course, so another officer was sent there eventually before I left and took that over.

When we got into the war, which of course wasn't too long after -- I got there in December of '40 and in December of '41 the war started. We were all called into the office at the time. There wasn't much for us to do until we were all called in anyway. We talked it over and we were brought to the realization that now we were in a different situation and there was a war going on.

About that time a submarine was reported down off the Texas

coast, down off Port Aransas. There was a submarine all right. I don't think it did anything except scout the area or something like that because it didn't shoot or sink any ships and there were plenty of ships around.

But I was told by the District Commander to go down to Port Aransas where we had a lifeboat station on the beach, which had been transformed sometime past to a lookout station for activities of submarines or anything else that might show up. So I said, "Yes, Sir. What shall I do?"

He said, "Never mind. Just go down there. When you get there, let me know and tell me what the situation is."

So I went down and I had a hell of a time getting there. I went in my own car and there were places along the way where they weren't allowing cars to go through. I was in uniform but they wouldn't let me go through anyway. After a while I got it cleared up so I did go through and I got down to Port Aransas and got out to the lifeboat station to see what was going on. They said that they had seen a submarine. There was then a lot of activity going on.

The Navy had that air station at Corpus Christi and there was a great deal of activity going on there. I stayed at the lifeboat station for a couple of days and then I was directed to come back. I guess there wasn't anybody doing my job back at the office so . . .

Q: You had to go back and report to the District Commandant what you had seen.

Adm. R.: Oh yes, I told them what I had seen. I told them that I hadn't been allowed through the road. I guess they cleared those things up a little later.

During this time, too, we were beginning to take in boats to be used for whatever purpose the Navy required.

Q: You requisitioned civilian boats then.

Adm. R.: Civilian boats. A fellow named T. Y. Awalt, who was a captain, and I were the first ones to be assigned to this job and we were very busy inspecting these boats. We were taking them in, crew and all.

Q: Did you go around to various anchorages and look over the . . .

Adm. R.: Whenever we went somewhere, we would go because a boat had been offered. Then we would go to see a specific boat. We took in a lot of boats. In the time that I was involved in that, which was maybe six months, we probably took in 60 or 75 boats.

Q: Were they all offered or were some requisitioned?

Adm. R.: In the beginning, they were only offered. Later on, we did take some in that -- from getting to know the boats we knew that there were some that looked good and they would be useful to us. There weren't too many of those but there were a few of them.

And we took those too.

In the case of those that were offered, we usually also got the owner and the crew with them. They would come along with them. They were made temporary reservists and we would give them an appropriate rating to serve only in the boats, and to operate the boats.

Q: And then the owner would stay with the boat.

Adm. R.: They would stay aboard. We'd make them get a uniform and they would stay there. Then we would put some other service people aboard too, who were not temporary reserves, because the authority of the temporary reserves was limited. So we had to put regular people aboard too who had authority to make arrests and board other boats and things like that.

Q: What kind of compensation was provided for these people?

Adm. R.: They were paid in the same way that a regular member of the Coast Guard was paid, according to the rating that we gave them. And of course, the maintenance of the boat -- we picked that up and their fuel, and so on.

There were a few people who offered to operate and maintain their own boats and pay their own fuel, too. We accepted such offers on the condition that we could put our people aboard.

Q: Was there some kind of a formal contractual arrangement?

Adm. R.: Yes, and we guaranteed in the contract that we would return the boat in the end. When we were finished with it and didn't need it any more, we'd return it in as good condition as that in which we received it. This, of course, led us to an awful lot of trouble at the very end because we did a lot of offering and we added a lot of things to those boats. We'd stick on the guns and all sorts of things. In not many cases did the boat turn up to be as good as it was. We had much trouble at the end of the war.

Q: What about those that were requisitioned? Were they compensated?

Adm. R.: Yes. We acquired those things for the government eventually and people were paid for them. We acquired a lot of very good vessels such as Vincent Astor's yacht through Astor's yard. Was it Normahal?

Q: The Normahal. Vincent Astor's.
You did that in addition to your communications duties?

Adm. R.: Yes. I did a lot of communicating at night.

Q: And in the last six months that you were there you were actually in war and that was a hot area, was it not, for the operation of German submarines?

Adm. R.: We did get more people but a lot of the people we got were right off the streets. We got a fellow. We went to see his boat. He was a man who owned a hotel over in Pensacola. We went over to inspect his boat and he was a young fellow, probably 35 years old. He wanted us to take his boat and he wanted to come with it and he said he wanted to do more. So he came over to the office and discussed the matter with other people who were on a higher level than I was. They took him in and made him a lieutenant, junior grade, and they sent him to some schools and he turned out to be a real good officer. Billy Harbison. He turned out to be a fine officer and he served for a good many years. He came in as a temporary reservist and then he became a regular reservist and he stayed right on. I think when he finally got out he was a commander. By that time, he had left the district and had served aboard ships and all kinds of things. He served on a DE at one time.

We got a lot of very good people. But we got some that weren't worth getting, too.

Q: Would you, for the sake of the record at this point, distinguish between the temporary reservist and a reservist?

Adm. R.: The temporary reservist was a fellow who, as the thing was finally set up, could come in under a lot of circumstances. He could come in to serve part-time, he could keep his regular job, and then serve as a guard on the dock for a certain number of hours during the night. He could be paid or not paid, and he was at the mercy of the people who were running it. He could be dropped as a temporary reservist at any time and I don't think there had to be a reason either. You know, if you just didn't need them. You could say, we don't need you any more. So as a temporary reservist you were finished.

A regular reservist was on the same basis as a regular member of the Coast Guard, except that he could be put on inactive duty. But he still retained his status as a reservist if he was put on inactive duty. And he was subject to all of the same regulations and requirements as a regular member of the Coast Guard. He was subject to all the discipline and orders and all that.

Q: But a temporary reservist was also subject to discipline when he was actually at work.

Adm. R.: When he was actually at work, yes.

Q: When did it come into existence?

Adm. R.: It started in Philadelphia and I think it started in early 1942. It might have started a little earlier than that, I think it probably did. It probably started in '41. I know it did, because we took in some people when I was doing this boat thing. We took in people as temporary reservists. I would say that it started in the last half of '41.

Q: This was due to the expediency of war.

Adm. R.: Yes. The port security thing made a big thing out of this. The Coast Guard was given the job of port security. This required security measures on the water and also on the docks, and we needed large numbers of people. So we got these people that were working part-time and there were just thousands and thousands of them.

Q: These were men that were not young enough for the draft?

Adm. R.: In some cases they were people who were not eligible for the draft for other reasons, you see. There were quite a few of them that were young. But they might have had jobs that exempted them or they might have had physical conditions that would have exempted them.

Q: So the Coast Guard had to lower its standards then.

Adm. R.: Oh yes. As far as temporary reservists were concerned they all got in if they had two legs. And we had some that had members missing. I don't know what the final number was. When I left my job in New Orleans, I went to Washington and I was in charge of enlisted personnel. So I had some connection with this business of temporary reservists. When I left I think we must have had a couple hundred thousand temporary reservists.

Q: Do they continue as a classification during all of World War II?

Adm. R.: Yes, I think so. But it did change. Toward the end as we built up, the Coast Guard itself got up to about 170,000. When we got enough people trained, with proper physical characteristics, and people that we could direct to do things and depend on them to do it, we let a lot of these temporary reservists go. So I don't know how many there were at the end of the war but I'm sure there were some.

There was a fellow named Marks who started the thing. He started it in Philadelphia in the port security end of it, anyway, and he was put in charge of it and was brought to Washington eventually. He was made a captain, a temporary reserve captain. He, in the beginning I think, ran the whole thing and then later on somebody else came in and took over. But he stayed on and I think he was in Washington during most of the war. He had a business in Philadelphia, too.

Q: Talking again about communications as they operated out of New Orleans when you were there in '42, you might say something about the background of the Coast Guard in terms of communications and their traditions in that area.

Adm. R.: The Coast Guard has always had a good communications system, probably necessitated by the need that came up during prohibition. But anyway, every district had at least one fairly good-sized radio station with the capability of transmitting and receiving over great distances, and at least one communications center which was well manned and operated on a 24-hour basis. This had been going on for a number of years, during all of the time that I served in the Coast Guard. We always had had good communications.

Q: The very nature of Coast Guard duties demanded this sort of thing.

Adm. R.: That's true. When we were involved in search and rescue, communications became important because it was necessary that we communicate with other units, Coast Guard or not, in order to get them involved in some of our searches, and tell them what the situation was.

There have been quite a few rescues at sea that have been accomplished by other vessels because the vessels were directed by Coast Guard units which were involved in the search and while running down certain leads, weren't able to run down other leads and asked merchant ships to run down these leads. There have been quite a few rescues made that way.

I think the Coast Guard has over a period of years developed the capability of using civilian facilities in carrying over its duties.

Q: What special efforts were made to train communicators because of the need for them in the Coast Guard?

Adm. R.: You mean during the war?

Q: I mean as a general rule.

Adm. R.: Our radiomen went to Navy schools. We trained our radiomen in Navy schools. Our officers were also trained in Navy schools in communications principles and so on. A good many of our officers later on, as our system got bigger, were brought up within the system.

For instance, I never went to a Navy school but I was very familiar with our own communications system and with the Navy communications system, too, because of my connection with it aboard ship as a communications officer and then by the time I got to be the communicator in New Orleans, I had had a lot of experience in communications aboard ship and in other capacities ashore too. You don't have to be a communicator to get involved in communications aboard ship. The commanding officer is probably more involved than the communicator is.

When I went into my job as communicator in New Orleans, I guess I had in the office with me in the Communications Center about six, maybe eight radiomen. By the time I left, which was a year and a half later [May of '42], I probably had about 30 involved in the Center which had expanded a good bit by then and in the ship control center, the place where we kept track of the movements of the ships. Then, of course, there were some other people there who were plotters and file keepers and so on.

But we grew awfully fast and we had a hard time getting

trained people and had to do a lot of the training ourselves on the job.

Q: It was an awfully hot spot.

Adm. R.: There was a lot going on. It's possible it was the same in other places too. But there was a lot going on down there.

Q: That coastal traffic was the target of so many German submarine attempts.

Adm. R.: Yes, of course, and that straits of Florida was such a narrow place, you know. And everything going into the Gulf, almost everything, goes through there, and leaving the Gulf goes through there. But they can go down around Cuba but that adds so much to a voyage that in time of war you don't want to waste that time.

Q: Did you have any special contact or liaison with the Navy commander in San Juan who was particularly concerned about this whole traffic and the submarines?

Adm. R.: No, I didn't directly. I guess that such communications would have been with the naval district commander in New Orleans, that was 15 down there. We had an air station down there and we had a couple of ships assigned in that area. But Puerto Rico in the beginning at least wasn't a big area of operations for us. I expect that such communications from the Commandant of the 15th Naval District and others in New Orleans would have been through the Naval District. He would have passed the word through him.

I don't think we did much in the way of direct communication with them. We might have done a little, but not much. Of course, we handled a lot of Navy communications but the Navy Communications Center in New Orleans was also hooked up to our radio station. So our radio station would handle traffic that I would not see in my office. I would see anything that came through our Communication Center but it could get to our radio station without going through my communications center.

Q: In May of '42, as we said, you left New Orleans to take up quite a different tour of duty, quite a different experience in the realm of personnel.

Adm. R.: Which I had never had anything to do with before.

Q: How did you happen to get that particular assignment?

Adm. R.: I have no idea. I just got a set of orders and went. I think it was because the Chief of Personnel who was a man named Jiggs Donahue. He knew me because he was a football fan and he had attended a lot of games that I had played in, so we knew one another.

Anyway, he was the Chief of Personnel and when I went to

Washington I was assigned to Enlisted Personnel Assignments, it was called at that time and that's all it was, just assignments. We didn't keep the records. We did have to do with some of the activities in connection with promotions and so on, but the job that I went to was Enlisted Personnel Assignments.

Q: Were they assigned as individuals or en bloc or what?

Adm. R.: By the time I got there they were doing it en bloc. They had been individuals usually.

Q: You said that the man in charge of that division was a Lieutenant Commander Allison.

Adm. R.: He had at his desk a warrant officer, a chief petty officer who was a Chief Yeoman, and one civilian, and that was all. But his staff hadn't enlarged at all during this time, during the time since the war began, and he wasn't a man who would try to get any more.

When I went into his office to report to him, he had a stack of personnel folders alongside his chair that must have been that high.

Q: That must have been three feet high.

Adm. R.: There must have been 400 of them. They were the personnel records of first class petty officers in the Coast

Guard who had been recommended for promotion to chief. This was at a time when they needed chiefs. He had these things there and his desk was just stacked with papers. I don't know how he could tell where anything was. And every once in a while he would reach over and take one of these things and put it on top of the pile and he'd open it up and look at it and he'd look all through it. After he got finished he would take a piece of paper and he would write on it whether he recommended that this man should be promoted. Then he'd send that out, put it in his outgoing basket and then he started working on all this other stuff. After a while, he'd get another one of these and in the meantime, six more would come in.

Q: I can see why you were assigned there.

Adm. R.: He was pretty old. He retired not long afterwards. At that time you had to retire when you were 64 and he was pretty near 64 and he showed his age. He had been in the life saving service at one time and had been brought in in 1915 when the life saving service came into the Coast Guard. So that's his source.

Anyway, I relieved him.

Q: May I interrupt with a question at this point? It might be a good place for you to comment on officers who are capable of serving in peacetime and yet when war comes, they are really not so capable.

Adm. R.: I think most people when the thing is thrust at them will adapt to the situation. They'll improve their methods or they will get more people to help them or they'll do something in order to take care of themselves. But there are some who won't do that, who will just go along at their steady pace and do what they can at that pace and just let the work pile up. There were quite a few people like that.

Q: They're more adapted to peacetime endeavors.

Adm. R.: Yes, that's their pace. They set that pace in peacetime and they're not willing to change. In wartime, I found out you can't do it that way. You may not think everything is well reasoned out when you act but at least you act if for no other reason than to get rid of it.

Q: The tempo was changed greatly.

Adm. R.: Anyway, I relieved him. I asked him a lot of questions about what's the job and all that. I really gave up when I relieved him because I don't think he knew what the job was then. He knew what it was when he took it over and he told me that, but this pile of papers -- he said, "Well, I get through them some time."

Q: Meanwhile the whole Coast Guard operation was being held in abeyance.

Adm. R.: Anyway, I did relieve him and I went to see Chief Donahue and said, "This is hopeless. I've got to have more people or I'm not going to be able to handle it in there."

He said, "Okay." So I said "I would like somebody who was connected with personnel who can act on these promotion folders that are alongside my desk. I don't think that I should be doing that anyway. There's too much detail in each folder. Somebody else should be doing it." So he said okay and he named the guy. So I had them take that pile out.

Then after I had been there a short time, they assigned the records to my office too. They sent people. They were mostly the people who were keeping records then, who were civilians. But this was getting to be a big job too. They were getting more people in, some civilians and some military people. About that time we began to get girls -- SPARS.

So we got a lot of those. By the time I left, we had 80 SPARS working in records. We had some of them working in other jobs, too.

Q: They had been trained in Orlando at that time, or was it later?

Adm. R.: They had been trained by the Navy. The first SPARS we got were Navy girls. They were girls who had agreed to come into the Coast Guard, so they shifted. From WAVES they became SPARS.

Q: The Commander of the SPARS was also in the Navy.

Adm. R.: Yes. Dorothy Stratton. We got a lot of them and they were pretty good. They lived in barracks that were just SPAR barracks, you know. I guess they weren't used to that sort of thing. Maybe during training they could do with it but after they got out and went to work, they didn't like them. They never did like these barracks.

Q: Were they over on the mall?

Adm. R.: We had half a dozen places in Washington we rented. We had officers assigned there to keep control of the places. But the girls were escaping and pretty soon they were bringing boys in. We had all kinds of trouble. Gee whiz, they were more problems.

Q: They were very useful as your office workers, were they not?

Adm. R.: Oh yes, sure they were. I was so happy with the work they did and their willingness. They were in there to do their part. There were a few sour apples among them, but most of them were very good.

I had a lieutenant who was assigned to me, a woman. She came from the University of Wisconsin and she was pretty close to Dorothy Stratton. Anyway, she was assigned to my office and she was a marvel. She was just great.

Q: Were the SPARS inspired by the same idea that the WAVES were? That they came to release a man from a desk job to be an active participant?

Adm. R.: Yes, I think so. I think that was taught to them. And of course, the ones that we got from the Navy were really brought up that way. We opened up our own recruit training station down in Florida. I think it was in one of the hotels down there. And of course, we trained officers up at the Academy, the Coast Guard Academy. They put a bulkhead across the corridor and said women on one side and men on the other. I don't know what we would have done without them. We had to have them. We were really scratching for men. After a while we had so many people that perhaps as individuals their assignments and their activities weren't too well handled, not in all cases, because there were so damned many of them, you know.

The same thing I suppose was true of the women, too. But the supervision of such large numbers, after such small numbers, hits you pretty hard.

Q: And you expanded so very rapidly.

Adm. R.: Yes.

Q: Tell me about some of the problems in this personnel office because this was one of the places where it was crucial.

Adm. R.: At the time I went there, we were in a building called the Liberty Loan Building. As you go down 14th Street toward the 14th Street bridge, it was the last building on the right. I think the building is still there. It's not a very big building but, anyway, that's where we were. You notice a road goes through a tunnel through a building down there? That's the building. When I got there, the corridors were full of file cabinets. The corridors were about half as wide as they should be because of the file cabinets that were out there.

So somebody arranged for the Southern Railway Building which is where the Coast Guard was before it went to where it is now. We moved there while I was there. That was the greatest relief, you know. We moved in there and had all this space, you know. Of course, space was an awful problem in the Liberty Loan Building. So we moved into this other place and it wasn't long before we started to pile things up out there, too. But we started off with a lot of space anyway.

My desk down the Liberty Loan Building -- the chief yeoman was in the room with me and so was the warrant officer and there were file cabinets all over the place. When we got down to the other place, I had a room about as big as this, but I was in there by myself. The SPAR was sitting just outside and I had another officer, a man, and he sat just outside there. From there on there were quite a few people in a big room.

But we did have room for our file cabinets and about that time we started putting records on these wheels, you know -- cards on wheels. This was a big help to us in keeping track of what was going on.

Q: This was the first step in the direction of the computer, wasn't it?

Adm. R.: Right. We had a girl working on each wheel. She kept those records on that wheel.

Q: On what basis were your assignments made? Tell me about that.

Adm. R.: We stopped doing it by name except in special cases where somebody had to have some guy ready. We did it by moving groups from one district to another district or we'd send a detail to a place where they were training a crew of a ship. And somebody else would fill in with other people until we got that and that crew would be there and would be trained in the details of the ship. They would have had other training before, of course, in their specialties, but they would go to this place. And then the whole lot would go to the ship, or other unit.

Q: But this was placing a lot of the responsibility for deciding to the officer on the spot then, was it?

Adm. R.: Oh yes. We never said -- I say we never said, but we probably did -- but anyway, it wasn't our idea. If in the Third

District they wanted a Yeoman Second Class to serve in the Port Security Office and they wanted somebody with port security experience, we would say to the First District, we would take this Second Class Yeoman who is now assigned to your Port Security Office and send him to the Third District for assignment to the Port Security Office there. This is the way it was done, you see.

Before, the orders would be to send usually a man by name, maybe who was just about ready for assignment to a certain place in the district. We didn't do that. But of course this meant that the districts had to build up their organizations.

Q: It was decentralization, wasn't it?

Adm. R.: Yes, we were getting out of headquarters and putting more of it on the districts, then they in turn were doing it further down the line. And we had to do it or we'd have licked ourselves in the war.

Q: It called for a great deal of administrative ability, didn't it, in order to run this expanding office?

Adm. R.: If it did, I didn't realize it. I was doing it a day at a time, I'll have to say, when I started out. After while I got a better picture.

Q: Well, you were on-job learning.

Adm. R.: Well, I'll tell you, my biggest job was to get rid of some of the things that I had to do. I had to get rid of them and give them to somebody else who could be responsible to me, of course. But I had to get rid of them in such a way that I didn't come anywhere near them in some cases, you know, because this was killing this guy Allison, who was ahead of me. I know it was killing him. I don't think he would have lived much longer the way he was going.

It required a lot of thought on my part I know. But I probably didn't have the proper kind of training to go into such a thing and set it up on a real good basis. We had some good people around. We had a fellow who was in Headquarters -- his name was Carroll -- and he had been a pay clerk and I think he had lived most of his life in Headquarters. But he was a damned good administrator. He really had his finger on things. A lot of the things that he did might have been to his own advantage, that was what a lot of people said about him anyway, but he was a great guy. And I used to go to him and talk to him about a lot of things and he told me a lot of things. I was grateful to him for a long time after that. The poor guy -- he lived throughout the war and then one day he had a heart attack and died. But luckily he lasted through the war; he got us through that!

Q: When you went in, your office was handling roughly how many men for assignment? And tell me how it grew.

Adm. R.: When I went in there, I would say that the Coast Guard then was around 20,000 enlisted men. I was there from May until the following July or August or something -- I forget what day I left.

Q: October 1943. From May '42 to October '43.

Adm. R.: At the end of that time I think we must have had 120,000.

Q: So that was the expansion -- from 20,000 to 120,000.

Adm. R.: Yes.

Q: And did the Coast Guard stations multiply accordingly?

Adm. R.: Yes. The things that really grew were the Port Security Stations and, of course, ships. But our ships -- when we sent our people to the ships, we still handled the personnel matters for our ships and all. For ships that we manned for the Navy -- our own ships which were then operating under the Navy anyway, of course. So we ran into some difficulties because we would have a need to send a group of people to a ship. So we'd gather them and send them. Then it turned out if we'd send them to Honolulu and the ship has gone to Australia or something like that. So we had some difficulties like that.

Q: Your vaunted communications broke down.

Adm. R.: Boy, yes. You see, we weren't sending the ships; we were just sending the men. We'd send the men and the Navy would send the ship somewhere else.

Q: When you talk about port security, how large a contingent of men were required to operate in a given port? Say, in Baltimore, for instance.

Adm. R.: Three or four hundred. New York was much bigger. I don't know how many they had. I'd say they had about 1500.

Q: And these ports multiplied throughout the country, on both coasts?

Adm. R.: Well yes. Eventually we even had some out on the Great Lakes. They didn't give us the problems the others did. But both coasts, yes. And the Gulf. The Atlantic, the Pacific, and the Gulf port security was a pretty important matter then. The Navy was particularly concerned about port security and didn't want to take it themselves. We had it and were handling it and it was going all right. They didn't want to go at it, but they were a little unhappy about the fact that we weren't putting enough people into it. So we put more and more in and I think we held it down to pretty reasonable portions, I guess. In New York we operated out of Ellis Island.

Q: Did you take over the immigration facilities there?

Adm. R.: Yes, we had the government buildings.

Q: What about the -- did you have any control over the assignment of men for specific training, or was this done elsewhere in the Coast Guard? You had to be cognizant of it.

Adm. R.: There was a separate division in the personnel office for training, which encompassed the training of officers and enlisted men. They would set up requirements for a certain number of people, you know, for a certain kind of training and they would say how many and what qualifications they needed and so on. We would then furnish those people.

Then we would forget about them until they were trained.

Q: But then you came into the picture again.

Adm. R.: Then we came in again, yes. We would come in at the end to tell them where to send these people that had the training.

Q: They called upon you first for a certain number of men for a specific training and then, once the training was accomplished, they called on you to take over and send them to the various destinations. This became a very complicated thing, didn't it?

Adm. R.: Yes, it became a complicated thing, but we worked pretty closely with them. There was a captain named Arthur Morrill who ran it and I used to spend quite a bit of time with him on this matter of getting people to him and taking people from him. He would base his requirements, of course, on requests that came to him, the need for certain people. He would handle those requests and determine what he needed in the way of personnel. He would come to me with those things and then, in the meantime, in the course of his job he would get lots of information on where these people ought to go when they were finished. We would talk this over between us -- we would work this thing out. But we would send them; we would order them out.

Q: But his office was a kind of clearing house for the requests that came from the fleet units and so forth.

Adm. R.: That's right.

Q: You didn't handle that phase of it. The requests did not come to you.

Adm. R.: No, anything like that went right to him. We would discuss it in the course of our daily discussions, but he was responsible for those things, yes.

Q: Since you were under the Navy as such, were there any requests from the Navy for blocs of men?

Q: Yes, I'm sure there were. In the beginning, our first experience, rather than manning ships for the Navy -- Navy ships -- we furnished people to attack transports. We did this because we had a lot of good boatmen in the Coast Guard. People from our lifeboat stations and aboard ship we always maintained a pretty high standard as far as operating smaller boats and so on.

They needed these people for landing craft on these attack transports. So we furnished a lot of people to the Navy for those things. They would tell us that they wanted us to furnish the boat crews for a given transport, then they would say what numbers and what rates and so on. So we would order those people to that ship.

Then if they needed to replenish those crews, we would get requests to replenish. They lost some of those crews, of course, in attacks and so on, and they lost them for other reasons too, I suppose. Then we would replenish those crews. during the time I was there. Maybe later on we must have run out of these people from the lifeboat stations after a while -- we didn't have too many.

Once we had manned the ship -- for instance, we manned a lot of DEs -- as a matter of fact, I served on one. When we came into port, we always went to New York. I would go -- or somebody on my staff would go to the District Office and tell them what we needed in the way of personnel before our next trip. The District Personnel Officer would give us people out of a receiving station that he maintained in New York. He would give us people and fill our needs.

Q: The receiving station was a kind of a pool then?

Adm. R.: Yes.

Q: Was there any sign of friction between Coast Guard personnel and Navy personnel serving together? Was there any problem there?

Adm. R.: Well, there really wasn't too much of that -- later on, anyway. In the beginning, when we furnished the boat crews and the Navy furnished the rest of the crew aboard the attack transports, there was this mixing. But there wasn't very much mixing of crews other than that. We would man a ship, you see, completely -- from commanding officer all the way down, we manned the whole ship. I don't think that there was much trouble between those boat crews and other people on board the ship.

Q: That didn't constitute a problem for your office then.

Adm. R.: No, it never became a problem.

Q: What about men whom you had assigned en bloc for various duty that turned out to be unfit? And this is inevitable sometimes. Would this come back to you?

Adm. R.: Yes, we had cases like that where the people were unsatisfied with the numbers or the quality of the people, both. But there isn't much you can do about things like that. Just because somebody complains about a personality of a man that goes to them, I wouldn't take any action on that.

Q: No, but I was thinking more particularly of somebody who was assigned to a combat ship and who cracked up -- that sort of thing. What could you do about that?

Adm. R.: Well, we had a number of cases of people who cracked up. We would remove them at the first opportunity and replace them. In the case of the DEs, we did that in New York when we got there through the District Personnel Officer. We'd say this guy can't do the job, and he would handle it.

Q: Would you say something about the system of promotion in wartime as you experienced it in this particular division?

Adm. R.: We changed our personnel regulations in such a way that promotions could be made by commanding officers in most cases.

Q: On the spot promotions.

Adm. R.: On the spot, yes, to fill vacancies, the commanding officer could promote the people he had available to promote.

Q: A "raise your right hand" procedure?

Adm. R.: Yes. Of course, he had to determine their qualifications in some way. I think we did away with the business of written examination for promotions. There used to be written examinations for all promotions, but we did away with that. I think we even did away with it for promotion to Chief Petty

Officer for a while, but then brought it back for promotion to Chief Petty Officer. The fellow couldn't make up his own written examination but he had an examination that he could use for promotion to things like Chief Petty Officer.

Then maybe at one time toward the end, we left it with the District.

Q: To handle the examinations.

Adm. R.: Yes. The District who was handling their personnel, they would handle this examination.

Q: But it all had to funnel back into your records.

Adm. R.: Well, it had to come back into our records, of course. Those wheels were spinning all the time. There were more changes going on in a fellow's career. Between transfers and promotions and misbehavior and all this kind of thing.

Q: Promotions came much more swiftly, did they not?

Adm. R.: Oh yes, of course they did. And there were some problems with it, too, because if a guy was real good and his commanding officer wanted to push him, he would go too fast some time. Once the guy is promoted, you can't do much about it. But you can lay down the law and tell them that there are certain guidelines about the length of time a fellow should serve before he gets promoted again and things like that. We had such problems.

You see, we manned a lot of LSTs. Now some of those LSTs that we manned served in groups or squadrons, or whatever they called them -- I don't recall what the smallest operating group was now -- but they would operate with Navy manned LSTs.

Q: They did in the Mediterranean, didn't they?

Adm. R.: I'm sure they did in quite a few places. We manned a lot of LCILs. But in those cases, we manned the whole group of LCILs -- we manned the whole thing.

So the guy in charge of the group of them was a Coast Guard officer who was familiar with our own policies and so on -- our own desires. But sometimes when one of our ships would get in with a group of LSTs that were Navy-manned, we would get some odd situations because the guy running them was a Navy officer that didn't know and probably didn't care either what our ideas were about how these personnel should be handled.

Q: What was your relationship with the draft for enlisted men? Not enlisted men, but drafted men who served in this capacity.

Adm. R.: A man who was drafted who wanted to come into the Coast Guard could choose the Coast Guard -- at one time, when I was there, anyway -- he could choose the Coast Guard. To begin with, we weren't involved at all. But then we did get involved later on because . . .

Q: You mean you used up all your reservists?

Adm. R.: Yes. We couldn't get any more people in the reserve. We needed more people. And so then we did a few, but we never got very many people out of the draft. We sent some of those requirements to General Hersey a few times.

Q: Did you requirements differ from, say, the Navy requirements?

Adm. R.: I don't know. The Navy never leaned too heavily on the draft either, I don't think. I think the Navy, because of their larger numbers, must have needed more than we did. I'm sure they needed more than we did. But our requirements weren't very high and as a matter of fact, I think we might have gotten along without the draft. But we were more or less required to say that we would take people from the draft.

Q: Then these draftees who opted for the Coast Guard became your charges in your particular office and their files were there.

Adm. R.: Yes. That required a little arranging. This didn't happen while I was there but I can see the problem. I don't know how they handled it but I know they had to be kept in a different file from the other ones, because their tour of duty wasn't going to be the same. There were a lot of differences.

I don't think I ever served with anybody who was drafted in the Coast Guard. Of course, I could have but didn't know it.

Q: Tell me about this growing problem or record-keeping. You outgrew the Southern Building.

Adm. R.: Yes. Of course, we eventually outgrew the other place, too. We eventually had to hire some more buildings and moved some offices out of the Southern Railway Building. We had the Southern Railway Building except the top floor. The top floor was the Narcotics Bureau. I don't know how that came about but anyway, that was the way it was, right from the beginning. While I was Commandant, they (the Narcotics Bureau) moved out of the Southern Railway Building and we got the top floor. But in the meantime, we had rented a good many places - I say a good many, I mean half a dozen places - in Washington, where we had various groups stashed out to themselves.

Then, of course, the thing that brought it to a head - maybe it didn't bring it to a head but it brought it to a head as far as we were concerned, we knew we had to do something - was that they decided to tear down the Southern Railway Building and make a parking lot out of it.

Q: This was post-war.

Adm. R.: Oh yes, this was while I was Commandant. That was, of course, when the Transportation Department got into the picture. They built the building and we moved into it.

Q: During the war now, while you were still in this personnel job, what about the calls on you for the assignment of men for the traditional services of the Coast Guard?

Adm. R.: You mean like the lifeboat services?

Q: Yes.

Adm. R.: Most of our units were involved otherwise than their traditional roles. Most of the lifeboat stations also had some sort of job in connection with port security or some other additional job. Most of our lifeboat stations had expanded crews for this reason. They used their vessels for other purposes, too. They used their vessels for patrol and things like that more than they did in the normal course of events. I don't think there was any difference in the handling of personnel for those units then. We sent part of a crew to an LST. If they needed some in the lifeboat station, we'd send them.

The Districts were responsible for handling through their receiving stations these things like a lifeboat station. And each district had a receiving station where they had a group of men who were assigned to this receiving station for assignment by the district. They would work from there.

They would use this group they have in the receiving station to fill school billets, and to fill vacancies, I suppose, in their own office and their lifeboat stations and things like that where they had a primary district interest. They'd use them for other things too. When somebody would come to them and needed men, as we did in New York, they'd fill that bill and if they couldn't fill it then they would be the ones to get in touch with headquarters and get a draft to fill the needs.

Q: In terms of Coast Guard aviation, were there any problems in assigning personnel?

Adm. R.: No.

Q: Weren't they involved with flying boats on patrol along the coasts?

Adm. R.: They flew PBYs and . . .

Q: That's what I mean.

Adm. R.: But filling those billets was a minor thing compared to the other business because it was small. And of course, our aviators have always been trained in the Navy. They've always been trained at Pensacola or Corpus Christi.

I think we have since, at some time or other, set up some training ourselves for helicopter pilots. But I think their basic flying training has always come from the Navy.

Q: During World War II, I know there was a flurry at one time and a great concern lest the German submarines were landing spies along the Atlantic coast in particular. Did the Coast Guard get involved in that? Did you have to furnish personnel to try and act as counterspies or what-have-you?

Adm. R.: Until the war and continuing through the war, there has always been a beach patrol from lifeboat stations. During the war, this was beefed up and we used horses, for some of those patrols.

Q: Along the lonely dunes.

Adm. R.: Yes. And I don't know in how many cases we actually caught anybody, but we did catch a couple of men on Long Island Sound who had been landed by a submarine.

Q: They were actually saboteurs, weren't they?

Adm. R.: Yes, that's right. They landed from a submarine and their purpose was to blow something up. The people from the lifeboat stations caught them. I think it must have been luck because patrolling the beach is such an impossible thing, you know, to patrol effectively. You had to have so many people and they patrolled for so many miles.

Q: I suppose there had to be close coordination between the locating and spotting submarines off the coast and the beach patrol then.

Adm. R.: Yes. I suppose those people had to have some special kind of training, I don't know. But you know, the question of the horses -- we did use horses for a good many of those patrols and I think we may have quit it by the end of the war but at least we did it in the beginning of the war and we did it for some time during the war.

But we had a lot of dogs. And we had to have people get a lot of training in order to handle those dogs. These were in connection with port security and the docks, and also in connection with other guard work. For a while, we furnished guards at certain factories that were making certain things. We furnished the guards and dogs.

Q: At least the guards came under your purview, but not the dogs.

Adm. R.: Well, the dogs did. We had an office in headquarters that was responsible for this group of people who were to work with dogs and their dogs. I think a fellow who is now retired, Admiral Mauerman, had something to do with that. He later was Superintendent of the Academy; he was a captain at the time, and he later became an admiral and he was the Superintendent of the Academy in the '50s.

We furnished people who were guards in the cryolite mines in Greenland and this was before we actually got into the war. I don't know whether it continued afterwards or not, but we did it before hand, I know. I know we were not in the war because of a detail that I will bring up in a minute.

But they were allowed to do this by the Coast Guard on the

assumption that their connection with the Coast Guard was temporarily done away with. It didn't exist any more. But they were promised that at the end of this tour of duty up there, that they would be brought back into the Coast Guard and that their time up there would count as time they had served in the Coast Guard. This was an agreement that was made with these people. It wasn't a large number of people but it was maybe 25 or 30 people.

It led to difficulties later on because it's an illegal thing to begin with and slipping it through was a little hard to do. I think that it was finally arranged so that this was done and the people were brought back into the Coast Guard and the time was some how or other given to them as credit for retirement and pay purposes and things like that.

Q: Who owns these mines?

Adm. R.: They were operated in Greenland. You remember, before we got into the war, one of our ships went up into Greenland and went into some place up there and captured a German weather station, the personnel and all - captured the people and the whole works. So the Germans were operating around Greenland and everybody knew it. And the cryolite mines, of course, were important to the aluminum industry, isn't it? Anyway, it was . . .

Q: Were they privately owned mines or were they owned by the

Danish government?

Adm. R.: They might have been owned by the government. I'm not sure about that. I'm not sure who owned them, but they were in Greenland and they were operated in Greenland, not by Americans, and these people -- I don't even know how we got involved in that except that we did have people that were assigned up there before the war in Greenland. We had a base called Bluie West One and Bluie West Two, I think, and these people I think came from those bases and probably knew the people up there and the proposition was made. And somehow or other this deal was made . . .

Q: These were Coast Guard people.

Adm. R.: They were Coast Guard enlisted men and they were put on this job up there. Now it may be that the people at Bluie West One or those bases down there realized the need for these people and volunteered to do this. Then after doing it, they decided they couldn't do it any more and then the idea came of getting these other people, getting these people to stay on in this other category.

So the Coast Guard wouldn't be running the thing but the Coast Guard was running it in the beginning, I think. This is a thing that actually happened. The Coast Guard enlisted men went to work as guards up there and they were not subject to the Coast Guard any more while this was happening. In effect, they were discharged from the Coast Guard.

Q: But they did get credit for being there.

Adm. R.: Later on, yes. This was the agreement that was made with them.

Q: You do strange things in wartime.

Adm. R.: And these people showed up again in the Coast Guard after they had finished this job. I may just be guessing when I say that they got credit for the time that they served up there, but they came back and they served in their ratings that they held before. There was one guy who was a chief radioman, I think, who was among them. He may have been the leading light among them, I don't know.

Q: You must have had a very special office within your office for the special cases.

Adm. R.: Well, this was a thing, of course, that wasn't handled in my office. I think it might have been done in the Commandant's back room or something like that when it was done, or some other big wheel's back room. But it was done.

Admiral Iceberg Smith was the guy that was running that business up there in Greenland and he might have done it. He may have made some promises he couldn't keep, too.

Q: What was the Coast Guard, and particularly the enlisted personnel, relationship with the intelligence service?

Adm. R.: We had our own intelligence service. We still have. We have a close relationship particularly with secret service, but also with narcotics and the FBI. We still do, or we did anyway, run the target range for secret service over at the Treasury Department. I think we probably still do that. We had a very close relationship with all of them.

We were very close to Navy intelligence. During the war, our intelligence activities got to be pretty big because of the port security thing. We got involved later on in one of these things. In our records, we made anybody who wanted a port security pass fill out a form. One of the things we had to fill in was organizations you belong to and all that. If you belonged to any of these that were listed as subversive, he didn't get the card. This was a matter that was carried out by our intelligence people. We had to stop that. We had to stop this question about the subversive organizations and all that kind of thing. So we have no record now. If some communist wants a port security card -- I don't know whether we issue port security cards any more or not. If we do, they are only in certain cases.

But now if a communist wants something from the port security office, we don't know if he's a communist and we can't ask him if he's a communist. And we can't do anything about it if he is, I guess.

Q: That's an infringement of constitutional rights.

Adm. R.: Yes. We got involved in that quite a long time ago. As a matter of fact, I think Al Richmond might have been Commandant at the time. Maybe it was just about that time.

During the war, we set up throughout the world a number of Hearing Units. Their purpose was to handle disciplinary cases in the Merchant Marine and other Merchant Marine things that turned up, but principally it was disciplinary. We had these things all over. A classmate of mine was stationed in Perth, Australia, one of them was in India, and there is still one of these things in London and I think there may be one in Amsterdam or one of those places in The Netherlands or Belgium, around in there. We had one in Germany in Bremerhaven.

Q: This was prior to the war?

Adm. R.: No, this was during the war.

Q: You had one in Bremerhaven?

Adm. R.: No, we have it now, because I visited the place.

Q: During the war, did you have one in Murmansk?

Adm. R.: I don't remember that.

Q: All those important convoys went into Murmansk.

Adm. R.: Yes. But they were for the purpose of handling Merchant Marine disciplinary cases. If a skipper had a complaint against a member of a crew, he would make his complaint when he arrived. Otherwise, the thing would go on so long before he might get back, you see, to where there was a Hearing Unit in the United States that this thing could go on forever. In some cases, the Hearing Officer would give punishment of some kind to the Merchant Marine man who was involved, or he might make note of it and refer it back to the home port for a further hearing when he got back. But he would act on these things in order to clear the disciplinary records of the ships.

Q: This must have been an awfully tough assignment. A hearing officer.

Adm. R.: Yes, but Merchant Marine Inspection Officers are involved in these things all the time. They are involved in disciplinary hearings.

Q: And they have, I think, complete acceptance from the labor unions, the maritime unions.

Adm. R.: I suppose.

Q: How did the Coast Guard train people for a particular assignment like that?

Adm. R.: We ran - I was going to say that school in New London where we trained Merchant Marine officers. Captain Covert

Wendland's experience would have been there because he was assigned to that school. He was one of the instructors there. He was a classmate of mine. And he's the one who was in India.

Q: They must have experienced some particular problems in various parts of the world.

Adm. R.: There was problem upon problem in the Merchant Marine crews during the war and these units were set up in order to handle these problems. The ships so often were away for many, many months before they got back to where they could get to a regular unit, a regular Hearing Unit, on these matters, that they set these things up in order to dispose of them.

Some of the people that they had hearings on were sent back by other ships.

Q: I've heard various stories from   people about problems with Merchant Marine personnel and their insistence upon observing work rules and that sort of thing in combat even, in combat areas.

Adm. R.: Yes. We had a unit in Saigon that listened to Merchant Marine disciplinary problems during the Vietnam War. I think that was the same sort of thing. They had other jobs, too, but they had that as one of the jobs.

Q: These Hearing Units each had a court reporter stationed there and you tell me that you trained them?

Adm. R.: We trained them for use in our courts and also for this use. You know, it was somebody who could take down a hearing and most of them worked with machines.

I had a Chief Yeoman who was temporary there. He wasn't my Chief Yeoman, as a matter of fact, but I had served with him before. His name was Pocorney and he was one of these people. He had been in one of these Hearing Units.

Q: You might tell me, Sir, about your relationship with the Commandant when you were there in Washington.

Adm. R.: As personnel officer? Well, the Commandant was Waesche and I didn't see much of him. I saw a lot of Admiral Donahue. The Commandant was otherwise engaged, I guess. As I said, he spent a lot of time, I know, over in the Navy Department and I rarely saw him around headquarters. I don't know if he ever saw me.

Q: He's one of your famous people.

Adm. R.: He was one of the greatest we ever had. He thought big about the Coast Guard and he thought a lot about maritime affairs and he involved the Coast Guard in them. He is the fellow who was Commandant and I think had most to do with it, that got the Lighthouse Service into the Coast Guard. He also, during the war, had Merchant Marine inspection brought into the Coast Guard as a temporary measure. Later on, it was made permanent, of course. But originally it was done as a temporary measure and the purpose -- this probably has something to do with the authority for these Hearing Units -- the purpose was to bring this Merchant Marine inspection business under military authority where there could be some control over it during the war.

Anyway, he did both of those things. And those things, I think, are now, or for many years were, the bread and butter jobs of the Coast Guard. These are things we could always fall back on. Search and rescue is wonderful and our reputation is probably built on search and rescue, but if they did away with search and rescue, the Coast Guard would continue on the basis of these bread and butter jobs. Other things have been added since, of course, but that business of maritime safety and aid to navigation -- there is a definite national need, a world-wide need for all of this.

Q: And a continuing one.

Adm. R.: A continuing one, of course. If we didn't have those things, I think we sometimes would have a hell of a time justifying our search and rescue activities as the basis for the Coast Guard.

Q: One other thing, when I think of Admiral Waesche, is his contribution to the development of the helicopter, his vision in seeing this as something that you . . .

Adm. R.: Yes, he had a fellow named Kossler working for him. I think I might have mentioned him when I was talking about the Academy before, because Kossler was an instructor there. He was the guy who pushed and pushed and pushed on the helicopter. He was an electrical engineer and he eventually wound up in headquarters and while he was there, he was in aviation and he really was a helicopter man. This was all during Waesche's time. And Waesche was a great advocate of helicopters.

Q: At a time when the Navy wasn't interested.

Adm. R.: No. We did all the early development on helicopters. The Navy didn't do it; they didn't want anything to do with it. Neither did our aviators, most of them. We had a guy named Erickson who was an aviator who was sold on helicopters. The other aviators would hardly talk to him because he always brought it up and he was always nasty to them about it. But he thought helicopters were wonderful and he was right.

During the war we manned so many different kinds of ships and did so many different things. We manned attack transports fully and other transports.

Q: For amphibious operations.

Adm. R.: Yes. And destroyer escorts and frigates. We had about three or four divisions of frigates, I don't know how many exactly. The name frigates has covered a lot of different kinds of ships in this time.

Q: The World War II frigates were small escort ships.

Adm. R.: About like a DE. The LSTs and the LCIs. Then we built some new 255-foot cutters during the war and manned those.

Q: Where would they go?

Adm. R.: Mostly on the West Coast. Maybe all on the West Coast.

Q: Were they a very special design?

Adm. R.: They were 255-foot cutters and we may still have a few of them in operation. We had one in operation down here in New London since I retired because I visited it. As a matter of fact, I have a nephew who enlisted in the Coast Guard and he served aboard and went to Vietnam in it. I was down the dock to meet him when he came back. But that one is now out of commission and I think most of them are out of commission. But they are about 30 years old now.

Q: What was the experience that went into the design of those particular ones?

Adm. R.: I don't know what led up to that kind of ship because the last ships that we designed before that I think were the Secretary class ships and these are completely different.

Q: Wherein do they differ?

Adm. R.: They are a shorter stubbier thing and they are not as fast. They have a very quick and easy roll, there is too much motion in them. I think it was a poor design. It was a design that was arrived at during the war and it might have been a hasty one, I don't know. But their purpose, of course, was to replace the Secretary class ships with a smaller ship to do the same job. And they were supposed to be able to do that. But they are not as habitable and they weren't as good by any means as the Secretary class ships. As I say, there may be a few of them still operating and I know that there are a couple of the Secretary class ships still operating. I know the TANEY -- I think she's stationed in New York. And there may be another one on the West Coast.

I don't think anybody was very happy about the design of the 255-foot class after it was completed and in use for a while. It wasn't big enough -- they did weather patrols. They were too small for all the equipment they needed for the weather patrol plus the other duties they were required to do. They just didn't have the room aboard.

The power was steam, like a steam turbine I guess. They weren't a complete flop. They were used.

Q: Were they turned out by the Kaiser Shipyard?

Adm. R.: No. I can't remember the name, but it was on the West Coast. There might have been some built on the East Coast because there was a pretty good number. There might have been a dozen or fifteen.

The icebreakers, the WIND ships. Of course, two of those we turned over to the Russians.

Q: They wanted all of them, didn't they?

Adm. R.: They wanted all of them, yes. But they got two and that was pretty late in the war that that happened, because when it happened, when they got the second one, the engineering crew came to the MACKINAW. I was then skipper of the MACKINAW. This was in 1945. They came up there because our power plant was identical. They came up there for training in the operation of the ship. The Russians came up to the Great Lakes. So we had them on board the ship for a month or so. They didn't have anybody that spoke English, but we had a Coast Guard officer who spoke Russian -- they brought him in for this job. He was our go-between. I don't know how much they got out of the training but he worked like hell trying to get the word back and forth.

Then they left from there to Seattle and went right aboard the ship. I guess when they got finished with that ship they hadn't learned much about taking care of it because it was in pretty bad shape when they got back.

Q: They turned them back, did they?

Adm. R.: Oh yes. We got them back.

Q: They were lease-lend but they were turned back.

Adm. R.: Oh yes, we got them back. There were four of them -- well, more than that because there were some that went to the Navy, but four would go to the Coast Guard -- the NORTH WIND, SOUTH WIND, EAST WIND, and WEST WIND. They got, I think, the NORTH WIND -- maybe they got the NORTH WIND and the SOUTH WIND. And we got them both back. They got two and we kept two. And we got the two back, in very bad shape. The engines were shot to hell.

Q: You just mentioned weather patrol.

Adm. R.: We took on weather patrol as a result of the war. In the beginning we got some ships out of the Great Lakes to run the weather patrol. They were old freighters -- they were really old, they were really beat up old things. And this is the way we manned the original weather stations.

One of them at least went on patrol. Captain Charley Toft, who had been a classmate of mine at one time and resigned and then came back again in the next class, which was 1930, was the skipper of that ship. They went to sea and they knew the ship could make maybe 9 knots or something like that -- it would just barely go along. It was very old and when we got it, I suppose they must have done some work on it. I don't know how many patrols he made but anyway, on one patrol, we never heard from him again. He just disappeared. He might have been shot down, he might have been torpedoed or something, but I don't think the Germans were bothering our weather ships. I think that they wanted the reports as much as we wanted them.

I never heard of any other weather ship being attacked. This one just disappeared. These were ships that were built for operation on the Great Lakes.

Q: Yet they were operating in the ocean area.

Adm. R.: They brought them up for this purpose. They brought them out for this purpose. They brought them from the Great Lakes to operate on the weather station.

Q: What kind of equipment were they carrying? Weather equipment?

Adm. R.: I don't know what they did at that time. They must have sent up balloons; I imagine they did. I don't know what the equipment was.

We mentioned a lot of the things that were added to the Coast Guard during the war.

Q: It was a watershed time for the Coast Guard, wasn't it? Before and after. So many duties added to it.

Adm. R.: Oh yes. It was a tremendous number of duties that were added during the war. The older type of duties stayed there, too. So it grew up into a great number.

One of those that I haven't mentioned is the LORAN stations. Of course, they became very important during the war. I don't know who worked on the development of the LORAN stations, but we got into it early, I know.

Q: Was it purely Coast Guard?

Adm. R.: The operation was, yes.

Q: I mean the development of it?

Adm. R.: No, it wasn't. I think somebody else really started it and the Coast Guard got into it very early, before really much development, and took hold of it and did a lot. It has done since most of the development. Of course, it's been rivaled by other things like OMEGA and other systems, but LORAN has held on and is now the accepted means of navigation for all of the United States forces -- Air Force, and others.

But during the war, we built a great number of these stations and they were very useful. The kind that we built originally didn't have a great range, but they had a pretty good range -- about up to a thousand miles almost, I guess. They were very useful in the handling of convoys -- the directing of convoys and so on. So we had large numbers of them and we manned all of them. In the course of development, a LORAN station was developed for operation from a truck. In some of the invasions in the Pacific, these trucks were sent ahead and were landed at places and set up on islands so that they could be used in the approaches to the invasion of those islands or other islands -- other islands I guess mostly, although I think there was at least one case where they landed a truck on an islad that was occupied by the Japanese. But in a good many cases, they were set up on other islands that were not occupied and used in the approaches to these invasions.

Of course, this is one thing that has developed to such an extent now that that old type of LORAN station is either finished now or it's about to go -- those were called LORAN A stations and these are LORAN C stations, the present ones. These are very sophisticated stations and are very powerful. They have a long range. They work on a different frequency, a much lower frequency than the others so there is less likelihood of there being an error in their transmission. They are very accurate over long spaces.

They have done a lot of work on the development of transmitters -- not transmitters, but antennas for these things. At one time, our antennas for the LORAN C station had to be one 1350 feet high. This was an engineering feat in itself to rig that up, of course. We had a lot of those and we still have a good many of them now. I think now when they build a new station they supplant that with an array of smaller antennas. But some of those big antennas went over in hurricanes and storms.

Q: They are really vulnerable, I would think. Top heavy.

Adm. R.: Yes, and there were at least two that tumbled. One of them really for not much reason except a defect.

Q: So they experimented with towers.

Adm. R.: They have experimented and they are replacing these big ones with arrays of antennas and smaller which will be less vulnerable than the big tall ones.

Q: Did our enemies during World War II have anything similar to LORAN?

Adm. R.: I don't know. I don't think so.

Q: It was a highly secret thing at that time though.

Adm. R.: Oh yes. In the beginning it was very much that way. Now, of course, it's available to anybody who wants to buy a receiver.

Q: I've got a book here with diagrams of some of it.

Adm. R.: As a matter of fact, they are doing their best to develop a receiver that will be available to people for as small an amount of money as possible. They're down pretty low now.

I bought some stock in a company. Some guy that was interested in starting up, and I bought 150 shares of the stock before he had even gone on the market.

Q: I hope it's prospered.

Adm. R.: I paid seven for it - the last I heard - it's not public yet - the last I heard he was offering stock options to his employees for twelve, so it's gone up some anyway.

I think that more and more people are taking on LORAN C now. I'm pretty sure that they are almost at the end of the LORAN A stations now. LORAN C will be a much more economical thing. Each station, of course, is a more expensive place than the LORAN A station but you don't need nearly as many stations. You can cover the world with a much smaller number.

We erected a chain during the Vietnam war. Two of the stations in Thailand and one on the island off the southern coast of Vietnam where they had these calls.

Q: Down near Camrahn Bay.

Adm. R.: Yes, I guess so. Anyway, one tower was down there. They used them. The Air Force used LORAN in their approaches on the bombing runs and their scouting and things like that. My son was assigned out there for two years, I guess. He was in Bangkok and he was in charge of the operation of the stations.

Q: You said off tape that the Coast Guard had very little to do with the Korean War.

Adm. R.: But toward the end of the Korean War, we sent a detail over into Korea and their purpose was to guide the formation of the Korean Coast Guard. I don't know how many people we had there. We had a captain in charge of it. His name was Captain Si Perkins, who later became a Rear Admiral and is now retired on the West Coast. He was in charge of it in the beginning. They acquired the vessels I guess through the United States for the formation of this thing and built it up. Then later on, when the Korean Coast Guard was established, after a couple of years of their being over there, our group left and almost immediately the Korean Coast Guard became the Navy.

Before that, they were not allowed to have a navy by some agreement. They had agreed anyway not to build up a navy at the time. But they were allowed to build up a coast guard, which they did. Then they changed it and called it the Korean Navy. I don't know what the South Korean Navy amounts to now but that was the beginning of it anyway. That was about our part in that, I think.

In the Vietnam business, we did quite a lot over there, but you probably have heard from other sources. We began - this was during my administration as Commandant. We began by sending 26 patrol boats, 83-foot patrol boats over there. Originally, 13 of them were to go to Danang and 13 to Phu Quoc which is a mile on down in the South.

These vessels were transported overseas on board other ships. They were hoisted aboard and taken over there. 85-foot patrol boats. Then they were placed in the water and trained in the Philippines. The first group who was trained went to Danang. I made a trip over there about that time and visited the group which was in training in the Philippines, that had completed their training. And then went up to Danang and visited those up there.

Those vessels apparently did a pretty good job in the particular cast for which they were sent over there, which was the prevention of smuggling of arms and munitions from North Vietnam down to the people who were on their side.

Q: Smuggling along the coast. The Viet Cong.

Adm. R.: Yes. And they did, besides that patrol and their operations, they did a good bit of bombardment work. They had an unusual gun aboard. It was one that was developed for use aboard those vessels. It was a mortar which worked off the mount of a one-pounder which was part of the regular armament of this boat. They used it in many cases in short-range bombardments.

Then of course, later we sent our larger ships over there to engage in the other patrols off shore. One of the 83-footers was shot up by an air force plane - a U. S. Air Force plane which mistook it for an enemy vessel. But they made runs on it and they killed two or three men aboard the ship and beat it up pretty good before they were finally called off.

The result of that was an improvement in communications so that we would be able to talk to the airplanes as they were approaching us. Before that we couldn't. Their communications had to be through a shore station and all this happened before communications were established finally so the guy stopped shooting at them, but he had done the damage.

The other vessels, the bigger vessels, alternated in their patrols over there. That didn't happen while I was still on active duty. That came along afterwards. So I wasn't very closely involved in that.

Another thing that we set up rather early was ammunition loading detachments and unloading detachments over there. The Coast Guard supervised loading and unloading of ammunition in Vietnam for certainly the first part of the war.

Q: That was quite a task. And then you cooperated with MSTS?

Adm. R.: Yes. This, I suppose, came out of our experience in port security at other times. This is, I think, why we were singled out for that job.

Q: Sir, in October of 1943, I suspect it was, you left the Enlisted Personnel Division in Coast Guard Headquarters and you became Commander of the Escort Division 45 Unit of Task Force 60, escorting U. S. convoys. Tell me about that. That was another vastly different operation.

Adm. R.: Yes. There were six ships in my Division. When I left Headquarters, I spent a period of time in St. Augustine at a school the Coast Guard ran down there which was an antisubmarine school.

Q: Oh, they had their own.

Adm. R.: We had one in St. Augustine. I spent not a very long time in there, but we sent our prospective commanding officer and our prospective division commanders down to this school. I didn't stay there long because I was going from there to Miami to the Navy school. So after a short time in St. Augustine, which I thought was really a very good school, I went on down to Miami to the antisubmarine School. I spent about a month there, I guess.

Q: What was the difference in the two schools?

Adm. R.: I think that our school may have duplicated a lot of -- our school at St. Augustine may have duplicated a lot of the Navy school. But I think that our school was intended for commanding officers and antisubmarine officers and so on. So was the one at Miami except that it also had certain things set up for people who were going to be in a position of division commander and so on. That is what I was really after. And that is what I did at Miami.

I spent about a month there and then . . .

Q: What particular things did you learn in a school like that? As a division commander?

Adm. R.: The organization of convoys, methods of screening, types of screening, and matters of that kind. We worked problems on the boards or we pushed buttons and so on setting up certain situations where there was a submarine off of here, how would we set up our screen in the combat situation. There were many things of that nature.

Then some of the nuts and bolts, too, of arranging for your ships for supplies and repairs and things of that nature.

Q: You weren't so much concerned about ordnance and that kind of thing, as you were with the overall . . .

Adm. R.: Yes, the handling of a group of ships and putting them in the right positions to combat certain situations. This was the main business there.

When I had finished there, I went to Galveston where one of the ships for my division had just been finished. It had been built in Houston, it was in Galveston taking on supplies, and I boarded that ship and sailed in it to Bermuda, where the rest of the division already was. They were engaged in ship exercises down there -- individual ship exercises. After a couple of weeks of that, then we engaged in division exercises, maneuvers, and so on, simulated situations. And we worked on live submarines down there too -- chasing down a submarine, you know, and simulating attacks and so on.

Q: And all the time you had to be cognizant of the possibility of the German submarines.

Adm. R.: Oh yes, we did. And this was made very plain to us too. It was a very interesting and I think a fruitful thing as far as I was concerned. I learned a lot in that situation down there.

There was a Navy captain that was in charge of all the training and his name was Maderos. He was a pretty sour kind of a guy, but he knew what he was talking about, and he was pretty insistent about what he was talking about, too. There was one situation that I thought was amusing.

We had pretty frequent conferences and we had a conference every morning early, about seven o'clock. One morning a ship had just arrived -- a DE -- from New York for training, and the commanding officer was in on this conference. He had come down in very bad weather. So Captain Maderos had told him to make a report on the performance of his ship during this thing and he did. He said it was a most uncomfortable trip. He said, "We rolled 65 degrees."

Some fellow in the group said, "You couldn't have rolled 65 degrees because the stability of a DE disappears at 56 degrees."

The guy said, "I'm glad nobody told me that."

Q: Where were your headquarters? At Hamilton?

Adm. R.: We were anchored and there was a repair ship down there where Maderos's headquarters were aboard, and that was where the conferences were held -- on this repair ship. We were anchored in clusters to buoys all around.

Q: In that harbor?

Adm. R.: Yes. We were within sight of Hamilton.

When we were released from that, then four of the ships in my division were sent into Norfolk for some reason. I can't remember what it was. It might have been for an alteration or something, because they were always altering these ships -- adding torpedo tubes or adding something else. Then two of the ships, one of which was my flagship, went to New York to escort some tankers down to Texas. That was my first real experience with a real convoy.

One other ship was assigned to me. So I was the escort commander with three escort ships.

Q: Three escort ships and how many tankers?

Adm. R.: There were about a half a dozen. It wasn't a big convoy; it was a small convoy. It was about a half a dozen, I think. We carried out that job and then we returned to Norfolk and picked up our first convoy. The escort was made up of a division of Navy destroyers and my division of destroyer escorts. The escort commander was a fellow named Captain Nickerson and he rode aboard one of the Coast Guard cutters which was on escort duty named the BIBB. Those ships were used for that purpose during the war to a large extent. The escort commander rode aboard them because they had better communications facilities and they were more comfortable, too. That was another reason why he rode on it.

We took on the escort of a convoy of about 120 ships. Our destination was the Mediterranean and it was a slow convoy. The slowest ship in the convoy was expected to be about 9 knots. So that was the speed of the convoy, 9 knots. So we were quite a long ways under way from Norfolk.

Q: It was a huge convoy, wasn't it?

Adm. R.: Yes. All of those convoys were big. They were all over 100 ships. I don't know if any of them were more than 120, but I know that first one was a tremendous big thing. They really spread out all over the place.

Q: What were you carrying in the convoy?

Adm. R.: It was a variety of things. There were two Navy tankers in the convoy, in the middle of it. And later on, we picked up an aircraft carrier -- one of these escort carriers. It rode along with us and it was in the middle of the convoy, too. It would, on occasion, shove off and go somewhere. I think they were engaged in killer duty. They would go off and meet their ships somewhere, then they would go on a run where there were submarines reported. In a convoy like that, of course, it's like a city, when you get that many people - you've got a lot of people involved in this thing and all sorts of things are happening. People are hurting themselves and getting appendicitis and things like that. We had a doctor. He wasn't the only doctor in the convoy, in the escort, but he was the only doctor in my division and the division of Navy ships didn't have a doctor. There was one on the BIBB and one in my convoy. And that doctor was on board my flagship; he was on my staff.

So he made, I would say, an average of two trips a day to other ships by high line.

Q: He had an exciting voyage, didn't he?

Adm. R.: He did. I had never seen this done. We had transported all sorts of things back and forth between ships in the course of our training and all that. But I had never before transported a person back and forth. This doctor was new at it too. He was a public health service doctor. The Coast Guard manned the whole thing, furnished the doctor and all, and that's the kind of doctors we had - public health service doctors.

So when it came time for this, he hadn't done this before either. He was asking questions about it. We said to him, "Doc, you don't have to worry about it. This is a commonplace thing. We do this sort of thing all the time. We just haven't done it with you aboard, that's all."

Q: It was extremely safe.

Adm. R.: Yes. "There's no reason for you to be worried about it." So he finally shoved off. I don't think he -- maybe he got his feet wet -- but it wasn't any worse than that. And he got over to this other ship and he fixed up whatever it was he had to fix up over there. Then he came back. As he came back aboard, we said, "We're sure glad to see that works. It's the first time we ever saw it." He didn't speak to us for a while. He didn't trust us in anything after that.

Q: He'd give you a dose of strychnine or something. Were you attacked in any way by submarines?

Adm. R.: No, we were not bothered in any way by submarines. But we got into the Mediterranean, just inside of Gibraltar we were attacked by aircraft which attacked every convoy that came in and went out. They came out of southern France. We knew they were coming, long before they got there. It was quite a run down there for them, the airplane speed being what it was at that time.

Q: What were they? The Folk-Wulf? German?

Adm. R.: They were German aircraft. There was a variety of them. Before they got anywhere near us, there was one that was called the Master of Ceremonies and he would circle around up over the top of us, way up beyond gun range. He was up there watching us and guiding these other people in.

This happened every time we went over or left. This guy was up there and I guess they probably took radio bearings on him or something that steered them in. That's how they found us. They would come at night or in the daytime. I think they preferred to come at night because then we didn't have anything to shoot at, you see. They came out, and there must have been about 12. They were dropping bombs and shooting up the ships and all that kind of business. A couple bombs hit ships. They didn't do an awful lot of damage, but they did a lot of shooting up around on the decks of ships. Every ship in the convoy was shooting just as fast as they could shoot.

We had set up a smoke screen and it was fairly effective, I think. But these guys were flying through it and every ship was just shooting all the time. There were about a half a dozen people in the convoy that were hit and they think it was by bullets that were fired by ships in our convoy.

Anyway, we came through that and we didn't lose any ships and nobody was killed in a convoy, but there were half a dozen people who were injured. Knowing, of course, that these guys were coming, there wasn't anybody exposed except those who had to be exposed. So we continued with that convoy to Bizerte and there the British relieved us off Bizerte. They took the convoy on to the other end of the Mediterranean, and maybe from there down through the Suez. But there were ships dropping off all along the line.

Quite a number of ships left at Oran and we had a couple of other places along the line there in the Mediterranean. So I would say that when we turned it over to the British we probably had about 100 left.

Then we went into Bizerte, tied up at the dock, and we were there about a week, I guess. Then we came out and relieved the British of a convoy going the other way that was almost as big as the other one. Again we were attacked by the aircraft just before we hit Gibraltar. No submarines bothered us then either. We got out and we went all the way back to the United States.

Q: This was a convoy en route to the United States.

Adm. R.: Yes, these convoys went Norfolk to the Meditterranean. We weren't bothered by submarines at that time, either. It's surprising how many false reports you get - whales and sharks and other things. But we were/attacked by any submarines.

When we got about a day out, the escort commander split up the convoy and he went into New York with about three-quarters of the convoy and he gave me the others to go into Norfolk. So I took them into Norfolk and headed out with my escorts and went up to New York, too. We went into the Navy Yard at New York, which is what happened after every one of these things.

We went into the Navy Yard at New York and the shipyard people descended on us. They began ripping things out and putting new things in and we had nothing to say about it. They didn't even tell us what they were going to do if we didn't go up there and ask them. We didn't have torpedo tubes so they put torpedo tubes on. I don't know if it was that time or another time, but they did put them on. They changed antiaircraft guns and gave us a different kind of depth charges. They did all sorts of things like that.

Q: In the implementation of all of this, did they also give you experts to show you what to do?

Adm. R.: They came aboard and explained things to us, but we had people who by that time were pretty well trained in these things and when we finished with them, as a division we left and went up to Casco Bay. There was further antisubmarine training and training as a division in general operations and all that kind of business - underway training. And we did that for a week or ten days, I would say.

Then we were let go from there and we went down to Norfolk and picked up another convoy. This happened regularly every seventy days. We left Norfolk exactly 70 days after our previous departure.

The first convoy was uneventful as far as our submarine business was concerned. After that, the next couple of times we did have contact with submarines.

On one occasion, I was in the rear of the convoy with two other ships. They were stretched out across the convoy and an aircraft reported a submarine that was running along about ten miles behind us on the surface. So we took out after it and we spent several days trailing that submarine. We had a contact now and then but we never were able to make an attack because of the weather and a lot of things. Finally, it disappeared as far as we were concerned. So we then left and went back.

Q: Were you beneficiary of the Tenth Fleet communications on submarines? Washington.

Adm. R.: Yes.

Q: I understand that was very helpful.

Adm. R.: Oh yes, we got all kinds of reports on submarines. It seemed like most any time it wasn't a surprise to see an aircraft come out -- B-24s came out quite a bit and would circle around and they would look here and there. Then they'd disappear and a while later, maybe a day later or a couple of days later, another one would come out. So we were not left alone in the middle of the ocean. They were watching us all right.

During the time that I was aboard that ship, our closest contact with a submarine came in the Mediterranean as we were coming out. We were running at night in the Mediterranean and our lead ship, the one with the escort commander aboard came on a submarine on the surface. They spotted the thing on the surface and it was up in front of them. They headed for it to ram it and the submarine managed to get down. Of course, the convoy just kept going; it went right over the top of the submarine. The submarine fired three torpedoes while it was under the convoy and then was left astern. I was again in the stern and I was left with two ships to trace it down.

So we stayed with it and we made some attacks on it. We didn't get it but we made attacks on it and we kept track of it. Every now and then we would lose him and we would spread out and search and we'd pick it up again. We were there three or four days, I think, with this thing.

Then a division of Navy destroyers came from somewhere -- I don't know where -- and they relieved us of this thing and they picked it up. They got him. And we returned to the convoy and two or three days later, they got the submarine. This, they say, was the last submarine in the Mediterranean. It was reported to me as the last one in the Mediterranean. Last German submarine.

This fellow hit two ships. He hit one in the bow with a torpedo and that ship had to go into Oran for repairs. The other ship was also damaged in the bow but continued in the convoy, but it was hit.

Our greatest activity, it seemed to me, was rounding up stragglers. A lot of ships were coal-burning then, you know, and some of these ships were carrying coal, and some of the ships that burn coal were carrying coal. But they didn't want to touch their cargo and they didn't want to burn up all their coal before they got where they were going either. So they'd hang back, you know. We were always after them to pour on the coal and get up in there where you belong.

On a couple of occasions when a guy would drop back like that, we would hang around back there and circle them because sometimes they would get so far back that they were beyond the protection of the screen.

Q: Didn't the skippers have any concern for their danger?

Adm. R.: I don't think they realized it or else they had more concern for their fuel than they did for their danger.

On one occasion at least or a couple of occasions, we simulated attack and dropped back there. And you should have seen them get going. They'd pick up speed and go up in there, back up in their place, you know. One guy almost went through the convoy, and came out the other end.

Q: Playing games.

Adm. R.: On one occasion as we were coming back there was a tanker that was manned by the Coast Guard -- it was a Q-ship -- it was a tanker and it was equipped for antisubmarine warfare. It simulated being a straggler, trying to get a submarine to approach it and attack it so that it could attack the submarine.

That thing met us one time and was staggering along behind there. We'd drop back to check on him, you know, and talk to him on the blinker and he'd talk back to us. It turned out this fellow was a guy I knew. His name was Jordan. He had been a Warrant Officer and had been promoted and he became a commander, and he was in command of this ship.

I think that was the only one of those ships that we manned. There must have been others that were manned by these Navy people.

Q: Acted as decoys?

Adm. R.: Yes, they were trying to get some submarine to do something to them. They had a lot of guns. He unveiled his guns on one side -- they had a false rail that concealed their guns. He lowered the rail and there were about four or five guns along the railing. A submarine attacking a decoy like that would come to the surface and get himself a good aim before he fired a torpedo and they were ready for him on either side.

Q: How many convoys did you help escort?

Adm. R.: About five or six, I guess.

Q: And didn't lose any ships in the process?

Adm. R.: We didn't lose any ships, no. This fellow Nickerson who was our escort commander was very favorably inclined towards the use of smoke screens. We had been directed during all of our training to be sure how to use our smoke equipment and get it in good condition and have it ready to go at all times. We always used smoke screens in that area where we were likely to be attacked in the Mediterranean. We always covered the thing as much as we could with the smoke. We had pretty good smoke equipment. It was white smoke and it came from an affair on the stern of the ship and would blossom out an awful mess.

Q: It would envelope the whole ship?

Adm. R.: It would envelope the whole convoy. We ran away from it. We didn't allow it to envelope ourselves. We tried to stay out of it. We had to work out a mooring board problem to see just where we should go and what course we should go in order to have this smoke blow across the convoy and we would stay away from there ourselves.

Q: This sort of thing you learned in the submarine school?

Adm. R.: Yes.

Q: That was an exciting assignment then.

Adm. R.: Yes, it was an exciting assignment. We were surprised that we didn't have more action. But I guess we had enough. Come to think of it, we got our convoys there without losing them anyway, and that was the purpose.

Q: This was actually after the peak of the German submarine threat?

Adm. R.: Oh, that was after the peak, yes. This comes along in late '43 and during '44.

Q: Was there any concern for possible German raiders? Any XCLs or whatever they were that they operated in the Atlantic?

Adm. R.: Yes, we thought about them but we never had any warnings of any and we never saw any. I'm sure we would have formed up and attacked it if we had seen any but I don't know what would have happened to us because they probably were more heavily armed than we were. Our biggest gun on ships that I had was a 3-inch gun. We had torpedo tubes so if we could make a run on them we could shoot torpedoes. Our biggest gun was a 3-inch gun and there were some of the later DEs that came out that had a 5-inch gun up in the bow. But ours were 3's as they all had been before ours came out. We had two 3-inch guns, one forward and one aft.

One of the Coast Guard manned ships, not in my division but in the division ahead of mine, was torpedoed by an acoustic torpedo in the Mediterranean. He was running down a submarine and the fellow fired an acoustic torpedo and it hit him right in the stern. It blew the stern off the ship. There was a gun tub back aft with her 3-inch guns and there were about eight or nine men up in that gun tub attending the gun, preparing to attack, if this fellow came to the surface and most of them were killed. There were quite a few people on the ship that were killed.

Another DE manned by the Coast Guard was torpedoed in the North Atlantic and was lost with all hands. I think they were the only Coast Guard DEs that were lost. There were some others that were involved in affairs with submarines. A fellow who was recently the Superintendent of the Coast Guard Academy named Jack Thompson was credited with two submarines, I think.

Interview #3

Admiral Edwin J. Roland, USCG (Ret.)

March 29, 1976 at Old Lyme, Connecticut

Interviewer: John T. Mason, Jr.

Q: It's mighty nice to see you this morning, Admiral. You were talking about the convoy duty in World War II when you were with this Coast Guard unit and your flagship was the VANCE.

Adm. R.: I think we had about finished my account of that kind of duty. But the last trip we made was an interesting one. We ran across a submarine in the Mediterranean which was said to be -- after the thing was over -- the last German submarine that was still active down there. This was in November of '44.

Our escort commander's ship nearly ran it down. They came across the net after dark, she was on the surface, and as a matter of fact, they attempted to run her down after they had sighted her, but she escaped and submerged and fired a couple of torpedoes and hit a couple of ships, each of them in the bow. It didn't sink either one.

Q: These were merchant ships?

Adm. R.: These were merchant ships in the convoy. The ships got into Oran and we continued without them. But I was assigned with the VANCE and two of the ships from my division to hunt this submarine down. We were at it for a couple of days. We made contact occasionally and we made attacks. But the Mediterranean is a difficult place because of layers of water at different temperatures. It's a difficult place to do this. But at least we did stay with them for a couple of days.

Then we were relieved by a division of destroyers. They took up the search. We had made contact just a short time before and they took it up and we returned to the convoy. About two days later we got word that they had gotten him.

Q: Was the VANCE equipped with depth charges?

Adm. R.: Oh yes. Our DEs were antisubmarine ships. We were equipped with depth charges and all kinds of antisubmarine equipment. We were well equipped.

Then on the way back when we were about half-way, one of my ships sent me a message that really puzzled me. It spoke about the flowers in Toledo, Ohio, and wished that I would enjoy them. Now I had no idea what he was talking about. His radioman had intercepted a broadcast that contained my orders and the orders were to go to Toledo where this ship was being built. I had no idea what the fellow was talking about and I made some crack about the flowers in other places are just as good as Toledo. It was a day later that I found out what he was talking about and it was my orders to leave the VANCE and go to the yard in Toledo.

Q: What was the date of that?

Adm. R.: It was in November, the late part of November, somewhere around Thanksgiving, of 1944.

We continued on with this convoy and I was relieved when we arrived in New York in December, the early part of December. I was relieved by a classmate of mine who was the commanding officer of one of the ships in the division.

Q: Before you go to your new assignment, I have a couple of questions I'd like to ask you about convoying duty and about the units of the Coast Guard. Would you say something about personnel, Coast Guard personnel on convoy duty? I don't think you talked about that.

Adm. R.: We manned one hundred percent of the ships that we did man and we had five divisions of six ships each. I had one division -- Division 45. I was the division commander of that division.

Q: The sailors were reservists, many of them, or what?

Adm. R.: Oh there were lots of reservists, yes.

Q: What proportion of them were reservists?

Adm. R.: I would say that the proportion of reservists must have been, at that time of the war, seventy-five percent at least, maybe eighty percent. We had a majority of reservists -- people that we took in and trained. Just like the other services, we were largely reservists. By that time, which was the end of '44, we had been in the war a couple of years.

Q: The Coast Guard had several categories of reservists. There were special reservists and regular reservists?

Adm. R.: We had temporary reserves. But temporary reservists only performed certain kinds of duty and they didn't go overseas and they didn't man our ships. They manned patrol boats and they manned yachts that were taken over. Some of the temporary reservists were the owners of the yachts that were taken over. They performed inshore duty and duty ashore.

They formed quite a large part of the dock forces and things like that. They performed part-time duty. They might work four hours a day or they might work one day a week or they might work almost full-time. There was a great variety in the number of hours that they could spare for this. They wore a uniform and they had police powers and things of that nature.

We had other people operating with them in most cases -- regular officers and more highly trained reservists who were in charge and were full-time. But they filled in gaps.

Q: But that's the distinction. The part-times were the temporaries and the others were the regular reservists.

Adm. R.: Regular reservists were full-time just like the rest of us. The only difference was that they were brought in as reservists because they didn't intend to spend careers and there were certain privileges that a regular has that would have been expensive to hand over to the reservists so they didn't do it.

Our reserve policy is the same as that of the Navy.

Q: I also wanted to bring up this point: in reading the history of the Coast Guard in World War II, a statement is made that the Coast Guard never relaxed its attention to the duty and assistance of people in jeopardy who needed rescuing. How did this pertain when you were on convoy duty?

Adm. R.: Our principal duty when we were on convoy duty was with the convoy. We were there to get the convoy where we were taking it. We weren't there for any other purpose. If somebody was in distress and usually it was because we were attacked, then sometimes we would be sent or sometimes a Navy ship or anybody might be sent in order to pick up survivors and things of that nature.

One of the things that we did a good bit during this escort duty was picking up people who fell overboard. In convoys as big as these that we had -- up to 120 ships, like a small city, you know -- lots of accidents happened. We always had two or three ships at the stern of the convoy -- the others were spread out in the screen ahead and down the sides -- but we always had some astern and those astern had doctors aboard and would go up to ships where they needed medical attention and transfer their doctors or transferred the patients aboard our ship and carried out that duty. Also, they were there for the protection of the rear of the convoy. It occurred frequently that we would get radar contacts after dark. Submarines which were trailing the convoy would come to the surface and we would pick them up and then take out after them. But the escort commander would never allow us to go too long on a hunt like that because he wanted to keep this screen. If there are some tagging along and making themselves seen it might be for the purpose of getting part of the escort away so others can come in and raise cane.

Q: Yes, they act as decoys by trailing along.

Adm. R.: So we picked up lots of people who had fallen overboard and, in some cases, they were pretty drunk too. These were seamen on the merchant ships who would be having a party or something and one of them would go overboard. We picked up several that way.

There were a few that we lost and never saw again. But we did pick up quite a few.

One time -- also on this last convoy -- after we had searched for the submarine and had been relieved and returned to the convoy, I made a report of our search, a written report, which was to go to the escort commander. When the thing was all ready, we went up alongside the flagship and maneuvered to pass this message over. It was in a watertight container with a line on each end of it. So we passed the line over and let them take it over and then they would detach it and we'd pull the line back in again. When the thing was done, in the beginning, they heaved the line over and it didn't quite make it. Our end hadn't been attached yet, and the damned thing fell in the water. We had a serious-minded boatswain's mate who was in charge of this thing and here this thing was going by. I was up on the bridge and I saw this thing going by -- and the boatswain's mate -- I saw him start out down the back and he went all the way to the stern of the ship and he went, boom, right overboard. He went right out and swam over and picked that thing up. Nothing was going to happen to it, it was in a watertight container. It was lighter than the water so it was going to float, but he wasn't going to let any spies get it before he got it. We were very serious about this thing and the report was a secret thing and he knew all these things, you know, and he was being very careful.

So we had to go up ahead and come back down through the convoy and pick this guy up. By the time we got to him to pick him up, he was at the end of the convoy. The convoy is a couple of miles long and all these ships were going by him, but nobody was doing anything about picking him up. Of course, we were heading for him. But it was a kind of hairy experience because we had this fellow in the water and he didn't have a life jacket on. He was swimming. And we were maneuvering down through the convoy in the opposite direction. It was always a little bit frightening because you don't know what somebody is going to do about it.

Q: Did he get a citation for this?

Adm. R.: Did he? Well, he got bawled out first thing. But then, I think he did get some sort of a letter of commendation.

Q: That brings up the question of the communication within the convoy from the escorts to the merchant vessels and to the commodore. Would you talk about that a little?

Adm. R.: The ordinary maneuvering material was just passed by word of mouth, by voice radio -- short-range voice radio.

Q: This was not considered a hazard where the enemy submarines were concerned.

Adm. R.: No, because of the fact that it was low-powered stuff, and it was necessary to do. The other, of course, would be to tap it out in code, to encipher it, then send it and decipher it and there usually wasn't time for that sort of thing. So this was the solution. It worked all right because it didn't go much beyond the convoy. The power wasn't up.

Any other traffic was usually by blinking light. Traffic back to the United States or to some other place in a distance was handled by the ship that was the guard ship. They would get this traffic by blinking light and then they would set themselves off somewhere a couple of miles and they would send it, they would broadcast it.

But within the convoy _most_ of what was done was done by voice radio and the rest of it by blinking light.

Q: And sometimes by line.

Adm. R.: Oh, yes. There was lots of that. Like my thing, you see. It was a written report that was probably four pages long -- a fairly long report. It would have been difficult and tedious and not as exact if it was done the other way. This was a commonplace procedure. We'd pass these back and forth between ships all the time -- engine parts and all sorts of things.

Q: And what about people?

Adm. R.: Oh yes.

Q: There was traffic of that sort then.

Adm. R.: Yes. We had a doctor I think I told you about.

Q: Yes, you did tell me about that.

Adm. R.: He made almost a trip a day, I would say, and maybe more sometimes. He had never done it before and he got so he didn't think anything of it.

Q: What about the facilities on the Azores? You talk about the convoy going back to the States. What sort of facilities did we have on the Azores that were helpful to convoys?

Adm. R.: There were aircraft flying out of there. But we didn't see much of them on these runs to the Mediterranean. The convoys that ran up north did see them. They did come out with them. We would see an airplane now and then which would come along and fly over, just checking the area, checking the convoy, and checking to see if there was anything nearby.

Q: Was it a flying boat?

Adm. R.: Yes, these were big ones. Nothing that would have been much help to us if we were being attacked. But at least they were there keeping track of the thing. It was a comfort to have them and I think they were probably pretty useful. As far as I was personally concerned, I didn't see any direct results. I'm sure that if there was information that he would come over. We didn't communicate with him at all unless there was some very good reason for it. He would just come and he would circle. I'm sure that there was information that got back to the escort commander by broadcast. We received communications by simply copying broadcasts. It wasn't two-way. There were scheduled broadcasts. And we would receive communications that way. And that was the thing, you see, where my orders were -- that we hadn't picked it up on our ship, and this other fellow had on his ship, you see.

That would eventually get to me because the guard ship would see that this material that they collect in the boardcasts was distributed to anybody involved.

Q: A daily bulletin service.

Adm. R.: Yes. There were regular news casts, too, that we would get, dot-and-dash, you know. Our radiomen were always alert to get those because everybody was looking for the news. So everybody copied that.

But for business, there was one ship -- anybody could copy -- but there was one ship that was the guard ship and he was responsible for getting it.

I was relieved in early December and had a couple of days leave to go home and I reported to Toledo about the 15th of December and the ship went into commission on the 20th of December.

Q: You got there just in time.

Adm. R.: Just in time, yes. I didn't know much about this ship.

Q: It was a very special, new type ship, was it not?

Adm. R.: Oh yes. Well, we had some big icebreakers that were somewhat like it but this one was built for duty on the Great Lakes. It had the same power.

Q: This one was named the MACKINAW.

Adm. R.: This was named the MACKINAW and it had the same power plant that the WIND ships had, the big icebreakers. But it was a bigger ship in length and width but it didn't draw as much water. It's best icebreaking draft was $19\frac{1}{2}$ feet. The other ships were ten feet deeper than that. But a ship with that draft wouldn't be useful on the Lakes because it couldn't get in most of the harbors.

Q: It had to be shallow draft.

Adm. R.: It had to be shallow draft so this ship was built differently than the others. And it was different in some other ways, too. For instance, we didn't have condensers and evaporators and things like that for turning salt water into fresh, because we were going to operate in fresh water. We had a water plant aboard that was like a water plant in a city. It took water from overboard and ran it through this purifier and that was our water, which was a great advantage. This was a very good-sized ship.

Q: How many tons was she?

Adm. R.: She was about 5200. Her tonnage was not much different than the tonnage of the WIND ships, but it was spread out more and didn't go so deep.

Q: Incidentally, what is the ordinary depth of ice on the Great Lakes where you would be operating?

Adm. R.: During the time that I was up there I would say that we didn't see any ice that was more than four feet thick. But the difficulty with ice up there is different than it is in the Antarctic and the Arctic, where they have this tremendous thick ice. Up in the Lakes the ice storms come and it breaks up the ice and piles it up. During tests that we made one time -- we had a party aboard from Washington that came up for us to make tests -- they had probed over the side and they found ice as far down as thirty feet. But this was mixed with water, you see, not solid.

But it clogs the intakes, you see. This is the difficulty that ships always run into that aren't prepared for breaking ice. On the MACKINAW our intakes were along the keel, right down at the greatest depth. Most of these ships have their intakes three or four feet below the water line. So this was a great advantage to us because it was always clear water down there, some ice, and it would clog up but we had devices for blowing it out if it did clog up.

Q: Inasmuch as this was a special design that came along and was building during the war, I'd like to ask a question: I know that we were building icebreakers for the Russians. Was there any feed-in from Russian experience with icebreakers which was supplied to a ship like the MACKINAW?

Adm. R.: I'm sure there was some, but I don't know the details of it. The Russians, of course, took some of our WIND ships.

Q: They wanted all the icebreakers we could turn out.

Adm. R.: Oh, they wanted them all and they did take some. We trained an engineering crew aboard the MACKINAW while I was there for one of the WIND ships. Our power plant was identical. So we had them aboard for about a month, I think. We found one Coast Guard officer who could speak Russian and that was our only translator aboard. So he was up day and night while these people were there.

Q: Was that happenstance that you found somebody who spoke Russian?

Adm. R.: He was sent to us as part of the deal but he was the only one. Of course, there was an awful lot of communication after a couple of days by signs and taking a guy by the arm and leading him on and doing something.

Q: There was always a possibility of error by that kind of thing.

Adm. R.: Oh, of course. Anyway, we went into commission on the 20th. Then during the time after I arrived and the 20th, we had trials. We went up the Detroit River up the St. Clair River up into Lake Huron and then came around back down.

Q: Was this to test the icebreaking ability or was this just to test the engines?

Adm. R.: I think it was just mainly to test the general operating characteristics of the ship -- the steering and everything. They had a lengthy series of tests that were run on all the equipment aboard.

Q: With shipyard people.

Adm. R.: With shipyard people, but there were Coast Guard people, too. All of the inspection force was aboard -- the Coast Guard Inspection Force that was at the building.

Q: At that stage she hadn't been turned over to the Coast Guard?

Adm. R.: No, she still belonged to the shipyard.

Q: What was the shipyard in Toledo?

Adm. R.: The American Shipbuilding Company. The ship didn't become our property until the 20th of December and that was also the day that we went into commission.

Q: During the trials you were the skipper -- potential skipper -- but you were not actually in charge during the trials?

Adm. R.: No. I had a free hand. I could go anywhere I wanted to watch anything . . .

Q: That must have been a great help, wasn't it?

Adm. R.: Oh, it was a tremendous help. I should say.

Q: What was the complement on board?

Adm. R.: When we started out, we had about, I would say, 225 people, which is much greater than the number now.

Q: That was a wartime complement.

Adm. R.: It was because in wartime, of course, they always put about twice as many people aboard as you need. Anyway, it was a new undertaking for us. The ship was electric driven -- a diesel electric -- and there was a lot of electrical equipment aboard the ship. So we had about 35 or 40 electrician's mates aboard.

When the thing finally shook down and got into a peacetime operation later on, they wound up with about eight electrician's mates. You see, we had all these guys that were all over the place checking things and just seeing if everything was going to work out the way they thought it was going to work out and all that. We were well loaded.

We had no guns.

Q: No guns. You were operating in the Great Lakes alone. Was there a proviso for installation of guns in case she operated somewhere else?

Adm. R.: No, I think not. It would have been difficult, maybe impossible to send her into salt water because she didn't have the equipment to handle salt water.

On these trials we checked everything out. We had the whole crew aboard then, so they were all getting shaken down into their

Q: Had they been trained in special schools for their various functions?

Adm. R.: Yes. For instance, these electrician's mates either had been operating electrician's mates somewhere or else they were people who had been sent to school to become electrician's mates. Then they were all put together in a receiving station somewhere -- I think it was Cape May probably for that crew -- and they operated as a group there. They were lectured and drilled and worked with models and drawings on this ship and became thoroughly familiar with the way the ship was put together and the purpose for which it was going to operate and all that.

Q: You as the skipper -- were you cognizant of the scope of their training?

Adm. R.: I didn't know anything about these ships. I knew we were going to build an icebreaker but I didn't know when we were going to do it. No, I didn't know what was being done.

Some of the officers who went to the ship were with them.

Q: What sort of a cadre of officers did you have?

Adm. R.: There was one other regular officer -- he was the engineer. All of the others were reservists. In the engineering force -- that's another thing -- we wound up with about seven or eight officers in the engineering force. And about half of those were people who had been warrant officers and had been promoted during the war. Then there was the engineer. The rest of them were reservists.

On deck, all of the deck officers were reservists, except me.

Q: I would think this would have placed an added burden on the skipper's shoulders to have an overabundance of personnel on board.

Adm. R.: Yes. We had some people who had come into the Coast Guard as reservists and wanted to go to sea, but they were needed ashore, you know. Two of them were stationed in Toledo as captain of the port force there. They had never been aboard ship and they came aboard as watch officers. Of course, I didn't let them stand watch. We had three or four people who had stood watches and they stood watches and I spent most of my time on the bridge when I was aboard the ship in the beginning until we got well shaken down.

Q: Until you were confident of your personnel.

Adm. R.: Yes. We had all kinds of talent among them. There were lawyers and all kinds of businessmen, you know. There were people who had more money than they'd ever need and things like that, but they were just like everybody else. There was really all kinds of talent in the enlisted force, too.

During the war there were lots of cases. Huntington Hartford was an enlisted man in the Coast Guard. We didn't have anybody named Huntington Hartford or anybody as far-fetched as that. But we had a lot of enlisted men who were seamen and men like that.

We had a fellow -- a Senator from Rhode Island -- Senator Claiborne Pell. Senator Pell was a cook in the Coast Guard. He later became an officer and he still is a Coast Guard reserve officer. He may be retired by now, I don't know. He got to be a captain. While I was the Commandant people kept coming to me about when are we going to make Pell an admiral? But we didn't have many admirals then.

Q: She was destined for what was termed the task on an unprecedented scale of icebreaking in the Lakes. Do you want to talk about the scope of the duty that you had?

Adm. R.: Well, the importance of the thing was that they wanted iron ore. As a matter of fact, they even went so far as to build a railroad up from Escanaba in Lake Michigan up to Duluth on Superior, up in that area. So they wanted us to extend the season as much as we could at both ends.

Of course, we were getting there in the middle of winter so there was no extension to be done right at that time.

Q: I take it that in peacetime these routes were not kept open in the winter time.

Adm. R.: No. There were a few ships that operated on the Lakes. There are some car ferries that used to operate across Lake Michigan. That was the main line of the grand trunk was across Lake Michigan and car ferries. They went across from Ludington to Green Bay and also from Grand Haven and the next town north over to Milawukee. So we had some work with them.

As a matter of fact, that earlier icebreaker that I mentioned I was on up there, the Escanaba - we used to work with them, too.

Q: They were much lower down in the Lake.

Adm. R.: Yes, that was in Lake Michigan. They were better icebreakers then, than the Escanaba was, anyway. But we did work with them and help them when they got stuck.

Anyway, after going into commission, we spent a couple more days in Toledo, taking aboard stores and things. Then we left and went up into Lake Huron and operated up there in the ice for a while, just testing things, checking things out, and arrived at our home port which was Cheboygan, Michigan on the Straits of Mackinaw, on the 30th of December.

Q: How did she perform in Lake Huron?

Adm. R.: She is the best ship I have ever been on for the purpose for which she was built. We never ran across any ice that stuck her. Well, it would stop her for a minute, you know, but never ice that stalled her from doing the job she was out there to do. And if you put full power on her and headed her into anything, she would go right through, slow down but go ahead. The idea of an icebreaker is a little different than is required on the Great Lakes but she's built with a cutaway bow and her sides are completely half-round. There's no straight up and down under the water at all.

The idea is that she will ride up on the ice and break it down. There was a propeller in the bow of the ship. The idea of that propeller was that the ship rides up on the ice, the propeller pulls water out from under that ice and thereby weakens the support of the ice and allows the ship to break it down.

Q: Now this would happen where the ice was no deeper than four feet, but if it got down to thirty feet, how would that function?

Adm. R.: They put those things on the WIND ships, too. After some operation they came back and just cut them off because they would run into icebergs and they used to get all jammed up. It would just break them off. They had trouble with shafts and bearings and they'd lose their wheels, of course.

Q: There must have been some special steel used in these.

Adm. R.: Oh, yes. On the MACKINAW - that ship has hit ice with that propeller, very heavy ice - this stuff piled up, you know, very heavy blocks of ice - has hit it so hard that the propeller would stop. And then it would start up again. There is still the same propeller on that ship, in the bow, that there was in the beginning. The same propeller is still there after 30 years.

Q: What a record!

Adm. R.: Yes. That propeller was not very good as a propeller. It was more built like a big club - it had the general shape of a propeller but it was built to stand something like that.

Q: It really had a different purpose, didn't it?

Adm. R.: Yes. The other propellers aft - there were two propellers aft - they were standard propellers made of good material and they were very rugged and stood up for a long time but they have been replaced, I suppose, several times.

Q: Now, when the bow propeller was operating as it was intended and went up on top of the ice, how much weight approximately would be applied to that ice at that point?

Adm. R.: I don't know. Of course, it was combination of the force that was applied - the weight and also the push of the ship. But it had to be a couple of thousand of tons, I would say. The ship would ride way up. The ship would ride up to the extent to where you would see this propeller sometimes. The propeller was a six foot propeller - I mean a twelve foot propeller in diameter. There's six feet above the shaft and when the ship was lying dead in the water, I would say that that was probably six feet below the surface. But it would come up when the ship would ride up. It would come up so you could see it. So there was a lot of weight. And there was a big tank in the bow which in icebreaking trim you kept full for that purpose and to have that extra weight up there, you see.

The ship also had heeling tanks. There was a 200-ton tank on each side and they were connected by 24-inch pipe. There was a big electric propeller pump in there that would pull this water back and forth. You could pump 200 tons of water from one side over to the other side and back again in 90 seconds - to get side-wise rolling motion of ship.

Q: That's what a heeling tank is.

Adm. R.: Yes. And this tank in the bow and a tank back aft near the stern were also connected so that you could trim the ship. But that didn't amount to so much. You could heel the ship probably about eight or ten degrees with these tanks.

Q: Was this a new type of equipment for an icebreaker?

Adm. R.: It was on the WIND ships. And I think that the Finns and the Russians probably had it before then, too. It wasn't a new development but it may have been better. I don't think that you needed to do it that fast. We had a tremendous pump on this thing to pump that much water back and forth in ninety seconds.

Q: Did it have to be pumped in that length of time or could it be delayed?

Adm. R.: Oh no, you could slow it up. We tested that a good many times. We didn't really need this heeling business much. We used it occasionally because it did help, but we could have broken any ice that we came to without it, I know.

In the summertime, one time we went up into the mouth of the St. Mary's River and anchored the ships to test equipment. One of the things we tested was these heeling tanks. On the top of each tank on the main deck there was a cover - a safety valve, a heavy metal cover probably two-and-a-half to three feet across - and if you pumped too much water into the tank, this safety valve would lift up and allow the excess water to flow out. We did that one time. This one time in the first summer that I was there. We had too much water. You only need 200 tons but we probably had a good bit more. So when we heeled over and the water began coming, this thing opened up. I had seen it open before so it didn't bother me. But my son, Eddie, was aboard - this was in 1944 so he was about 7 years old - he saw it and his eyes were as big as saucers. There was water gushing out and it came up a foot high all over the deck. He looked at it, you know, and looked at it. After we finished our tests that day, we had an assistance call down in the St. Clair River. A ship had gone aground on an island down there.

So I had Eddie aboard and I didn't want to go back and put

him ashore, so we went down. On the way down it turned dark and I said to Eddie, "Now, you go down to the cabin, Eddie, and you sleep in the bunk in the spare stateroom. I'll be down pretty soon to see you."

He said, "Okay." So he went down and after a while I went down and there he was, up in the bunk, and he had a life jacket around him. His head was hanging out of one end and his feet out the other. I said, "What in the world do you have that thing on for, Eddie?"

He said, "Well, after what I saw this afternoon there when you were testing that thing, I don't trust this ship."

Q: He really thought she was on the way to sink.

Adm. R.: He didn't know what was going to happen next.

As I said, we arrived on the 30th of December of '44 at Cheboygan and, of course, this was the day before New Year's Eve. The next day they had a big welcome thing and they had a banquet that night in the only place that was available for a crowd and this was a big bar, really, where they had it - the Gold Front in Cheboygan, Michigan. There were several people who got up to speak. Skippers of the car ferries from up a way a little bit, at Mackinaw city - they were there and they both got up and spoke. And other people who were in the steamship business around there were there. Everybody was doubtful about the MACKINAW, about whether she was going to be able to do the things that people said she was going to do.

Q: You mean because this was an operation that had never been accomplished before?

Adm. R.: No, they could see that she might be a good help all right but they didn't think that she was going to be better than their car ferries. The two car ferries that operated across the Straits of Mackinaw, up at the west end of the Straits of Mackinaw, up at Mackinaw City, were icebreakers. They both had bow propellers, too, and one propeller aft. But they weren't very high powered and they often got stuck - frequently, almost every time they crossed in the middle of winter, they would get stuck. They'd work themselves out.

Q: So applying that experience to the MACKINAW, the new ship, they were doubtful about her.

Adm. R.: They didn't think she was going to be able to do it. The skipper of the St. Marie, when he finished up his talk - and he said some complimentary things - he said, "Captain Rowe and I want you to realize now that if you ever get stuck, let me know, and I'll come with the St. Marie and get you out."

Q: How did you feel as the skipper of this new ship? How did you feel about that?

Adm. R.: Everybody laughed, so I laughed too. But it wasn't very long . . .

Q: Were you apprehensive about her ability to perform?

Adm. R.: Well, I wasn't as sure as I was a little later. I hadn't been up through where they operated, which was the worst part of the Straits. I hadn't been up through there - I didn't know what was going to happen when we went there. I knew we were going to get through because these other ships got through but I didn't know if we would get through better than they would or not.

Q: What was the potential iron ore traffic that you were intended to assist? How many ships?

Adm. R.: There must have been 20 companies and I would say there must have been 75 ships - big ships, 600 feet long.

Q: And you were the sole icebreaker for them?

Adm. R.: Except these car ferries. Before we got there, in the spring they closed down this car ferry operation and the steamship companies rented these car ferries in order to get them up through the St. Mary's River, to help them after the ice had broken up. But to get them into the corners and all that, they'd hire those ferries.

Q: When you were engaged in breaking ice and making a channel for these iron ore ships, how much time was allowed before the ice would form again?

Adm. R.: A good bit of the time in that heavy piled up ice, we would go through and ships would be following us and they would immediately get stuck before they had time ever to form again, because this slush would close in on them and they would lose their water suction.

So then we would circle and we would get behind them and we would run as fast as we could up past them and as close as we could and that would break up a wide path in the ice and then they would be able to get going again. So whenever we were taking ships through it was likely to be that way in the heaviest part.

Q: How many ships would be shepherded at one time?

Adm. R.: At one time, I would say as many as ten or twelve. But usually after we got going with say ten or twelve, after you've gone a few miles they would be strung out and there would be one or two of them that were up close with you. Then you'd take them out until you got away from the bad ice and let them go, and then come back and get a couple more and bring them through.

Q: You were like a mother hen with her little chickens.

Adm. R.: Oh, yes. It took a long time to do this. The St. Mary's River was a very difficult place and the channel not very wide. Getting them up through there was very difficult in the beginning, but having done it once and having run it a couple of times, then you could be pretty sure that they would be able to work their way along.

Then we would work in what was called Whitefish Bay, to the west of the Sioux, at the eastern end of Lake Superior.

Q: What sort of draft would these iron ore ships have when they were laden with iron ore?

Adm. R.: The limiting draft in the river was about 20 feet. They would come down to within a few inches of that. They'd be just this much above bottom. They'd load all they could, board all the iron ore they could. It really wasn't very much iron ore either when you look at the piles.

Q: Iron weighs heavy, doesn't it?

Adm. R.: Oh, there would be a pile here and a pile here and a pile here and space around them. In a 600 foot ship they probably had around eight holds. There would be a big pile in this hole, a big pile in this hold, but not anywhere near full. But they had to have a ship that big in order to support that much weight.

Q: Tell me about your first job.

Adm. R.: Our first job came - we left Cheboygan on the 3rd of January, so it was not much time from the time we arrived and had our celebration until it would be enough for people who had been to parties on New Year's Eve to get over them. So we left on the 3rd and we had to go up the St. Mary's River and there hadn't been anything up through there all winter from the time they closed traffic which was the 7th of December. So it was frozen solid and we had to go up through there and then go through the locks and go up through the Superior Harbor.

There were three new transports that had been built for the Navy up there. They were small transports, probably about a couple hundred feet long. So we went up to get them and brought them back.

Q: These were personnel transports?

Adm. R.: No, they weren't. They were AKs, cargo transports. We brought them back down and took them through the locks.

Q: Were they laden with anything?

Adm. R.: No, they were empty. They were ballasted. They performed pretty well. We got down and took them through the locks.

Q: Was there any particular difficulty with the locks in freezing?

Adm. R.: Yes. I'm going to mention that. The operation of the locks, I think, was the reason why they hadn't thought about a bigger icebreaker out there before. They had decided that the locks could not be operated in the wintertime. Now, a couple years before the MACKINAW went up there, because of the desperate need for iron ore, they decided to keep open a little later.

Their normal closing date was the 7th of December and they stuck strictly to it. If a ship was out at the west end and didn't get back by the 7th of December, he had to spend the winter. He had to turn around and go back to Duluth and spend the winter there. It didn't run through.

A couple years before they had decided to keep the locks open. The locks get filled up with ice and you have to open the gates and the gates get fouled up by this and you have to manhandle that ice with poles and with pikes in order to get it out of the way so you can get the locks open. Then you've got a jammed-up lock and you've got to get through. So this was a hell of a job and it was a tough job when we went through this time. But we did get through.

The time before when they tried it, they opened the gates and while they were opening, ice had formed on the hinge of the gate and it lifted up the gate and dropped it on the bottom. The gate came right off and just fell down to the bottom. There they were.

Q: No lock.

Adm. R.: There was no gate for the lock and they were stuck. There wasn't a damned thing they could do until the next spring when the ice went and they could get hold of that gate and take it up and put it back in place. So they had good reason for thinking that they couldn't do this. They have later devised means of preventing that. I don't know what they do about handling the ice in the locks now, but they now stay open through December.

Anyway, when we went through and got these people and came back, nobody had ever done it before, nobody had ever gone through those locks in January before that happened. We took them down and when we came out of the St. Mary's River and headed across through the Straits of Mackinaw. Then we had our first encounter with this ice that the car ferries had.

Q: That stumped them.

Adm. R.: Yes. So we ploughed right through, we hardly even slowed down. We went right through it and we got these transports out past the path where the car ferries run and the car ferries were stuck in there. So I had the transports stopped and we ran down alongside the car ferries and circled them and then came back and got the transports again. And the car ferries went on. We broke them out and they went on to the other side. They never said another word about our icebreaker. I sure was happy about that. That wasn't long after they had me on the pan.

Anyway, we took these AKs through and it's about eight or ten miles across the north end of Lake Michigan there, a string of islands. We took them out and headed down. From there on it was easy. There wasn't very much ice in Lake Michigan. We took them down to Chicago and tugs picked them up and they took them through the canals down there to the river and they went down to

New Orleans. They did whatever work there was to do around and then they shoved off and went out to the South Pacific. So that was my first . . .

Q: Tell me a little more about how you operated through the locks. How you got through the locks, it being a very formidable task.

Adm. R.: Of course, yes. Our beam was 74 feet, four or six inches, I'm not sure which. The locks are 80 feet. So when you go into the locks with the MACKINAW, you're practically touching the sides. So it was a little difficult to do but we didn't have much difficulty doing it. We used our wheels to pull and shove ice and we piled up ice in the locks, messed it up a good bit. But when we got in and they opened the other end, then we were able to push the ice out the other end.

Q: How did you circumvent the difficulty with the hinges on the locks?

Adm. R.: I don't know what they did. I don't know how they worked that out. They must have used some kind of heaters on there. That was what they eventually did. They wired so this ice would . . .

Q: They had already perfected some kind of technique.

Adm. R.: I don't think they had done it then. I think they used some other temporary measure at the time, because they didn't have any intention of continuing this, you know. They did this simply to get these three transports through.

Q: But they were not optimistic about iron ore ships going through.

Adm. R.: No. All the rest of the time I was up there, they didn't do it any more. Those big ships out there are not built to operate in ice anyway. They have straight sides, so they have an awful drag on the sides when they are trying to get through.

Q: They were really built for summertime traffic.

Adm. R.: Yes, that's what they were intended for.

Q: What was the possibility of using rail traffic from Duluth to get the iron ore out?

Adm. R.: Well, it was too expensive, I guess. They built a single cable rail from Escanaba up to the mines and they got some out that way. But it wasn't enough. They weren't able to get anything like what they wanted. It either had to be a full-scale railroad operation which they apparently weren't ready to tackle, or else by ship.

Q: What kind of a navigator did you have on board?

Adm. R.: Well, my executive officer was a fellow named Hopkins and he was a reserve officer. He was a very serious fellow and a hard worker. His experience had been aboard landing craft, LSTs, and he was all right. I was satisfied with him. He did as well as he could do under the circumstances. He was a pretty good pilot.

Q: But you spoke about the numerous little islands dotting the area up there in the rivers and the straits and it occurred to me: what is the rule in the Coast Guard when a skipper runs aground? Is it the same as in the Navy? Does he ruin his career?

Adm. R.: It's supposed to be but I don't think that the Coast Guard has ever been that way about it. As a matter of fact, you know that great big ice breaker, the POLAR STAR? The biggest thing anybody ever heard of? A fellow named Vensko is the skipper of it, was the skipper of it. He was selected to be a flag officer. But he was still a captain and he had been assigned to this ship. He was assigned to it and was in the yard where they were building it when he was selected.

So when the ship was commissioned and they had their big party and all that, he took it away from the yard and headed for his home port to tie it up and I'll be damned if he didn't put it aground. He was aground for over a day before they finally got it off on a high tide. He had already been selected. Nothing ever happened though, he's still selected.

Q: They wouldn't rescind that. Does the Coast Guard have a court of inquiry if something like that happens?

Roland #3 - 234

Adm. R.: Sure. Any time you touch bottom there's a board.

Q: It seems to me that operating in an area such as you were operating in the same kind of rule couldn't apply.

Adm. R.: No. I know that we had that ship aground, but we had enough power so it didn't make much difference. We drew so much water in this place -- you know, coming down the St. Mary's River through a place they call the Rock Cut, in one place they have a separate downward and upward channel. They call that the Rock Cut and they just blasted it out.

Q: It was a made channel.

Adm. R.: Yes. It's only about 16 feet deep or something like that. So our best icebreaking draft was $19\frac{1}{2}$. So when we went through there we pumped out all the water and did everything we could to get her up. We could get her up that high all right and we'd go down through. But we were awful close to the bottom even then. We could get her up to about $14\frac{1}{2}$ feet.

Q: What extra precautions are taken in building an icebreaker to protect the hull, the bottom?

Adm. R.: Heavy plate -- that's the only thing. Of course, they are built with narrow frame spacing. The frame spacing was about 14 inches, I think, on the MACKINAW. The plating was about an inch and a half -- I think it was an inch and five-eighths -- for six feet below the water line and about a foot or two above where the ice would be. The rest of the plating was not that heavy, but was heavy plating. As long as you didn't hit a rock - if you hit a rock going at a good speed, I know that it would have punched a hole in her. But if you hit a sand bottom or something, you wouldn't have that difficulty.

As a matter of fact, the harbor at Cheboygan where we were stationed was only about 16 feet deep. The width of the channel was less than the length of the ship so we couldn't turn. They had a turning basin in there. In the turning basin there was only thirteen feet of water, so we couldn't use it.

Q: So you were fraught with danger all the time.

Adm. R.: We had to go in and then back out. After we had done it a few times, I did it the other way because I thought I might want to come out in bad weather some times or something, so I would back in. But the first time and for several times we went in head first and then backed out. Then when we got there if the weather was bad, we waited for the weather to get better and then we'd back in and tie up. Then we were ready to go, to head out. But the channel wasn't much wider than this ship either. There was no place to go. It was a real tough place.

They later dredged that channel and they've got about 18 feet in it now, I think, and the turning basin - now they have a good mooring place - the turning basin is where the ship is tied up now -- they built a mooring on the side of the turning basin. So the ship is out of the channel now and in the turning basin and they're in fairly good shape now.

Q: I trust that you were asked to make a thorough going report on the rules of the road for this area you were operating in, so those who came after you would know.

Adm. R.: Oh yes. Nobody that came after me had the same experience. After we got things going we always had somebody come up there and serve aboard the ship for a little while before he took command of it. The fellow who relieved me was aboard for a month and a half before he relieved me. Whenever there's been a relief since they've done that.

There's a lot of difference, you know, in the rules of the road in the Lakes and in salt water.

Q: Tell me about some of the differences.

Adm. R.: For instance, the fog signal is different. The fog signal up there is two blasts every minute. This is a bad rule because when you give two blasts -- and you have to have distinctive pause between the blasts -- you have a blast that is about a second and a half or two seconds, about two seconds, I think was required -- and then about a second and another two second blast. Then pretty soon you're blowing again. Your fog horn is going too much. You can't listen. After your fog horn stops, you can't hear for a while anyway. And other people are doing the same thing, too. I mean their fog horns are blowing all the time up there.

They have a rule of their own up there that bothered me for a while. The first time I ran into it I didn't know anything about it. I didn't know it existed. But if two of these ships are coming down the channel - and it happened to me in the St. Clair River - the two ships were coming down like this and I was coming out. So I blew a blast which meant that we would pass port to port and this fellow answered me. And this fellow following blew two, and he was over here on the other side of the channel. So he kept coming and I had to go between them. I answered his signal with two blasts, but immediately I repeated the signals and turned the searchlight on him and used the searchlight along with the signal for this one and then did the same thing for this one because I was giving them different signals. This is recognized by them. Some of the ships up there had at that time whistle lights and I think they all are required to have whistle lights now. Every time their whistle blows there's a light up in the mast - the masthead light lights up so that you know who's blowing the damned whistle and signalling because you're liable to get this thing.

Q: But in the fog is the whistle light visible very far?

Adm. R.: No, not in fog. It doesn't do any good in fog. This is just passing signals that they want that for.

Q: You spoke about the difference in operation in the Great Lakes in contrast with salt water. Using this illustration of the two blasts for the fog, what would you do if you were off the Grand Banks?

Adm. R.: You mean what would be the fog signal?

Q: Yes.

Adm. R.: It was one every three minutes. The only place I know where the fog signal is two blasts is on the Great Lakes, not any place else.

Q: Were you equipped with radar?

Adm. R.: Yes.

Q: How useful was radar?

Adm. R.: Oh, it was wonderful, just marvelous. We'd have been in an awful fix without it, especially in the wintertime. It snows so much up there and we'd come down those channels in the snow and you really don't see much.

Q: You really couldn't have operated without radar then.

Adm. R.: No. We couldn't. We'd have had to wait for visibility to go through some of the places you have to go through there.

Q: Did you lose any iron ore ships during your period up there?

Adm. R.: No. These people are very good ship handlers. They don't know beans about navigating. They probably know how to take cross bearings - they must know it although I don't think they ever do it. They do everything on time. In fog, they'll run for a certain length of time and then they turn whether they see anything or not. They have fairly frequent collisions up there but they are always in bad visibility. When they can see one another, they manage to handle their ships well. These ships are tremendous things - they're 600 feet long. Now, of course, they're bigger than that even. There isn't a tug within 100 miles of the Sioux and these ships all have to go through, they have to make the landing on each end of these docks and then go through. And there isn't a tug anywhere near it.

Q: The Coast Guard is responsible for safety on merchant vessels. This would also pertain to iron ore carriers, would it not? So what does the Coast Guard do about training these men?

Adm. R.: We don't do anything about training them but we have always required that they be licensed.

Q: The safety would be involved, however, would it not?

Adm. R.: Oh yes, safety is involved and one of the things which the Coast Guard has done is to now require ships to ship radio. Every ship now has to have radio. Most of them had them then, too. They would talk to one another. But now they are required to have it and they have to talk to one another in passing situations and so on. The channels are fairly narrow. I would say the maximum width of channel up there in the rivers is 600 feet and in most places it's less than that. So they have to talk to one another. And they are now required to talk to one another and they're required to have radio.

Before they didn't. The Canadians often didn't have radio on their ships. I have passed Canadian ships in the St. Clair River and the Detroit River where there was nobody in sight aboard the ship except one man standing at the wheel -- nobody else on the bridge and nobody else in sight anywhere on the ship. Of course, we require lookouts and we require an officer on the bridge, as well as the man at the wheel. I don't know what the situation is now, but that's the way it was then.

Q: As skipper of the MACKINAW, did you have any obligation or did you help in any way with the Canadian ore carriers or were they operating?

Adm. R.: Oh yes. They just got in line with our ships.

Q: So you escorted them, too.

Adm. R.: Yes. As a matteroof fact, one of the things we did -- the next thing after we took those transports was to go down to Lorain, Ohio, and pick up a minesweeper that had been built down there. We had some extra time and we had been notified that there were a couple of ships coming out of Georgian Bay in Canada, on the east side of Lake Huron. They were coming down, inside the

Georgian Bay, down the west side of the Georgian Bay.

So I didn't say anything to anybody and I probably should have because later on the District commander told me I should have - but we went in and went down and met the ships and brought them out through the ice. They followed us all the way down through the St. Clair River and the Detroit River where we went on our way to Lorain. The first commercial ship that we helped at all was a Canadian.

Q: Was there any compensation involved for the Coast Guard in doing this for Canadian ships?

Adm. R.: No, we were really testing our wings ourselves. We were just messing around - and there isn't compensation now either. But I doubt that we would ever send the MACKINAW in there to do that because of the chance of their being some kind of an accident. There is a good chance of their being an accident when you are icebreaking. You have to run fairly close to other ships and the ice pushes you and pushes them and you're quite apt to have an accident. I don't think that they would send us into a Canadian port to do that.

Q: In case of an accident would there be a liability on the icebreaker?

Adm. R.: Sure. We had only one accident while I was there. It was probably the following spring after the time that I've been talking about. We took some ships across Lake Erie into Buffalo.

We had two or three of them following us and they were not able to make very good time -- they were slow ships. So we were proceeding at slow speed and we came across a great hunk of ice, a big pile of ice, and it stopped us. Well, the next ship was a half a mile behind us, so I sent him a blinker and blew the danger signal on the whistle and all that -- and this thing kept right on coming. He was backing full but it didn't look like he was backing at all. He came right up and we had two big ironwood fenders out on the stern. There's a notch cut in the stern like this that we'd pull the bow of a ship that you want to tow up -- that you want to tow through the ice and you pull it up close. There's a big ironwood fender attached to the hull on either side of that notch and he ran into one of those and it just opened up the side of his ship -- you could walk through. It was probably as long as this room.

Q: Was he operating on blinders or what?

Adm. R.: Oh no, he was backing but he just didn't have enough power to stop his ship.

Q: And he insisted on going in a straight line.

Adm. R.: Yes. That's the only time we had an accident. We touched other ships, you know.

Q: What kind of agreement did the Coast Guard have with these commercial shipping lines to prevent any kind of suits and suing from accidents?

Adm. R.: Oh, they could sue us.

Q: They could. You didn't have some kind of written agreement with them to prevent this.

Adm. R.: No, they could sue us, just as they often do. Fishermen have sued the Coast Guard when the Coast Guard was towing them in on a distress case. They run out of gas, you know, and the Coast Guard goes out and puts a line aboard them and brings them in. And then some accident like that happens, some real accident - and they can sue the Coast Guard.

Q: How amenable are the courts to a suit of that kind?

Adm. R.: I don't think we pay very many of those things. But we have paid some. Probably in some cases we were pretty much at fault, you know. You're bound to be because there are so many cases where you tow somebody that you're bound to be at fault once in a while if there's an accident. The risk is great in assistance cases.

Q: I would think that when you undertook a service such as you did to help these commercial lines get the iron ore out in wintertime and wartime, that there could have been some kind of a contractual arrangement which would exonerate you from anything.

Adm. R.: Well, there isn't. I'm sure there isn't now. I know there wasn't anything like that then. We are not supposed to touch them, we're not supposed to be in that close to them.

Anyway, when we picked up the Canadians we were on our way to Lorain, and we got down there and here was a brand new minesweeper that they wanted to get out in the same way we got the AKs out, the ones down in Chicago. Of course, a minesweeper is a pretty paper-thin thing, you know.

So we got in there and I went over aboard the ship and just took a look at it. I said, "You're going to have to take it easy on ice because it's going to be pretty rough going." They said, "Oh, we know that, but it's an emergency. We've got to get the ship."

So I said, "O.K. We'll break the ice." They said that they didn't have the regular wheels -- they're twin screw and they're kind of small screw and they turn pretty fast -- those wheels on those minesweepers. They had taken off their regular screws and put on cast-iron screws. I didn't know that this had happened, and if I had I wouldn't have said anything because it wouldn't have occurred to me and I think the other wheels probably would have gone anyway. But anyway, they put those on and they thought that the others would get bent up.

Q: Cast iron would be much more vulnerable though, wouldn't it?

Adm. R.: Brittle, of course. Anyway, we started out. I don't think we got a mile and a half and they stopped. They didn't have a blade left on their wheels, not a blade. They were gone.

And we were a hell of a long way from Chicago.

So I said, "What shall I do?" I called the District Office -- I said, "We could take him in tow and tow him around. It's going to be a long trip."

Q: How big a ship was he?

Adm. R.: About 220 feet long. It wouldn't have been much of a problem. So we hauled them up into the notch -- it was a way to test the notch, anyway. We got him up in there and we started out. The ice wasn't too bad for a while, but pretty soon I got a call from the man and he said, "Boy, it is really noisy over here. We can just hear the ice go sliding down the side of the ship." We could hear it in the MACKINAW, too.

But anyway, I didn't think too much of it. I sent the exec over. He went over and took a look at it. He said, "They're coming along all right." Then after a while I went over. I went down in the engine room and looked around. It sounds like coal going through a scuttle when ice is going down the side of the ship. It's a terrible racket. I looked around and I could see a dent in the side. I said, "Well, here's one place. I don't know whether you had that before you left or what."

He said, "Well, I don't know either." I said, "The ice is going to get a lot worse than this." Of course, this was a young naval officer and he didn't have any experience in ice. He was probably a very competent sailor and all but he hadn't been in ice before. So we kept on going and we went all the way up Lake Huron and then we crossed over through the Straits and it was kind of tough going up there. We were making slow progress, but we had to push pretty hard with our engines in order to make the slow progress. So we were shooting these hunks of ice up against them from our wheels and I went over again and went down to look. Gee whiz! There were several places now bent in.

Q: Like a tin can.

Adm. R.: Yes. Holy smokes! It was too late to turn back, so we kept on going. When we got down to Chicago, it was like a washboard.

Q: You got her to Chicago, not entirely safely, but you got her there.

Adm. R.: Yes, I got her there and I caught a little hell on account of it, too, because the Navy complained about it. They said that they thought that a person running an icebreaker like that would have more sense than to do anything like this. I was still writing my report when that came in so I started my report over again and said I didn't tow them because I wanted to tow them.

Q: They insisted upon it.

Adm. R.: They wanted to be towed. Of course, it would never be done again because it's impossible to tow a ship through that heavy ice at a slow speed like that without throwing these heavy chunks of ice up against it. With a light ship like that something's got to give. So I said, "I'm sorry it happened. Maybe I learned something that I didn't know before." But anyway, I went on for about three or four pages on that and I didn't hear any more about it. It must have taken a long time to get that ship in reasonable shape. They did, and the ship left and it also went out to the South Pacific somewhere.

Q: But not on schedule.

Adm. R.: Not on schedule. I should say not. I guess they were in the yard at New Orleans for quite a while getting things wrapped up again. Probably her skipper caught hell himself.

Q: Did you have any other harrowing experiences up there?

Adm. R.: I don't think particularly, no. The first ships that began to run up there were the Bradley Line ships and they run out of Alpena, Michigan on Lake Huron. We started out with them and they are a little better, a little higher powered than the other ships and they carry phosphate more than they carry iron ore, although they carry either. We took them over into Lake Michigan and then about the time that happened and around the 1st of April we started on the regular run of traffic. Once those ships got up to the St. Mary's River, we were stuck. There was no place we could go for a while. We had to stay in the St. Mary's River and Whitefish Bay for quite a while.

After we got to the point where they could do this themselves or with the help of tugs and these icebreakers - these car ferries, they were still operating - then we got down and got into the Straits again and did some more breaking there. But the most important thing was to get the run from Cleveland and Lorain and those places and Toledo, into the iron mines at the west end of Lake Superior, and back again, of course.

After that had been done, then we were able to explore in other places like in the Straits and always the last place is Buffalo, New York. It piles up down there. Piles up at the entrance to the Niagara River. In my first spring, we were down breaking ice in Buffalo on the 15th of May.

Q: It's a weather belt, isn't it, along there?

Adm. R.: It's a cold place and besides the weather is always blowing toward Buffalo across the lake and ice just piles up there. Our solution was to mess around in the Niagara River and break it up there and let it get started down there and it clears up pretty quickly.

Q: How cold does it get in this area where you were operating in the wintertime?

Adm. R.: I was in Duluth one time when the temperature was 40 below. It was rarely that cold. Twenty below is common.

Q: And when does the ice go out?

Adm. R.: Ships start to run around the first of April and some before that. Those Bradley ships always started out early and made their way as they could. If there was an icebreaker to help them, great; but it there wasn't an icebreaker, they would do it themselves. They'd just hit it and they'd back off and they'd hit it. It might take them a week to get across the northern end of Lake Michigan - about eight or ten miles. But that's what they'd do. They just wanted to get going as soon as possible. The ice leaves around the first of April. There still is ice, but it's here and there and you can avoid a lot of it. Whitefish Bay is one of the worst places.

Q: It prompts me to ask another question, which isn't exactly pertinent to the story, but the union seamen on these merchant ships - do they get extra pay for ice conditions?

Adm. R.: I don't really know. I don't think they did then. You know they weren't all unionized at that time.

Q: They were not?

Adm. R.: Not when I was up there. They probably all are now. But they had a minimum wage rate of about $2.50, I think. It was a good place to work - everybody was looking for a job in the summertime -- college boys and high school boys and everybody. But they'd close up tight in the winter. There were no jobs in the winter and the skippers would all go down to Florida. At that time the skippers were paid around $18,000 and that was high pay then, thirty-some years ago -- that was a lot of money. I don't know what they get now but they probably get a lot more now. Of course, the ships are bigger -- they are over 700 feet now and they are wider. They have new locks -- they've widened the locks.

Q: And they operate most of the winter, do they?

Adm. R.: They operate more than they did. No, they don't operate all through. They don't operate in January, I don't think. But I think they could now -- with the MACKINAW.

Q: Well, actually the need for the steel is not that great.

Adm. R.: No, the need isn't like it used to be. There used to be a lot of coal. At the time that I was out there, ships would bring down iron ore and bring back coal and all through the winter there were two or three of these things that ran between Toledo and Detroit in order to keep the places going in Detroit -- carrying coal to Detroit and then they'd go back and get another load of coal. That was an operation that required some help, too. We had to go down and help them a couple of times. We had a 180-foot tender in Detroit and one in Toledo. Those 180-foot tenders are icebreakers of some capability and they were busy all winter long with those things.

Q: When you were operating your icebreaker in that area, did you have other duties that usually pertain to the Coast Guard? I mean navigation aids and that sort of thing?

Adm. R.: No, we didn't do a thing about navigation aids all the time I was up there -- not a thing. There were lots of tenders up there, up in the Lakes. There are lots and lots of aids to navigation, so there were a lot of tenders. They handled all that -- there were thousands and thousands of aids to navigation in the Lakes.

Q: Naturally there would be. But you had just a single duty.

Adm. R.: Yes, that's right. In the summertime we made cadet cruises and we went to festivals -- cherry festivals and things like that.

Q: Oh, they have those in the Great Lakes, too?

Adm. R.: Oh, they have a lot of them. We patrolled some yacht races. There's a Port Huron to Mackinaw race which is several hundred miles long and a Chicago to Mackinaw race.

Q: And these took place in wartime, did they?

Adm. R.: Yes. Of course, we were near the end of the war. 1944 we were commissioned; in '45 things were beginning to straighten out. Some of the reservists were leaving. I was only on this ship until about April of '46.

Q: Which would be something less than a year after the war was over.

Adm. R.: Yes, and during that time, our reservists were leaving.

Q: Well, the Coast Guard then, even though operating in the Great Lakes, had something comparable to what they called the Magic Carpet out in the Pacific?

Adm. R.: Yes.

Q: Men were released on points, were they?

Adm. R.: Yes. The same thing.

Q: Tell me what that did in your ship.

Adm. R.: Oh, it raised cain with our ship. We lost 75 percent of our crew and we were really having a tough time. It was worse for the fellow after me, of course. We didn't lose 75 percent while I was there, but when he got there -- he took command he didn't have very many people to order around.

Q: Of course, you said that you started out with actually an excess.

Adm. R.: Oh, yes.

Q: So some reduction would not be too much of a handicap.

Adm. R.: I think the ship is running now with a crew of about 140 or 135. We had a hundred more than that.

Q: Did you ever have any problem keeping them all busy?

Adm. R.: Yes. We had other troubles, too. We had some colored people in our stewards branch, you know, and the south isn't the worse place for the colored people. Northern Michigan is the worst. They couldn't get a haircut; they couldn't do anything. They wouldn't let them in the barroom. We'd have to go down to Detroit once in a while and let these people go ashore and have some liberty -- and get their hair cut, too. And this happened for quite a while. Of course, they are still bad up there but they will tolerate them to some extent now and they will take them. But two guys would walk down the street and the cops would watch them every minute -- oh, it was awful.

I went to see the mayor and the city council and talked to them about it and I said, "We're going to have to leave here."

Q: This was in Cheboygan?

Adm. R.: Yes. And Cheboygan was kind of down at the heels at the time. Our payroll was five times as much as any other payroll that they had around there and their congressman had worked and worked and worked to get the ship up there. The Coast Guard didn't want that ship to go in that little -- there were only 3500 people in Cheboygan and we came in there with 225 more and the ship was bigger than anything in town and there was more money on it than anything in town. The Headquarters wanted the ship to go to Detroit where it wouldn't be noticed so much -- it might be absorbed better. It went up there and there has been every year some move to get the ship out of that place . . .

Q: You mean on the part of the Coast Guard?

Adm. R.: On the part of the Coast Guard. But now, of course, they have built this new mooring up there and I went up last August and I broke ground for a new dock they are putting in there and a new recreation building that they are putting in and the city is doing it. So you know if you get things like that, you can't get out. So I guess the ship is going to be there for a while longer. The ship is now thirty-some years old. But you know, it looked to me like it's as good as when it was new.

Q: The Coast Guard really anticipated some of these problems with personnel before they went up there?

Adm. R.: I don't know. Nobody warned me about it and it descended on me when we got there.

Q: How did you handle your own men? I mean, the morale must have been affected by this.

Adm. R.: The men aboard the ship hated the place. Most of the men we had there were single or else they didn't have their families there. When we went to go into this place, there weren't any houses. The place Jane and I lived in was a shack -- it was a hell of a place. There just weren't any places.

Q: And no place for them to kick up their heels when they were on leave.

Adm. R.: The Gold Front -- that bar. That's the only place. The men hated it. It's better now because there's housing now and of course there are fewer Coast Guard now, too. So they don't stand out like they did before. You'd walk down the street and three-quarters of the people were in uniform and in this little beat-up town.

Q: What steps did you take to offset the decline in morale because of this situation?

Adm. R.: We would take them to other places, that's all. I fought for them. I visited the police station once or twice a week to get guys out -- and they were pretty good about that. If I went down and they had some guy, I could usually get the guy out. I did a lot of that. And we made trips to other places.

Q: Where they could have adequate shore leave.

Adm. R.: But there weren't any very close. We'd go up to Sioux but the Sioux wasn't very big either. Chicago was a long ways down the other end from Lake Michigan and Detroit was way down at the end of St. Clair River. We'd go to Cleveland and occasionally we'd make a trip to Buffalo, and there was a big demand for the ship to come so the people could see it. Of course, when we had the cadets aboard on the cruises, we were underway a good bit of the time.

I was away from home a lot of the time when I was aboard that ship. In the beginning there was a lot to do and we were exploring and finding things out anyway. Then in the summertime there were the festivals. Everybody wanted the ship for festivals and they were all over the place. And we were making cadet cruises, too.

Q: How long was a cadet cruise? This was in 1945.

Adm. R.: We made two cruises each year and it took about a month for each one.

Q: How many cadets would you have on board?

Adm. R.: Oh, a hundred.

Q: And what was your special obligation as a skipper for the cadets?

Adm. R.: The cadets came with Academy officers who took care of their training. We had to provide watches for them to stand and they did stand the watches. We had our own people keeping an eye on them but we gave them all the responsibility we could. I think it was probably pretty good experience for them because they were operating in traffic all the time, especially the first classmen and the ones that were on the bridge. We were operating in traffic all the time.

There was always a lot to do in the way of plotting and navigation of the ship. But as far as taking a sight you hardly ever have a horizon up there, there's a shoreline.

Q: When you had cadets on board were they concerned about aids to navigation? I mean, did this become a factor?

Adm. R.: They were concerned in the use of aids to navigation, sure. By that time we had a pretty good combat information center set up -- we had two radars by that time when they were there. We had a dead reckoning plotter. We had all these things that they could play around with. They were things that you don't really need up there but they are good on board a ship anyway. The radar, of course, is needed. But there was lots for them to do and all kinds of room to do it. The bridge was a great big thing and there were all kinds of compartments in the ship that we had no use for. They were there because the ship had to be a certain size in order to make a path wide enough and in order to get the proper draft, there had to be a lot of it on the surface.

Q: It was a roomy ship — somewhat different from the VANCE.

Adm. R.: Oh, Lord yes! What a difference! I don't think I was welcome on the VANCE because I used the cabin and the skipper used the emergency cabin. I guess he was glad when I wasn't around.

I had two winters on her (the MACKINAW) and I enjoyed the duty.

Q: Was the second winter easier and better than the first one?

Adm. R.: Oh, we were much better organized the second winter. We knew better what we had to do. That first spring, in '45, we had a pretty rough time. Then in the fall it's not nearly as bad. When they're closing the season - the ships are out before the ice gets all piled up.

Q: Their schedules are arranged so they don't . . .

Adm. R.: Yes. They close the damned locks the 7th of December so they ought to be out by then. The ice just hasn't formed to that great extent by that time, you see. So we had a little icebreaking to do. Then during the winter, of course, the car ferries were still operating over where we're going and that business down at Toledo was going.

Then the following spring which is the real tough time, we had had this operation so we knew what was coming up - we had the spring of '45 behind us and '46 went pretty well. We didn't have any real difficulties.

Q: Did you have any experience with rescue operations as a side line to what you were doing?

Adm. R.: No, none except searches for missing things. There aren't many things of that nature. Well, we had that one -- remember I told you about the ship that went aground down the St. Clair River when we tested the tanks. We had one or two others. But that was a grounding at a relatively slow speed and he just didn't have enough power to get off. So we went down and tied onto him and pulled him off. Then he was all right. He didn't have any damage or at least none that I knew anything about, nothing that was serious. He just continued on his voyage when we towed him off.

That happens occasionally on those rivers because they are narrow, you see, and every once in a while somebody loses steerage way for one reason or another aboard ship -- somebody dopes off and isn't looking ahead when he should be.

Q: I take it the current is swift too.

Adm. R.: Not too bad. In some places it is but not much. Up at the north end of the St. Clair River there's one bad place where there's -- you come in and there's a turn to the right and a turn to the left with a bridge over it. The current sort of goes down through there pretty fast and it sweeps you to the side.

So it's kind of a bad place. It's one of the things I always admired -- the way they take those big ships through there, with hardly any power -- and they go through all right.

They have their trouble where there's no reason to have any trouble. They've got to go out of their way in order to hit the things they hit. But they handle their ships so well that when they're alerted by something like that bad place in the river, there's no question about it they go right through.

Q: I see. I read that Lake Erie sometimes presents a problem because it's pretty shallow.

Adm. R.: Oh, the west end of Lake Erie is terrible. That's very shoal and it's very rough because it is so shoal. Of course, when it gets rough you're quite apt to hit the bottom. In order to get from Cleveland to Detroit, you have to go all the way across the Lake to a place called Pelee Point and head west. There's a channel along there that's probably 20 feet deep -- I think, as a matter of fact, they have dredged it deeper now, but it was about 20 feet when I was out there on the MACKINAW. And if you get in there with a ship drawing -- say the MACKINAW would be drawing 18 feet and you'd have 20 feet and it's rough, you bounce on the bottom. So it's a very bad place -- the west end of Lake Erie.

Then it deepens. It's not as deep as the other lakes but there's no danger of anything like that. It comes down to 30 or

40 feet. Some of them, like Lake Superior and Lake Huron -- they're hundreds of feet deep, lots of water.

Q: As a result of the employment of the MACKINAW up there and her obvious success as an icebreaker, did the Coast Guard go ahead and build others similar to her?

Adm. R.: No. There was quite a demand for it though and there were several studies run on what would be necessary to keep navigation open for various periods of time including throughout the year. Most of these studies wound up with about five or six MACKINAWs and at that time, of course, the money was beginning to get a little scarce and it wasn't wartime any more and the MACKINAW was really a relatively inexpensive ship. It cost a little over nine million dollars to build her and outfit her. If they tried to do that now, it would probably cost them $50 million.

Q: I'm sure of that. The studies were instigated by the Coast Guard and conducted by them?

Adm. R.: I wouldn't say they were instigated by them. They were conducted by us and others too, in the shipping business up there. The people in the shipping business in the Lakes were the ones who were really interested in more of this same thing. The MACKINAW was a great thing for them. They said that the first year that the MACKINAW operated in the spring that it saved them probably ten million dollars or it got them ten million dollars of business by getting the ships through that much earlier. They thought that we had opened up about three or four weeks earlier than they would have been able to get ships through without the MACKINAW. They added a little bit on the other end, too. They thought that it was worth that much to them and they thought that in terms of how much the ship cost that it was worth it. There's more to operating a ship than building it.

Q: Then they wouldn't be footing the bill for this.

Adm. R.: No, they are just ordinary taxpayers.

Q: It was a government service. Perhaps this is the place to ask you about the relationship of the Coast Guard with the Merchant Marine as such. The shipping companies.

Adm. R.: In the Lakes?

Q: Yes.

Adm. R.: It is a very close relationship, a very pleasant relationship, and a very effective one, I think. The last three presidents of the Lake Carriers Association are retired Coast Guard officers. Admiral Spencer, who is retired and lives here in Old Lyme, became the president of the Lake Carriers Association in 1947 while I was Chief of Staff in Cleveland. He came out there and he became president. Then when Jimmy Hirshfield retired, when I became Assistant Commandant I relieved him and when he retired he went out and relieved Spencer as president.

Q: He had his headquarters in Cleveland, did he not?

Adm. R.: Yes, the headquarters were in Cleveland. Then when Jimmy retired from that job, Paul Trimble retired from the Coast Guard -- he was then the Assistant Commandant -- and he went out there as president and he is still the president.

Let's see now. Paul went out there when Chet Bender became Commandant, which would have been in about 1970. And he still is president. He's a younger man than Jimmy was. I don't know how long he stayed out there. This is the result of a good relationship.

They get a lot out of the Coast Guard, of course, particularly in the icebreaking business, and beginning in about February they always want the District Commander and the Chief of Staff and anybody else they can get to come to their meetings -- their Lake Carriers Association meeting, because they want the Coast Guard to be familiar with their plans so that the Coast Guard can break ice better for them.

Q: So they were hand in glove with the Coast Guard.

Adm. R.: Very close, yes.

Q: I take it that the Lake carriers are somewhat different from

Merchant Marine ships in the Atlantic and Pacific.

Adm. R.: You mean the association.

Q: Yes, and perhaps they are better off, are they, or are they subsidized the way merchant shipping is?

Adm. R.: They weren't subsidized at the time I was out there. They were pretty well off. At the time I was out there, they were running an awful lot of old ships. You know, in fresh water ships last a long time and they had some real, old clunkers that they were running. The steel was still in good condition and it hadn't gone as it would in salt water. But when I was out there, of course, you didn't see any more coal-burning ships around the coast. But you saw a lot of coal-burning ships out there.

Q: Oh, really.

Adm. R.: Oh, yes. You see, a lot of these companies handled coal as a cargo going one way, you know. So it was a good deal.

Q: Tell me about the ships plying the Great Lakes in the fresh water: are they subject to the same sort of fouling of bottoms that happened in the ocean -- barnacles and that kind of thing?

Adm. R.: No, none of that. Our regulations call for ships, in some places, being in drydock every six months -- down in the Gulf, for instance. Not any more because of better paints, but speaking back to the time that I was aboard ships and on active duty. It was six months in the Gulf and a year up around Boston and it was a year out in the Lakes, too. But when a year came around on the MACKINAW, it was like a new coin. The paint was gone because the ice had taken the paint off, but the thing just shines like a coin. The only reason for painting isn't deterioration of the metal or growth on the ship, it's just to have paint on it -- that's all. You don't really need it. Anyway, they don't paint every year -- I'll tell you now. It was changed to two years and it might even be three years now.

I think that the MACKINAW is a remarkable example of how a ship is preserved in fresh water. It looks to me like it did when it came out in '44. It's just beautiful!

Q: Are there merchant ships under foreign flags in the lakes?

Adm. R.: Oh now, yes. Since the St. Lawrence Seaway, there are lots and lots of foreign ships now. There weren't before. There would be an occasional one, but they were small because I think the limit was about 250 feet in the old canal. Now, of course, they can get big ships in it.

Q: Does this present a problem for the American ships manned on the Lakes? Are they undercut in terms of rates and that sort of thing?

Adm. R.: I don't think so. A foreign ship can't carry cargoes between American ports.

Q: From one American port to another -- he cannot do that?

Adm. R.: No.

Q: It's got to be from an American port to a foreign port.

Adm. R.: Yes. A ship can come in with a cargo and deliver part of it in Cleveland and then go to some place else and deliver the other part of it, but it can't pick up anything from Cleveland and deliver it to this next place. What they deliver at an American port has to come from some place out of the country. Of course, there was a lot of objection to allowing them to come in from the sailors out in the Great Lakes because these people sailed under the International Rules of navigation and there's a separate set of Rules for the Lakes. So it was a question of the two getting together in the Great Lakes in such restricted circumstances, that had the American sailors worried. And they have had some difficulty. But I don't know how they've solved all their difficulties. Anyway, they have been solved.

Q: Can you give me an illustration of a point wherein they differ in their regulations?

Adm. R.: Yes. Fog signals.

Q: Oh yes -- which you've already given me.

Adm. R.: There are other things. There are a number of points. I just can't think of them now. The fog signal is one of the outstanding ones, of course. But there are quite a few. That's why they wrote a separate set of Rules for the Lakes. There's a separate set of Rules for the Lakes and for the rivers - the Mississippi River and some of those other rivers down there - and those and the Lake Rules are somewhat alike, but there are differences between them, too.

Then there is a set of Inland Rules that's for U.S. ships within three miles of the coast or within inland waters and then there are International Rules. As far as along the coast where the Inland Rules apply now to American ships and anybody who is sailing a foreign ship into those waters continues to use International Rules. But the differences are minor.

One difference has been in lights. That's one of the things out on the Lakes. Out in the Lakes a ship has always been required to carry a mast head light and a range light. In International Rules that was not the case - it wasn't when I was there, anyway. In the Lakes and in Inland Rules the range light, which is the light up on the aftermast, has to be all around - an all-around light. In International Rules that range light only is three-quarters of the the way around and it doesn't show aft. And those Rules require a stern light, but the Inland Rules in the Great Lakes, don't require a stern light.

Q: Now, with differences of that sort, I should think there would be difficulty and perhaps accidents on occasion when you have men on a foreign ship operating with one set and locally operating with another. There has to be a general knowledge of both systems.

Adm. R.: This is exactly what was bothering sailors on the Great Lakes. What arrangements they have made to overcome those difficulties, I don't know. But there have been international conferences and all kinds of conferences on this thing. But the Canadians and the United States have the same rules for the Great Lakes. They got together . . .

Q: Simply because they were operating together.

Adm. R.: Yes. They had to to protect themselves. So I'm sure now that they have solved in some similar way the problem with a Finn or a Belgian or somebody else. I don't hear anybody talking about difficulties out there any more. But they did talk about them for some time after they started out. I'm sure that they have cleared all that up and I think there are more and more ships coming in every year, too. Cargoes are coming from Japan. They'll come in and go to Detroit.

Q: I would think that a lot of the grain carrying traffic is through the Lakes too, is it not? The wheat to Russia and that sort of thing.

Adm. R.: I suppose it is now but it wasn't at that time because there wasn't any way out. This is one of the things that hit the city of Buffalo. It used to be the biggest grain shipping port in the world. But it isn't any more. The grain would all be shipped to the elevators there and from there would go by barge or by rail or some other means out of Buffalo to some other place.

Q: I suppose that was largely Canadian grain, wasn't it?

Adm. R.: Well, yes. There is a lot of grain cargo still carried on the Lakes and, I suppose, as you say, it probably goes right out now through that canal. And Buffalo doesn't have the same amount that they had before. I remember when I was a kid the grain elevators in Buffalo didn't mean much to me then but there were an awful lot of them. I don't think there are as many now.

When I was in the Great Lakes, I can't remember much in the way of labor difficulties on the Lakes.

Q: Because it was wartime for the most part.

Adm. R.: Well, yes. And before that I think it was largely not unionized. I think that pay scales have been pretty good on the Great Lakes and there were all kinds of benefits. But one thing about working on the Great Lakes is that a person from the beginning of a season until the season is over doesn't get ashore very much. They take one of these ore carriers up into Duluth and they run it under the shutes and I think the record is four hours for loading -- but the normal time for loading is about six or eight hours -- and then they are gone.

At the other end, they take longer, but not much longer, to unload and then they're off again. It's a regular production line. Those ships are going almost all the time. There is much more time underway then there is in port. So in the wintertime they give them a very thorough going over and get them in good shape and they just run them to death in the summertime.

I can't think of a strike among the sea-going people up there while I was there.

Q: You were telling me off tape about the manner in which they load the iron ore and cart it directly to the steel plant.

Adm. R.: Yes, and then they have these big, tremendous pickers that unload the vessels very quickly. They go day and night. You take it in there and those things are going day and night. The crew doesn't have anything to do with it except handling hatches and so on.

Q: Did you use planes in any way in connection with your ice-breaking operations?

Adm. R.: Yes. And I was just going to say we used this helicopter from the MACKINAW when I was back up there at that time. But we did use airplanes from Traverse City -- the Coast Guard station at Traverse City, Michigan. We did use airplanes to search out fields of ice.

Q: And they could spot fields of ice from the air?

Adm. R.: Yes, and we were in communication with them.

Q: What were they? Flying boats?

Adm. R.: Yes, the Albatross -- the amphibians.

Q: But during this period in World War II you were not using helicopters?

Adm. R.: When I was aboard the MACKINAW?

Q: Yes.

Adm. R.: No. We had no way of handling helicopters. But for this time when I went up there in charge, they had built a platform aboard the MACKINAW on the quarterdeck where the helicopter could operate from.

Q: That's something you are going to tell me about a little later, I think, when you went back for that particular operation.

Adm. R.: Yes, that's one of the things in Cleveland -- one of the things that happened in Cleveland when I was Chief of Staff.

Q: I guess we're about to begin the story of the post-war period, in April 1946 when you left the MACKINAW to become Chief of Staff of the 9th Coast Guard District in Cleveland.

Adm. R.: Yes, that was sort of an unexpected honor for me. I was the only District Chief of Staff who was less than a captain at that time. It only happened because Jimmy Hirshfield who was my good friend insisted on it. He really wanted me.

Q: He was the Commandant?

Adm. R.: He was the District Commander. So that's how that . . .

Q: And you were a commander?

Adm. R.: I was a commander then, yes. So I was pleased at the assignment.

Q: You had served with him before somewhere?

Adm. R.: I had known him from way before. I had never served with him on any station but I had served with him in New London. He had served at the Academy a couple of times when I was in New London and I had known him at that time. He and I were close friends.

So I was pleased to be Chief of Staff and particularly to be his Chief of Staff. If I was incompetent because of the lack of rank I could get away with it better with him.

Q: Tell me about the scope of operations in that District. That was a very important District, was it not?

Adm. R.: Yes, it was a large district. It took in all of the Great Lakes and the adjoining states. New York state was split and Pennsylvania was split so we didn't have all of those but we had all the rest of the states that were adjacent to the Lakes. We had a lot of lifeboat stations out there at the time and we had a lot of aids to navigation tenders. In the way of other ships, we didn't have as many as other districts but we were pretty busy in the bread and butter activities of the Coast Guard. We had an air station up at Traverse City which was a fairly good-sized station. I think we had about eight or ten planes up there and a couple of helicopters.

The operation at the Sioux was a sort of separate thing that I don't think we had any place else. They controlled traffic in the St. Mary's River. They had a series of stations along the river where men were assigned and they had telephones connected to the headquarters in the Sioux. The men would call and give the names of ships and which way they were going and the time so that we kept track so we could control traffic around the locks at the Sioux.

Q: How did the Coast Guard get into that control of traffic? Was it in the interest of safety?

Adm. R.: In the interest of safety, yes. And as I say, we didn't do it any place else that I know of at that time. That has ceased now. As a matter of fact, that ceased about the time I left up there I guess. The stations that were along the river were all removed. There was no intention of replacing them. I think probably the introduction of radio aboard ship had something to do with it - the fact that they were required to have a radio, so we could keep track of them any way - that had something to do with it.

But our greatest problem while I was there, I think was the ore carriers. Yachting was very important out there. There were tremendous numbers of pleasure boats around Detroit and Lake St. Clair and, of course, around Chicago too.

Q: You district included Chicago?

Adm. R.: Yes, it included Chicago.

Q: Of course, you would have lots of yachts and things like that in southern Lake Michigan.

Adm. R.: Yes. We had all the Lakes so we did include Chicago.

Q: Did you also have the river system? The Ohio River?

Adm. R.: No, that was in the District with headquarters in St. Louis. I think the numbers of some of these districts have been changed since. That is now the 2nd Coast Guard District. Our districts correspond largely with the Navy's district numbers except that they don't have a 2nd. So we have that one there and that's where we have used the number "2."

Q: You are both Coast Guard and Navy in that area?

Adm. R.: They include all the area in other districts. For instance, our 8th District starts down at the Gulf and runs up about to Baton Rouge. But theirs continues on beyond Baton Rouge. Their 8th District includes a lot more territory than ours does. Then they probably include some of our 2nd with their 13th in the southern part of California and their 12th along with San Francisco. They get it all in there included in their districts but they don't have a 2.

Q: You were a natural for this assignment then, because you'd just come from the Lakes.

Adm. R.: I had had, I guess probably, more experience than most people had in the Lakes. I had been on that other ship, you see, the ESCANABA. I was in Grand Haven and, of course, I came from Buffalo originally. That made it very fitting. But I think my experience on the MACKINAW that, if I had any experience that fitted me for the job, I think it would be that, because that was a unique experience out there and an important experience as far as operating in the Coast Guard in the Lakes. So I'm sure that my experience on the MACKINAW had a lot to do with my going out there.

Q: Tell me about that three-year period it was.

Adm. R.: During that time, it seems to me that one of the most important activities for us during the year was preparing for the ice season in the spring. I spent a lot of time discussing these matters with the people in the Lake Carriers Association. On one occasion - I think it was in 1948 - I was assigned to head up that operation. We formed a task group of the vessels that we had in the District that were capable of breaking the ice and sent them all up into the area around the Sioux and I rode the MACKINAW as the flagship and controlled their operations and dispatched them to various places where they might be needed.

It turned out to be a pretty busy season. It had been a worse winter than most and that may be why we planned to gather our forces to get the ships going again. I spent about a month aboard the MACKINAW at that time. In preparation for this affair, a landing platform had been built in the quarterdeck of the MACKINAW to handle a helicopter and a helicopter was assigned to the ship for use during this icebreaking season.

Q: As an observation plane?

Adm. R.: As an observation business, yes. It was a very useful thing. It could scout at pretty great distances and keep us informed of the best route to take out of the fields, particularly in the harbor and in the bay entering the locks from the westward. The pilot of the plane was Erickson, who was an important figure in the development of helicopter operations in the Coast Guard. He served with us during that whole time. It was very useful to us. He was a very determined helicopter man. He loved helicopters and thought they could do everything and he could do about everything with them. And he did. He flew sometimes when I didn't think he should fly. He did anyway, and he came back. He was a very good pilot and a very useful one. Now they have changed the quarterdeck of the MACKINAW. At the time, there were some hatches on the quarterdeck and the platform had to be built over the hatches so that the helicopter could land. Now they have flattened out those hatches so that the access to the spaces below is through a hatch cover that is flush with the deck. So now helicopters can land directly on the deck.

So the ship is available for the use of helicopters any time now. Before, the platform that they put on when I was up there was made of wood and it was a very cumbersome thing. When it was removed at the end of that season, it was quite a job taking it off and it would have been a very difficult job putting it back together.

Q: It had to be dismantled?

Adm. R.: It had to be dismantled completely. It was made of heavy enough stuff that it could take the shock of a landing by this helicopter, which was a pretty big helicopter.

Q: Of course, that was really in the infancy of the helicopter.

Adm. R.: Oh yes, it was.

Q: It was experimental still.

Adm. R.: Oh, yes. We didn't have very many helicopters in the Coast Guard at that time. This was a Sikorsky -- I think you call it an S-3 or something like that -- and it looked to me like a tremendous big thing. I had the experience of riding in the hoist and all that kind of business at the time. I haven't had to do it since.

Q: Did you feel at that time when you were using the helicopter, that it was an improvement over the Albatross which you had been using?

Adm. R.: Oh yes, much better. This was a much better deal. We had so much better control of it. It was coming back to the ship and coming to us so we could actually talk to the people and we carried the fuel aboard. We did the maintenance aboard. Everything for the helicopter was done right aboard the MACKINAW. The Albatross we saw when it got there and most of the time we didn't see it after that. We just talked to him on the radio and when he was finished, he went back. We didn't have control, actually control of those airplanes was from their air station. When the air station thought they should come back, they called them back. We used him when he was there but we weren't quite sure what he was going to do because we didn't have the 100 percent . . .

Q: You had direct command of the helicopter but not of the Albatross?

Adm. R.: Yes.

Q: Tell me more about that month on the MACKINAW then.

Adm. R.: I said that we had gathered our facilities and we also had the use of the car ferries. The car ferries were rented by the Lake Carriers Association for this period and they were directed to report to me and to do as I wished. They were very useful.

Q: How many were there?

Adm. R.: There were two of them. One of them was named the ST. MARIE and one was the CHIEF OUAWATAN. They were pretty good icebreakers and were very useful in the St. Mary's River early in the game. Then towards the end we brought one of them up the Whitfish Bay and it was very helpful up there. They were better icebreakers than our small icebreakers, better than our 180-footers.

Q: Did the crew go with them when they were leased?

Adm. R.: Yes, the crew went with them. We had nobody aboard, but we had communications with them. So it was probably a looser arrangement than would have been made now, but it worked out very well and we did get what we needed out of them.

We distributed some of our smaller icebreakers to places that we normally wouldn't have broken ice. One place was Ashland, Wisconsin, which is toward the west end of Lake Superior near the Apostle Islands and there are ore docks in there. They are not as large as the ore docks or as capable as the ore docks at Duluth and Superior, but they were used at that time throughout the year. We assigned one icebreaker, one 180-foot icebreaker, at Ashland and in the beginning we made a run in the MACKINAW into Ashland and ran alongside the docks and broke things up. Then we went back out to Whitefish Bay.

There never was a time when we had all of the icebreakers in one place, say in Whitefish Bay. We scattered them pretty much. Another place that needs early attention in icebreaking is Escanaba, which is on the west side of Lake Michigan, and tankers run all year from Chicago up to Escanaba -- oil tankers. We had in our normal operations when I was aboard the ESCANABA -- I mean the MACKINAW -- we had gone over and broken out the harbor in Escanaba from time to time inorder to allow these tankers to operate. They carried oil in there and there I believe it was carried by pipeline to other places up around Escanaba, Wisconsin.

The other car ferries that were still at that time running on Lake Michigan seemed to take care of themselves pretty well that year and we didn't need to do much to assist them. Our smaller icebreakers wouldn't have been able to do much for them anyway since they had enough power to work their own way most of the time.

Q: You said the purpose of your being there as Chief of Staff to Admiral Hirshfield was in connection with the Lake shipping owners. Your being there on the MACKINAW.

Adm. R.: Oh yes. In order to coordinate the work of the icebreakers, in order to get the ships through . . .

Q: That was not being done while you were skipper of the MACKINAW.

Adm. R.: No, it wasn't done before. There were a couple of small icebreakers up at the Sioux that were attached to the base up there. When I was assigned to the MACKINAW as commanding officer, those ships were never detached from that base and assigned to the MACKINAW. They continued to operate under the orders of the base commander. The MACKINAW operated on its own. So this was a new deal.

We didn't do it the next year because the next year turned out to be a very light year. As a matter of fact, I don't think -- the next year we didn't use any of the car ferries, the ST. MARIE or the OUAWATAM. We did it just about all with the MACKINAW the next year except in the local harbors where the icebreakers were assigned.

Q: I would think, too, that once you had effected the coordination and the units remained the same from year to year, it wouldn't be necessary to repeat.

Adm. R.: That's probably so, unless it was an awfully unusual winter, I would think that that would be so. I think that the operation could be pretty well worked too from the office at the base on the Sioux. The man who was assigned as commanding officer up there is a man who has considerable knowledge of traffic on the Great Lakes and he has a better location, I think, for gathering information and for communication with ships in the worse part of the ice right there. I think really that that might be a better place from which to carry on the control of the icebreaking.

Q: It was obvious in your case, with your particular know-how, that Admiral Hirshfield probably wanted to use that know-how.

Adm. R.: I think that's so. The man who was at the base at that time was the reserve officer who had at one time been the skipper of one of the ore boats. So he had a pretty good idea what was going on too. He was well acquainted with all the difficulties that those people would run into, having been stuck himself a good many times. He knew what it was like.

My tour of duty as the Chief of Staff out there lasted into 1949. That was a considerable length of time to serve in that capacity and I learned a lot and enjoyed a lot. The congressmen out there were very demanding at the time and I learned how to say no to a congressman and not sound as though I had said no and this proved to be useful later on.

Q: They were demanding in what sense?

Adm. R.: They wanted favors from the District. They wanted Coast Guard people to take their ships into ports for demonstrations and so on when they were needed in other places. They wanted to control operations of some Coast Guard units for the benefit of their own district rather than for the benefit of navigation.

There was a fellow that came from Lorain that was particularly troublesome to us. But I think in the long run we satisfied him. Running an operation like that is difficult when there are a lot of small communities that would like to have - Well, they have regattas and they have other affairs along the water where these congressmen interest themselves in these communities. This was the cast out there. I would say that these congressmen were probably good congressmen because they were so interested. But they were very demanding as far as we were concerned and they didn't quite see when we had a ship over here - we didn't quite see why we had it there when they wanted it over here.

Q: Tell me about some of the other duties that fell on your shoulders.

Adm. R.: Of course, as Chief of Staff I was responsible for the operation of the office. It was an office of a pretty good size.

We had a very busy engineering office in the place, particularly civil engineering because we had so many scattered units in the district. I think that I mentioned before that we had a lot of lifeboat stations. We had more lifeboat stations than anybody else in the Coast Guard. During that time there was a study being made of lifeboat stations and which ones should be closed up.

The group came out to our District and in each case the Chief of Staff of the District joined the group for the study within the District. So I went with them and we visited all these places. As a result, we recommended closing a good many of them. This was something we would have liked to do but is also the sort of thing that makes it difficult to manage a place where you have a lot of small communities. Because moving a lifeboat station from one of those small communities means something to them. It means something to their economic well-being if people move out and they don't have a facility that they had before.

Q: Once again it involves you with the Congress -- individuals.

Adm. R.: Of course. And of course, appropriations were the reason for this whole thing. I think that by that time facilities had changed so much that we didn't really need all the stations we had. We had them about every ten miles along Lake Michigan. By that time we had boats that were covering the ground a lot faster. So we did wind up closing quite a few stations but not as many as we recommended. They weren't able to get them all closed. I think we must have had probably 85 or 90 lifeboat stations in that District and I think we wound up with about 60 perhaps.

Q: How many men on the average would be assigned to a single lifeboat station?

Adm. R.: It varied some but in most cases I would say, on the average probably eight. They ran continuous lookout watches and continuous communication watches. The number of people that were necessary just for standing the watches, besides the assistance cases, was a pretty large number. It was eating into our money. We wanted to cut those thing out.

One of the first things we did and maybe they did it throughout the Coast Guard was to cut down in most places to a single man for the communications watch and the lookout. We moved the communications up into the lookout tower and the fellow handled the communications up there with telephone communications to the other parts of the station in case he wanted to talk to the officer in charge or somebody else.

Q: This was, of course -- when you get into '49 -- this was the time of economy in the federal government and cutting down in the Navy and elsewhere.

Adm. R.: Yes. This study was carried on throughout the Coast Guard.

Q: This was a Headquarters study.

Adm. R.: Yes, it was. It aroused an awful lot of congressmen all over, particularly down around the Carolina coast. People down there grew up in these stations, you know. The old families that had been in there for a hundred years. A fellow's son moved in when the father retired and it was all families running these stations. And there was a lot of that up in the Lakes, too.

Q: Tell me about the regatta business and all that that you got involved in in the summer, anyway.

Adm. R.: The most important regattas that they held up there were the long races -- the races from Chicago to Mackinaw Island and from Port Huron to Mackinaw Island. In the Chicago to Mackinaw Island there were maybe 100 boats at times -- a tremendous number of boats.

Q: Did the Coast Guard have to act as a referee in the races or what?

Adm. R.: No. Sometimes by special arrangement we would carry judges aboard. But we, as the Coast Guard, didn't make any decisions on that sort of thing. We simply were patrolling them for safety purposes. Of course, one of the things that happened most frequently up there in the Lakes was that people would simply leave the race and go into some port and tie up and have a party and nobody would know where they were. They would be reported to us and the Coast Guard would start a search. And it would sometimes take us a couple of days to find them. Some of these boats were tied up to a dock somewhere, enjoying themselves too.

Q: Involved in that was of course the observation of safety rules by the yachtsmen themselves, rules which you had imposed. Tell me about that. How did you go about that? It entailed inspections of each and every ship, didn't it?

Adm. R.: Oh yes. We didn't inspect vessels engaged in regattas for safety purposes.

Q: You did not.

Adm. R.: Not during the regattas. No, we never interfered with the operation of these things. Usually, of course, these things are sailing vessels and these long races were sailing vessels. So they are sealed off, you know. Their power is sealed off. So they are operating as sailing vessels, not as motor vessels, and a lot of the requirements on boats, most of the requirements on boats are applicable to motor vessels.

Q: With fuel-burning motors.

Adm. R.: Yes. And not so much the sailing vessels. There are a few requirements for sailing vessels but they are not like they are for the motor boats, not nearly as strict.

Roland #3 - 288

Q: I take it that each and every boat was required to have a requisite number of lifejackets and maybe a raft?

Adm. R.: Well, yes. As a matter of fact, in most cases the rules for a regatta -- the rules made up by the committee running the regatta would specify these things and they were well within our rules. But they would specify these things. Everybody was inspected for these things before by the committee. In some cases we would inspect a boat if we had some reason to inspect it. But the committees were pretty rigid about enforcing their rules because of preparedness being involved in running a race of that kind.

Q: Did you have any cases where you had to rescue a crew or anything of that sort from one of these racing boats?

Adm. R.: Yes, we did. We had one case -- this was not while I was on the MACKINAW or while I was Chief of Staff, but I was concerned with it. One of the boats was in difficulty and the word filtered to us in the District office and we gave it to the MACKINAW who immediately went to this boat and it was a 40-foot boat. They got there in time to get the people off it but they lost the boat. The boat sank. It had run into some floating object that they didn't identify and we weren't able to find out what it was. They said they ran into something and the boat filled up and sank.

Of course, there are always collisions in those things.

Somebody tries to cut off somebody else and they have a collision. I can't think of any cases where there was anything startling in any of those. I can't think of any lives that were lost in regattas up there while I was there.

One of the races that we patrolled was the America Cup races in Detroit. While I was skipper of the MACKINAW we went down for that patrol. I was present and watching closely when Guy Lombardo's boat went flying through the air and Guy Lombardo separated from it and went one way and the boat went the other way.

Q: An explosion?

Adm. R.: No, it hit something and went up in the air -- it must have been 20 feet up in the air, and came down like that.

Q: What an impact!

Adm. R.: Yes. And he flew out of the boat. One of the small boats that was patrolling picked him up.

There are lots of minor things that happen in a regatta but mostly the things that happen are minor. None of them seem to come to my mind at the moment. But whenever you have a regatta as big as either one of those long sailing races up there, there are bound to be some accidents.

There are, of course, many, many regattas. Every weekend there is a regatta on Lake St. Clair just north of Detroit and it's a very wealthy area and I guess everybody owns a boat up there. They are very active and they are very good boats and very good races. Of course, the same thing is true around Chicago. There are many, many of them around there. Just north of Chicago there is one place in there that is a very lively place.

Q: Lake Forest.

Adm. R.: Yes, around in there.

Q: What about your relationship with the Great Lakes Training Station?

Adm. R.: We hardly ever had any contact with them. But whenever we went to Chicago we always went -- well, this was long before, this was when I was on the ESCANABA and also when I was on the MACKINAW. We went to the Navy pier. There were always a few people there, Navy people -- of course, not many. When I was assigned the skipper of the MACKINAW, I visited Great Lakes Training Station a couple of times. But they were official calls that I was making and we had no official business with them. And as Chief of Staff, we had little to do with them either. They seemed to operate their own place pretty well and we were trying to do ours. So there wasn't very close cooperation between us.

Q: Was there any building of Coast Guard ships in your District at that time? You spoke of the MACKINAW being built in Toledo.

If so, would that come under your District's supervision?

Adm. R.: No, only as a support for the inspection party. But I don't think that there were any then. Earlier there were ships built for the Coast Guard in Bay City, Michigan, and of course the MACKINAW was built in Toledo.

We used to take the MACKINAW into drydock down at Manitowoc, Wisconsin. We had her in there a couple of times while I was aboard hereand of course she went in there fairly regularly, maybe once a year, during the time I was Chief of Staff. But they didn't build anything for us during that time.

Q: They were busy building submarines for the Navy.

Adm. R.: That's right, yes. They were going out through that canal.

Q: The Illinois-Michigan canal.

Adm. R.: Yes. I had forgotten about that, but it's so. When I left this job in Cleveland, I went back to sea as the commanding officer of the TANEY. I arrived there in about August or September of '49 and had a relatively short time out there.

Q: Was this something that you had sought as an assignment?

Adm. R.: I was happy to get it. I hadn't asked for it or thought about asking for any assignment, but I was very glad to get it.

As a matter of fact, it was the only assignment in my career on the West Coast and it was less than a year. I was only there until August 1950.

Q: You started to tell me, Admiral, about going on board the TANEY.

Adm. R.: I arrived out there in August or maybe September. Before I reported to the District Commander that I was there and had a short conversation with him and I went down to the ship which was tied up in Alameda and was surprised when I boarded the ship to be greeted by a young officer of the day who was Chinese. I didn't know we had any in the Coast Guard. His name was Jones, and he had graduated from the Coast Guard Academy. It was really a tremendous surprise to me. Nobody had told me in the District Office there was a Chinese aboard and I didn't know we had any anyway. He was a very nice young man though and I enjoyed his company.

The man who was the acting commanding officer -- well, the man who had been commanding officer died and his executive officer became commanding officer and was assigned. He was not simply acting commanding officer, he was assigned as commanding officer. And so he was the one whom I relieved. Then he received another set of orders which made him the executive officer again.

Q: So he was commanding officer only temporarily then.

Adm. R.: Yes, he had been commanding officer for some months. Maybe at that time they hadn't intended to send me out there or maybe they hadn't intended to send anybody out there. He was a commander and was a reserve officer. He wasn't about to be promoted and I think they wanted to have captains aboard those ships at that time. Maybe they were a little high in numbers of captains and I was about to become one. So I think that might be why they sent me out there to fill that billet with a captain.

Q: The TANEY was a cutter.

Adm. R.: Yes, she was a 328-foot cutter of the SECRETARY class, a very fine ship, a very good one. The best ships we ever had in the Coast Guard, except I guess the ones we have now -- the 378-footers are superior. But the BIBB class was what they called -- no, the CAMPBELL class, they called the SECRETARY class. We got them about in the middle '30s. They were beautiful ships and did a lot of work during the war. We lost one of them right at the beginning of the war. It was torpedoed.

So the TANEY, from the beginning, had served right where she was. Her station was Alameda and that was her first station and she stayed right there.

Q: What were her duties?

Adm. R.:   Principally weather patrol.

Q: And this was your first introduction to weather patrol, wasn't it?

Adm. R.:   Yes, it was my first weather patrol. There were three stations to be manned out there. I have served two patrols on one and one on each of the others. One was in the Gulf of Alaska and one of them was about a thousand miles directly west of San Francisco and the other one was about halfway between San Francisco and Honolulu.

Q: These are both mid-ocean points then.

Adm. R.:   All of them were well out at sea. My tours on the two off California were very pleasant.

Q: How long duration would you have a tour on a given station?

Adm. R.:   We were on station for three weeks and we used about a week or more going and coming.

Q: What did you accomplish when you were on station?

Adm. R.:   We carried weather bureau people with us. We had all the equipment for operating balloons and for getting signals from the balloons and so on, simply getting all the dope on the weather in the places where we were for forecasting purposes, of course. We did this 24 hours a day while we were out there and turned in all the results of our observations by radio to the beach and there it was incorporated in the forecasting of weather.

Q: Why were these three areas considered weather stations of importance? What would they contribute over another area in the ocean?

Adm. R.: There were other areas. The Coast Guard manned another one that was out beyond Honolulu, Hawaii -- out beyond Hawaii a little north of the line out there in the direction of Japan, another thousand, maybe two thousand miles past Honolulu. Then other observations were made in other places by other ships that happened to be passing through. But we had all of the fine equipment.

We had the balloons and the instruments that were sent up in the balloons for sending us information on the temperatures and so on at various altitudes. We tracked every balloon by radar and by theodolite and measured the wind forces at various altitudes up to as much as 50,000 feet, sometimes more I guess if conditions were right.

So it was a very professional thing that was being done by these -- we did the tracking, of course, but the weather bureau people were professional weathermen. We carried three, I think, on each cruise, who recorded these observations and set them up in the proper form for transmission. Then we did this in the Atlantic, too, you know. We manned about half a dozen stations in the Atlantic.

Q: These stations are constant, are they? What are the set of characteristics which determines a weather station in the middle of the ocean?

Adm. R.: This is determined not by the Coast Guard but by the Weather Bureau. They need observations from here, so they set up a station. They need another set of observations over here too, to go with these, so they choose them so that they have the best coverage.

Q: I just wondered if there was any special characteristic of a given spot in the ocean which may be better than any other given spot.

Adm. R.: No, I don't think so, as far as that is concerned. I think it was just coverage for them in their forecasts. The water all looks alike out there. We were required to stay within ten miles of the position. All of these places were within range of Loran stations so that we were able to control our positions pretty well. We were to stay within ten miles unless we were driven off by weather which sometimes occurred.

Q: The reason I'm asking this question is because I can see on the surface why a station in the Gulf of Alaska might be important weather-wise and I just wondered whether there was something similar if there was a spot off Hawaii somewhere.

Q: Oh, well, the one in the Gulf of Alaska was needed I felt, but the station that was about west of San Francisco was on a line from Seattle to Honolulu and there were aircraft flights along that line. The other one was halfway between San Francisco and Honolulu with aircraft flights over that. Also aircraft flights from between Los Angeles and Hawaii were within reach of our radar at the southern station.

We not only plotted weather but we also plotted these airplanes and gave them their positions. We furnished them with their positions and furnished them with local weather, too. We told them what the wind velocity was at various heights and the directions and whatever other information they might be interested in. Those were the most important things for them, of course.

And of course, we were there for the purpose of assistance if necessary. On two occasions the Coast Guard was on the spot when aircraft crashed out in the middle of the ocean. One was in the Atlantic. The airplane was in trouble and notified the ship and the ship left its station and headed for the aircraft. It was a trans-Atlantic flight and was heading for the ship but it couldn't go any further. It was out of what it takes to keep going, so they met and this aircraft circled for a while, while the ship - I think it was the BIBB. The skipper was Paul Kronk.

They made preparations by spreading oil on the water and by laying out a line of lights so the airplane would know in which direction to go to land. Then they stood by and the airplane came down and landed and broke up. The ship happened to be close by and they put their boats over and went over and picked up all the people that were in the airplane. There were something like 50 or 60 people.

The same sort of thing happened out in the Pacific on that southern station, the one between San Francisco and Hawaii. The BERMUDA SKYQUEEN was the name of the one in the Atlantic. I don't remember what the name was of the one in the Pacific -- airplanes had names then.

Bill Earle, who is now retired and the executive secretary of the Alumni Association down here at the Academy, was the skipper of the ship -- I think it was the PONTCHARTRAIN, a 250-foot cutter. They had the same sort of a deal in the Pacific. Theirs was an even smoother operation. The other one had happened first and was the first that we had had, so then there were studies and instructions and all kinds of preparations and they had all kinds of gear to lay out to mark a path for the guy to come down in and all that -- laid out in the right direction, considering the seas and the direction of the wind, so that they could land with the least effect on the airplane. And the same thing happened. The guy had to come down and he came down and landed farther from the ship but they got underway and luckily that time didn't fall apart. I think the wings fell off or something like that but it stayed afloat for a little while until they got up close and they got a couple of boats over and got over there and they got all the people off of that one. They had another big number of people.

Q: This happened when? In the early '50s?

Adm. R.: I would say -- I'm trying to think where I was when -- Kronk's happened I would say in the early '50s, yes. Certainly after the war. 1950, I would say.

Q: These two experiences constituted a new dimension to the Coast Guard's duty of air-sea rescue. They are in the age of the airplane now and traffic in the air, so something has been added to the Coast Guard.

Adm. R.: Yes, that's true. Bill Earle's case must have been when he was commanding officer so it had to be in the '50s.

Q: Has this dimension to the air-sea rescue service increased?

Adm. R.: No, this has never happened again.

Q: It's never happened again.

Adm. R.: There have been lots of airplanes reported in trouble and asked for directions for how to head and all that kind of business, but none has ever come down. If it had happened any more we probably would still be manning the weather stations, but we aren't now. Originally the purpose of these things -- they started during the war -- and the reason was there were all these airplanes that we were flying to Europe then, heading for the war.

Q: Military.

Adm. R.: Yes. Then it continued with the civilian planes. The principal purpose was to help them in their navigation, if they had difficulty with that. Then to give them this information on local weather from place to place all the way across, and help them in their navigation.

Now, of course, Loran is available to everybody; they know where they are. The planes are so fast that if they are blown off course they're not going off very far any way because they are going so fast in the direction that they are heading that it is relatively small. So there isn't the real need any more.

Of course, sometimes there was opposition to withdrawing these ships from aircraft people -- airlines. Then they began to lay off because they thought if we say that we need these things out there people aren't going to be so likely to fly with us. So they began to lay off saying anything more. Now, of course, it costs so much. It costs an awful lot of money to run one of these ships for a year and we had to have a lot of ships in order to man all these weather stations.

So now this has been discontinued. And another thing is

that there were agreements with foreign countries on this, too, that we would do this. As a matter of fact, some of the foreign countries manned some weather stations in the Atlantic over toward Europe. There were about three or four stations over there that were manned by other countries. France had at least one and maybe two and I think the Belgians had one and the Norwegians had one. So we had these agreements and the background was that these two cases had happened where everybody was saved in these two cases, and no case where there had been one when nobody was saved. So apparently we had been doing it all right.

But nobody now thinks there is a real need for this any more, including us.

Q: And the weather service was discontinued because of satellites, the development of satellites?

Adm. R.: That had something to do with it. That came into the picture too. That's right.

Q: When you were involved with the TANEY, you were in command there -- you were making a contribution as far as weather collection.

Adm. R.: Oh yes, I think there was a general feeling that this was a good thing to have these things out there. They were very useful flying these long expanses to have this weather picture, besides the incidental assistance. If a guy is going to fall down in the Pacific, chances are that he is not going to fall down alongside one of these things. So we couldn't have enough to cover the Pacific for assistance purposes or the Atlantic either.

Incidentally, there is the advantage of having assistance available closer than from the beach anyway. Now, when somebody gets in trouble I guess an airplane comes out and escorts them back in. I don't think they can do much about picking people up but they can drop rafts and things like that. So they are apt to replace the presence of the ship.

Anyway, the thing is gone now. We don't have them . . .

Q: It was an interesting phase to learn about while you were still . . .

Adm. R.: It was a pretty tough business on some of these stations, too. That station in the Gulf of Alaska was a mankiller. Gee, the weather was terrible. I had it in the winter but the weather up there is liable to be bad any time. The other two -- gee, we were on a vacation. We played volleyball and went swimming, fished.

Q: I suppose the weather gathering data in the Gulf of Alaska was hampered too by these sudden storms and bad weather.

Adm. R.: Of course. You had to be able to -- the balloons send out signals and they carry radar targets so we could keep in touch with them even if the weather was bad. But when it's blowing real hard, of course, the line would go up like this;

when the weather was good, they'd go up like this. It's a lot easier and you can carry them a lot higher this way.

It was an interesting thing. I used to go out and watch a lot of this stuff when they were doing it and watched them copying down things. It was really interesting and I think at the time a very useful thing, too.

Q: And that was the sole duty of the TANEY?

Adm. R.: Except in between. We'd go off to a regatta or to visit some Fourth of July celebration -- or we had a couple of assistance cases and a couple of searches, between patrols. We went down to San Diego for refresher training, shortly after I got to the ship -- Navy refresher training down there. So we were kept pretty busy.

Q: How did you manage your family arrangements when you were sent off on duty like this to the West Coast?

Adm. R.: Our children were at a stage in school where one of them was about to finish high school and one was about to finish junior high, so we decided that my wife would stay in Cleveland and would come out at the end of the school year when they had finished. So when I went out there I lived aboard ship. They stayed in Cleveland and I came home for Christmas for a few days. I had a week's leave, I think, so I got to see them at that time. Then about March I had another set of orders bringing me back

East so they never did get out there. If I had stayed out there, they would have come at the end of the school year.

Q: It would appear from your assignment out there on the TANEY that your counterpart to the Navy's BuPers was in operation balancing out a career and rounding it out. Is that case?

Adm. R.: Yes, I think so. We had just begun a little while before that to furnish headquarters with what we called our 'wish' cards. A wish card is a card that has a summary of background -- how much sea duty, how much short duty -- and some idea of how much East and how much West and so on.

Q: Prepared by the man himself?

Adm. R.: Prepared by the man himself -- and they still do this. You indicate on there if at your next assignment you are going to shore duty, where would you like to serve? If you're going to sea duty, where would you like to serve?

Q: This is where the 'wish' comes in.

Adm. R.: Yes. We had furnished these things and I had said on my wish card something about the West Coast at one time. I don't think I ever mentioned the TANEY. I think I may have said I would like to have a tour of duty on a weather ship. I had said on another part of the card that I'd like to have some duty on the West Coast. I think that wish card would have been sent in when I was in Cleveland and I think it said, if you are ashore, where would you like to go? And I think I might have said the Coast Guard Academy. So actually I did go to the West Coast and I went to a weather patrol ship and when I left there I did go to the Coast Guard Academy. So I got my wishes anyway.

Q: So it pays to notify them.

Adm. R.: It doesn't always work out that way though. I thought that this was a very good thing and I think that the things are carefully studied. I don't know at what level they are carefully studied but I think that they are studied and recommendations are made to people at higher levels on the basis of these cards. I don't think, for instance, that the Chief of the Office of Personnel reads all these cards and tells them to transfer this fellow -- but somebody lower down studies them and makes lists of people who want to do this and that. I think they make their assignments somewhat on that basis.

Q: I was amused to hear you say that you weren't quite certain at what level these wish cards were scrutinized and a man's record was studied to see that he was getting a rounded career and number of assignments. I was amused because as Commandant of the Coast Guard you were not initiated into this.

Adm. R.: No. It was done in Personnel. I know though from my experience as Commandant that it's now all done that way.

Every once in a while and maybe more frequently than I think, a person is transferred because somebody in a higher place said I want this fellow to go to that job and he doesn't hear anything about what was on his wish card. Say, maybe the Chief of the Office of Engineering wants a certain fellow to be running the Curtis Bay Yard -- Repair Yard -- and he has somebody in mind who is a good engineer and a good administrator and he wants him to go there, he'll say, "I want him to go there." And I think that when he says that it's quite likely to happen, no matter what's on the fellow's wish card.

Q: So this is a system of spot placements that's superimposed upon a regular system.

Adm. R.: I think so, yes. I do think though that there is weight given to this business of rounding out their career. In some cases it doesn't. This same son of mine hasn't had very much sea duty. You see, when he graduated from the Academy he went to duty on board one of the weather patrol ships and served about a year or so aboard that ship and then he was made executive officer of a 125-foot patrol boat and he served about a year there and then he went to a Loran station out in the Philippines. When he came back from that they sent him to PG training in electronics engineering, which is something that he wanted. But he went to that and he was three years at it. When he came out, they put him to work on Loran, the operation of Loran systems. He's been doing that ever since, until he got into the position where he's in now which is electronics engineering officer in the First District. Now when he leaves that he's going down to the other place. But you see he's only had a couple of years of sea duty right in the beginning and he has had none since and now he's too old for it.

Q: This says that specialization has come to the Coast Guard too.

Adm. R.: It certainly has. He has gone to this and he has stayed right with it. That's true and not all specialization. Lawyers, for instance. They get a better mixture of duty. I think law training is very good for a Coast Guard officer. I think it's good for anybody probably. It's a good kind of training to make you analyze situations and get to the basis of things.

I don't think there is need for as many lawyers in the Coast Guard as we have, so they get used for other things. But I think the training is just as useful in other things. I think lawyers make good administrators, so I think it's a good sort of thing. If I were doing it over and had my choice, I think I might go for that because I think it would fit me for so many other things that I'd rather do.

Q: Let me ask. When you were Commandant, did you engage in any spot designations for people whom you thought particularly qualified for a job?

Adm. R.: No, except for Assistant Commandant. I picked the Assistant Commandant. But I didn't pick specifically anybody else. I think other people might have and I don't object to that too much. You have to think of the welfare of the person involved, the person that you are transferring. But you also have to think of the welfare of the Coast Guard.

Q: Yes, I would think so. I would think it could work on occasion to the advantage of both.

Adm. R.: Yes, I think so. I picked both of my Assistant Commandants. Of course, I wouldn't want that to be done any other way. By that time, of course, a person's career has been rounded or not and it's not going to be rounded any more.

Q: It's reaching a zenith, so to speak. Well, you went back to the Coast Guard Academy, in 1950.

Adm. R.: Yes, as Commandant of Cadets.

Q; You said that you had put this on your 'wish' card.

Adm. R.: Yes, I said the Academy.

Q: And why did you want to go back to the Academy?

Adm. R.: Because I thought it would be interesting. I think that the Academy is one of the most important things as far as the Coast Guard is concerned for the advancement of the Coast Guard, the training of people as officers. I think it is one of the most worthy things we can do and the better it's done -- and of course, as Commandant of Cadets I had a pretty good crack at it for four whole years, too.

Q: And you had such a long relationship with the Coast Guard Academy.

Adm. R.: Of course, I had been there as a cadet and then I had another tour of duty there.

Q: Yes. And you had seen it through different stages of development, so this is a logical time to go back.

Adm. R.: Yes, I saw the very beginnings on the present location and served my time in the last location before this present one, so my interest -- I'm sure my interest was real and I'm interested in all of the activities that they have. I'm interested in their athletic activities and I'm interested in their academic activities and their extracurricular activities. So, I was glad to get another crack at it, particularly as Commandant of Cadets because the Commandant of Cadets, I think, has more influence on Cadets than anybody else -- or he can have if he wants to.

Q: Did you have quarters?

Adm. R.: Yes and it's the first time I ever did, too -- it's the last time, too. It's the only time I ever had quarters -- as

Commandant of Cadets.

Q: Perhaps at this point before you talk about your four years at the Academy, that you might tell me wherein the Academy of 1950 differed from your last tour there in the '30s.

Adm. R.: It differed in numbers, of course.

Q: How much larger had it grown?

Adm. R.: When I arrived there I would say we had about 400 cadets in 1950 and when I left in 1938 I would say we had about 200 or 250. So it had grown a good bit in numbers.

It spread itself out in its activities. The extracurricular activities had increased by a lot -- I mean extracurricular activities outside of athletics. But they had developed a glee club, for instance, which was a very good one and was gaining more and more reputation. They put on a fairly good number of performances of different kinds in the way of entertainment -- plays -- and at that time minstrel shows were pretty amusing and well attended and they did one of those each year for a couple years until some objections.

Q: A little raucous perhaps?

Adm. R.: No, because of the ridicule of the colored folks.

Then the arrangements of the affairs of cadets was somewhat better organized than it had been in the past. Like the arrangements for getting uniforms and for furnishing other things that the cadets needed. The establishment of a cadet store, for instance, where they could buy things.

Q: Was that tied in with General Services Administration?

Adm. R.: No, that was run entirely by the Academy and run by a Coast Guard officer. I had run that business when I was there in the '30s, but it was on a low scale then. You know, if cadets were to get uniforms we would call somebody up and have them come in and tell them to furnish the uniform. It had grown to a scale where we were doing a lot of it ourselves. And of course, their athletic activities had spread out greatly. They had really gone a long ways in athletics.

The war had something to do with this. During the war we had an exceptionally good football team. We had always been playing in the league we are playing in now, which has grown to be a pretty good league now -- Trinity, Middlebury, and occasionally Rhode Island--Yale and Brown and places like that --we had never had anything to do with them. But we had a good boxing team and we used to box and could beat Yale in boxing. But anyway, during the war we did beat Yale, we did beat Brown, we beat Holy Cross. Of course, they were big time -- we were small time really. So things had improved. But of course, after the war they slowed down again.

But they were still on a good scale. We had improved our

coaching -- we had much better coaches. We were getting people who were professional coaches, you see. Before the war, we had taken Coast Guard officers who were the best fitted we could find among our officers. But it was getting so that we didn't have to apologize for any of our coaches.

So all these things had improved. I think that the cadets were coming out of the Academy better trained for work they had to do. They were coming out with more ambition, too, because they could see in the future PG training and specialized work in the trades in which they were particularly interested.

Q: They could see a career.

Adm. R.: Yes, and that hadn't been so before. Before, you were an engineer or a lawyer or you didn't get any training. And there weren't many lawyers at that. But now nearly everybody gets something.

My own sons-- one of them got to be a marine engineer, naval architect and the other one got to be an electronics engineer. They never taught me anything.

Q: So it was a much broader scope, as you indicate, in the academic sense.

Adm. R.: Yes.

Q: And the faculty was . . .

Adm. R.: The faculty was improving all the time and of course, during the war the faculty improved a whole lot and we got people who came as instructors at the Academy and who became officers and who stayed and continued. One of them just died the other day. He retired in 1974 and he died just a couple of days ago. He came here as an English teacher and he wound up as dean. I appointed him as Acting Dean when I was Commandant and he retired in '74. He had a heart attack the other day and he died. But he was a fine man. He was well educated himself and a good teacher. And the same thing is true of a lot of others.

So everything I could see was on the up and up and things were improving here.

Q: When you got your assignment to the Coast Guard Academy, you knew what billet you were going into.

Adm. R.: Yes, my orders said that I was to report to the Superintendent for assignment as Commandant of Cadets.

Q: Then you had time perhaps to formulate a list of things you'd like to achieve while you were Commandant of Cadets.

Adm. R.: Yes, I had the time, but I don't think I went so far as to do that. I had been away long enough so I thought I would want to see what I could see there before I did all that.

I had some ideas on discipline and I don't mean that I thought you could clamp down more than we had. I thought that perhaps we had clamped down more than we should. I thought the cadets weren't doing enough and getting enough responsibility themselves as cadets. I didn't want to turn it all over to them and make it a country club or anything of that kind. But I had those thoughts in mind. I could see that there was a lot that could be done. Because the cadet organization had been changed a good bit.

When I had been here before, we had a couple companies of cadets. When I came back I guess we had about four companies or maybe three. I think we had a battalion -- we had moved from the company organization up into a battalion organization. So there was a staff of cadets. Before there had been a company commander and a company executive officer and the rest of them were all carrying guns or swords. So they had a battalion commander and a battalion executive officer and a battalion supply officer and a couple of other things -- I can't remember exactly what they are now. But these are people who could actually supervise some of the life of the cadets at the Academy and got good experience from doing it. They had a battalion adjutant, too.

For instance, the battalion supply officer, after I had been there for a while, took on the business of filling out the laundry contract for the cadets. There had been a laundry at the Academy but they had cut it out and had turned it out to a regular laundry. But the cadets hadn't had anything to say about that. One day there was a sign up on the thing that said the Mohigan Laundry is now the laundry for you and there are laundry slips available down below and pass them out or something like that. But after I had been there for a while, I had the supply officer take on that particular thing. He, as a matter of fact while I was there, changed laundries. I don't know why. I do know why, he told me why. But I didn't think it was entirely necessary to do it, but he thought it was and so he did it. Of course, it worked out all right. It was as good after he changed it as it was before. He probably learned something by studying the thing.

Also when it came time for uniforms for the new class, the supply officer didn't decide who was going to furnish the uniforms but he was in on all the contacts and he made suggestions about what we should emphasize in the contract we made and all that -- about fittings and things of that nature. So I could see things like that. But I didn't make a list of things that I was going to do. I knew that there were things that I would look into and I knew that there were other things that I would run across while I was there, too.

Q: That's quite interesting. What were some of the things that you did run across as the time went on?

Adm. R.: The handling of demerits was one of the things, and it was an important thing. The cadets had nothing to say -- after an offense was committed and demerits were assigned by somebody who had authority to assign them, then if a case was serious at all or if it wasn't serious, if the cadet objected to the demerits -- because the cadets could object to demerits, you see -- then the decisions were made by officers who were company advisers. But the cadets didn't get in on it. So we designed a disciplinary board on the staff who would review these things. In all cases where it was a serious matter and in cases where there was a protest. They would make a recommendation to me as Commandant of Cadets. I could turn their recommendation around but I didn't very often. They were as nasty as I was and probably a bit worse in some cases. They were pretty good at disciplining themselves if they had a chance to do it.

But if they didn't have anything to do with it, they were against all this stuff.

Q: It's human nature, I guess.

Adm. R.: Well, making the judgment was good for them.

Q: You, in handling some of these things, must have been drawing on your own experience as a cadet and later on on the staff.

Adm. R.: Yes, I'm sure I was, but I think that I was also drawing on other experience that I had too. If you're in the service and you have people working for you, you do have disciplinary power over these people. You can wreck a guy by being too tough on him or you can wreck him by not being tough enough. So you have to make decisions on these matters as you go along in the interest of the people involved and in the interest of the service too, of course. This is what I thought the cadets ought to be getting their fingers into.

Of course, they have more of that sort of thing now than they had when I came there. Sometimes I think it's too soft there. It's not as tough as it was when I was there.

Q: That prompts me to ask you if you noticed any change in the attitude of the cadets as such. I mean, times had changed. We were in the post-war period and freedoms were much greater, as I recall, for young people. You noticed this in the cadet body as a group?

Adm. R.: I don't think I do. Maybe there are some things but I think they are minor things. I don't think the cadets keep themselves looking as neat as they used to. I don't think -- they look a little bit sloppy sometimes. Maybe it's because their hair is a little longer. They don't have long hair. They were allowed to have their hair fairly long at one time and then somebody saw the light and thought they shouldn't let that continue so they did clamp down on that. Now their hair is in pretty good shape. It's good across the back and it has little sideburns, but they are short sideburns, not long ones. They really do look pretty good. A lot of them used to look like Marines.

I think that a cadet is likely to have his clothes look a

little bit /more rumpled than they used to. I think there was a lot of pressure put on cadets at the time that I was Commandant for keeping themselves neat. I don't think there is that much pressure now. They look all right. They look better than an ordinary group of people, I think. But I don't think that they look quite as neat as they did.

As far as their behavior around town, I think their behavior is pretty good, at least as far as I know. They don't seem to get in the newspapers very much. Of course, a lot of them have cars now. The first classman can have a car any time. It used to be that you could have it at the last part of the first year. Now he can have it any time when he's a firstclassman. I think that they may be getting into the second class now. Near the end of the second class you can have it. I've seen cadets names in the newspapers a couple of times for being picked up by the cops for traffic violations.

But they don't seem to get into other trouble. They don't get into fights and as far as I know, they don't break into houses and things like that like other kids do-- like some of the kids do. I think that in general their behavior is pretty good.

I think the reason it is is because they have a group of their own that insists upon behavior.

Q: A group that applies the rules to their peers and as you

related before, sometimes they are tougher than older people are.

Adm. R.: Sure. There was a cadet thrown out of the Academy a while ago for cheating on an examination. I don't think anybody had anything to do with that case except cadets until it came time to actually sever his connection. I think they handled all the dealings before that.

Q: What kind of honor system prevails here? Or is there an honor system?

Adm. R.: Yes, there's an honor system. I don't know what you mean by what kind.

Q: What are its ramifications?

Adm. R.: I guess maybe I don't know. Because there was not an honor system when I was Commandant of Cadets. We insisted that there was an honor system even though it wasn't an established honor system. We said that you are all responsible for the conduct of the cadet corps and for people in it and you should see that people besides yourself behave themselves. We didn't put responsibility on certain people as responsibility is on them now. They are required now, for instance -- if they see somebody climbing the fence -- going AWOL -- they are required to report it. I know that when I was Commandant of Cadets, I don't think any cadet ever reported another cadet for unauthorized liberty.

I think that some of them may have signed people in a liberty book. I'm not sure of that because I had no proof, but I think that that happened.

As I think back on what happened before -- when I was a second classman at the Academy, I had a roommate who fell in love and he went out one night. He said I'm not going to be back when liberty is up. There were two of us in the room. I said, "Well, what do you want me to do?"

He said, "If you have to make your report, how about saying I'm here." I said, "I'll see what the circumstances are. Maybe I can."

So he went out and I stuffed his bunk. I took a blanket and rolled it up and stuffed it in there. Pretty soon the OD came along and he'd bang on the door and throw it open and whoever was in charge of the room was supposed to say "All present, Sir." So he came down and he knocked on the door and opened it up and I said, "All present, Sir." He closed the door and he opened it again and looked in and he closed it. I don't know why he did that. I think maybe he knew the guy was out. But nobody ever said anything. But I did that myself, you see. I don't think that this would fit the system now.

But I don't think the penalty is the same either. You see, if he was absent and detected as absent, he would have been kicked out. Now they wouldn't do that. They would punish him and probably it would be a fairly severe punishment, but he wouldn't be thrown out of the Academy. So I think this has some bearing on what they do now and what I did then, too. I didn't want to see my roommate thrown out. But if I had been caught making a false report and he had been caught for not being there, we both would have been thrown out. Gee whiz! That's asking a little too much of me, I think.

Q: I think asking of his roommate, it certainly was asking too much. But it's a youngster not thinking of the consequences.

Adm. R.: I think that's why the guy finally closed the door. I think he knew there was something screwy in there. So he joined in the crime too.

That roommate of mine had been a cadet before in this class ahead of this fellow who was the OD that night. It was two years ahead of our class. I think they knew him pretty well.

Q: And they knew his ways.

Interview #4

Admiral Edwin J. Roland, USCG (Ret.)

Old Lyme, Connecticut, March 30, 1976

Interviewer: John T. Mason, Jr.

Q: It's good to see your smiling face this morning, Sir. Yesterday when we broke off you were dealing with your four years as Commandant of Cadets at the Coast Guard Academy. You were talking about the giving of greater responsibility to the cadets. I think you wanted to develop that subject perhaps a little more.

Adm. R.: When I was at the Academy I relieved an officer whose name was Olson. He was a captain at that time, he later became a rear admiral and is now retired. He had been on the job for four years and had been, as a cadet, a year ahead of me, so I knew him quite well. We exchanged information for a period of almost a week, I think, before I finally relieved him and he went on his way. He was an aviator and I think he left there and went to an air station somewhere as commanding officer.

He was probably the first aviator who had ever been the Commandant of Cadets. I know he was. And this was the beginning of a movement, I think. We hadn't had many aviators at the Academy up until that time and certainly none in the higher positions in the structure there.

Q: They had earned their spurs in World War II.

Adm. R.: I guess they did. Yes, we got so that we had to accept them and they had to accept us too.

A class came in while I was there -- a new class came in. It was, of course, quite an experience to greet these boys and to see the increased number. I think there must have been about somewhere near 200 in the class that came in that year. Of course, that was large compared to my experience before that. As a matter of fact, that was as many cadets, more than as many cadets as we had had during a good bit of the time that I had been there before.

Q: I recall that when you came in there was hardly anybody there to greet you or anything of the sort.

Adm. R.: Oh yes, when I arrived as a cadet, I should say. So it was quite an experience. We did the greeting with officers. There were only a few cadets around -- I can't remember how they happened to be there but some of the cadets were away on cruise at the time, probably all of them were away on cruise. There were a few who happened to be there for one reason or other -- sick, lame and lazy, probably. We made use of them in setting up the arrangements for this new class, but mostly it was officers who handled it.

We organized them into a couple of companies right away and set up these cadets that were there as company commanders. At that time, these cadets were required to attend a few classes --

refresher classes in mathematics in the summertime. But mostly their immediate indoctrination was in military drill and lectures on the military life and so on. It wasn't long after that, however, that the cadets returned and then they took over immediately.

At that time indoctrination of cadets throughout the whole year was in the hands of the second class. The first class, of course, had a hard time keeping their fingers out of it and actually did enter into it to some extent. But the second class had the responsibility and took on the job in accordance with the plan that had been prepared before. So really it doesn't take long to get a new class pretty well settled as far as the Commandant of Cadets is concerned any way.

Q: I suppose an important factor is their receptivity to the life. That's what they came for.

Adm. R.: Yes. They don't all accept it. At that time and still, of course, there are quite a few who don't remain. They immediately make up their minds that this is not for them. There were, I would say in that class, there must have been a couple dozen homesick cases -- usually they get over those things. But we lost within a couple of weeks maybe ten percent of that class.

Q: That's a natural culling, isn't it?

Adm. R.: Yes. As I said, this was not an unusual thing. That happened about every year.

Q: Was hazing at that time ruled out completely?

Adm. R.: No, it wasn't. It wasn't ruled out completely but it was on a pretty low level. It had been a very rigorous thing before. There were a good many people who were actually injured to some extent. I don't know of any serious cases but there were people who would get cuts and things.

For instance, one of the things the upperclassmen made cadets do was to "sit on infinity" and that meant to take a sitting with nothing to rest on except a bayonet which was upside down and resting against the cadet's rear end. There were some cases at one time of people getting cut and cut fairly badly. They were kept in that position for a long time. That sort of thing by that time was not done any more. At least it wasn't done to my knowledge and I don't think it was done.

A good many of the very rigorous things had been cut out but they were still orderlies to the upperclassmen. They ran their errands, they went to the canteen for them, and they arranged their laundry and things of that nature. I think it was probably a good thing that these cadets were required to go to some classes because it gave them a rest.

Q: Yes, from the drill.

Adm. R.: From the drill and from the other work that the upperclassmen had them do.

I got the battalion and company officers in to see me

immediately after the upper class got back. We arranged a series of meetings between me and the Assistant Commandant of Cadets and these cadets. We met twice a week. Actually we met on some other occasions when there was reason for it but as a routine we met a couple times a week to talk about their difficulties in managing the battalion and their gripes, the causes of their difficulties and what we had to do with it.

This was very productive. When the battalion was completely organized, of course, then we had set up some officers part-time. We didn't have them as a regular thing but we set up some officers as company advisers, one officer for each company, and they were included in these things too. They learned a good many things from what the cadets had to say. The cadets were a little reluctant in the beginning to talk about their troubles and why they were having them. Actually they opened up later on and it turned out that a good many of their troubles were caused by interference by officers with what they were doing and fear of interference by officers.

Q: Were these administrators staff officers or were they instructors?

Adm. R.: These were instructors who were assigned part-time for this thing. When this began to shake out, there was a better relationship and I told these officers that I didn't want them to be doing all of the necessary things. They should be available and they should step in when needed but I wanted the cadets to do everything that they could do in the management of the daily life of these cadets.

Then there was quite a bit at that time. Later on, of course, when classes began they were in class a good bit of the time and there wasn't so much of that. But this was the beginning of it and it wasn't long before the cadets began to assume some responsibilities without it being given to them and we had to keep our eye on that too, because pretty soon we would have been on the outside and they would have been moved into my office I think.

Q: They would have packed your bags for you and sent you on.

Adm. R.: Yes. So there were some disappointments in some of the decisions that had to be made that removed cadets from some of the activities that they had assumed for themselves. But it shook out pretty well. After while, too, we were able to get officers assigned permanently to this business of company adviser and this was their primary duty and they spent all day at it if necessary. They had some additional duties assigned to them, of course. But they were taken off of instruction duty and their business with the cadets became their primary duty and they became very well acquainted with the cadets and they learned a great deal about the cadets -- their personalities and their relationships with their families and all sorts of details about them. Who their girls were and it really got to be very good.

Q: This was the beginning of a new policy, wasn't it?

Adm. R.: Yes. In the end, we actually got a woman assigned as a -- well, we called her a cadet hostess at the time -- and she was a great help. She was the widow of an officer who had been in the class after me. Her name was Mrs. Sinton. She was a tremendous help as far as the social life of the cadets.

We had quite a few social events. We wanted the cadets to get acquainted with the people in the town and also with the people at Connecticut College. So we had a lot of tea dances and things like that in the beginning. This woman was wonderful in that respect, as a hostess. Eventually, she arranged a lot of things. Before cadets would have girls come to town from their hometown or some place to go to dances and it was always a hassle about where these girls were going to stay. There were no fixed places. This woman arranged in homes nearby where these girls could stay. She did many things like that and set up a very good system of that kind.

She was the first woman to work for the Academy in that way. There were secretaries and clerks, but she was the only one who had direct contact and had an influence on the cadets in their training at the Academy.

Q: I would assume that that has continued as a practice.

Adm. R.: It has continued. That woman continued for quite a long time. There is a different one now -- Mrs. Pope, who is the widow of a naval officer. She is in that job -- they don't call her hostess any more, there's another title. I can't remember what it is. But she is as effective and maybe more effective. I think she has a couple of people working for her now, doing the same sort of thing. Her office is next door to the chaplain's office which is a good place I think.

Q: They can work hand in hand.

Adm. R.: Sure, they handle the real difficulties of the cadets.

So the cadets were given more and more direct responsibility and they took the responsibility which previously -- they would receive reports previously and just pass the report along to a commissioned OD. Eventually we got the commissioned OD moved out of the barracks. He wasn't far off but he was out of the barracks and the cadets handled the actual maintaining of order and quiet in the barracks during study hours and so on, where before there was often an officer walking up and down the corridors all through the study hour.

Q: A policing officer.

Adm. R.: Yes. The people who were assigned as the company advisers were the regular duty officers. They had the duty for the Academy; as a matter of fact, they had the duty responsibility for all of the Academy, not just the cadet corps. Later that was changed. It was after I left that it was changed so that now there is a different duty officer for the routine things at the Academy, the things that don't have to do with the cadet corps, and there is also a commissioned officer who is the duty officer for the cadet corps. He still stands his watch in a different building, a nearby building.

Q: Who was the Superintendent of the Academy at this time, during this time of innovation?

Adm. R.: [Admiral] Arthur Hall moved in at the same time that I did. He is now a retired Admiral; he lives here in Old Lyme. He was there for the four years that I was Commandant of Cadets.

Q: And he was very much in agreement with the whole development.

Adm. R.: Yes, he was very much. He was doubtful about some of things. He was an old hand and was used to the other way of handling discipline.

Q: An authoritarian.

Adm. R.: Yes. But he went along with it all right. He could see the reasonableness of it. Another good thing that happened. Before I got there -- a year or so before -- a psychologist was assigned to the Academy. He was a Public Health Service officer. His name was Williams. He took a decided interest in all these matters too. His primary job at the time was in connection with the admission of cadets, entrance. He later became the Admissions Officer, but at that time he was not the Admissions Officer. As a matter of fact, there wasn't anybody who was called the Admissions Officer, but he later became that. He took a very active part in this business of setting up responsibility with the cadets and discussing with the cadets. He was very good. He had been in the Air Force during the war as a reserve officer and then at the end of the war he was released by the Air Force and he went to the Public Health Service and came to the Coast Guard. This probably happened in '49 or '48 that he came over to the Coast Guard and went to the Academy. He stayed at the Academy until about two years ago when he retired.

So he has grown up with a lot of changes in the Coast Guard Academy at that time. He took a strong, active part in these changes. He was very favorably inclined toward giving them more and more and more responsibility -- more even than the rest of us were. Since he hadn't had the experience of going through the Academy as a cadet -- I don't know where he had gone to school but it was somewhere else where he had had complete freedom.

But he was very reasonable about it and I guess I said, very effective. He had a lot to do with our final arrangements. In the end, the cadets did many things -- they ran the military drills without the presence of an officer even on the field. Before we had had all of the officers on the field right with their companies, correcting the position of the arms and so on, actually a drill master. All this stopped and the cadets became these things. They appreciated the fact that they could do these things.

Q: And were their standards equally as high?

Adm. R.: Oh, I think so, yes. I think maybe even higher because they were on top of these things all the time and they followed them up. A lot of the drill at the Academy then, and now even, is done outside of drill hours, you know, in the corridors in the barracks. If somebody is sloppy about handling his rifle, an upper classman gets him out in a corridor with his rifle and gives him 15 minutes or extra work at this.

Q: The drill on the field is for the show.

Adm. R.: And more and more. The cadets get very little drill actually on the field, except for the reviews. In the beginning when a class comes in they are out on the field a good bit. But after the academic year starts, they don't get out there very much any more except for reviews. And the detail work is done in the barracks by individuals -- to individuals and by individuals who observe these faults and do correct them.

I think probably they are as good now as they were before. At one time, the curriculum included three hours a week of military drill and the cadets got credit for it, academic credit. Now there is nothing like that. Three hours a week and besides that the reviews.

Q: I suppose that three hours of credit for drill wouldn't help you in getting academic standing with the association of schools, would it?

Adm. R.: We put it in our transcripts as -- it wasn't called drill; it was called military tactics. Of course, there were other things that were included in it. There were a few lectures that went into it besides drill, but the main thing -- the hours that were set aside in the schedule were just for drill. They would come out at the beginning and have a drill for the hour and then they would go back in and this was all they did. They didn't get any lectures then except "Move your butt right," "Get in step," and "One, two, three, four."

So the cadets really took over that business pretty thoroughly then. And then there was a change in the drill manual during the time I was there. We used the Naval Drill Manual. They oversaw all the detailed change from the way drills were carried out. It used to be that there were a lot of movements like "Squads left," and "Squads right," and all them. This was dropped while I was there. It was a simplification and an improvement, I think, and there weren't individual squad movements. There was no such thing as that except when a squad was drilling by itself somewhere. But whenever, by the new manual, there was to be a movement, it was a movement of at least a platoon and probably a company movement.

So there were lots of these changes. And the cadets did most of this themselves. There were officers looking over their shoulders, of course. We continued our interviews with the cadets with the cadet officers for all the time that I was there. And the interviews continued to be productive. They always thought of more things that they thought should be changed.

Q: Always developing problems.

Adm. R.: Yes. At that time, there was an Academic Board which took care of everything. It took care of disciplinary cases and the academic records of the cadets and so on and it sat and heard all cases where there was a possibility of serious disciplinary action or dismissal or anything like that. It was composed of the Superintendent, the Assistant Superintendent, and the heads of departments. There were about a dozen people on the board.

It met frequently because there was occasion to meet pretty frequently. That system continued while I was there. We formed some other boards. For instance, we formed an Athletic Board that took care of matters of principles involved in our intercollegiate athletics and so on and also our inter-class and inter-company athletics. There were other boards formed too. They now have quite a few boards for different purposes. There is a separate Disciplinary Board now, separate from the Academic Board. The Academic Board considers only academic cases. So there's quite a change now.

But while I was there that one Academic Board supervised all of these things.

There were some other boards formed at that time. Boards principally to review the curriculum. We had been recognized from the time I was a cadet by the Engineers' Council for Professional Development, which is one of the best recognitions for an engineering school. I don't know how we happened to get that recognition in the beginning, but while I was Commandant of Cadets the Engineers' Council for Professional Development came to the Academy and inspected our system and our curriculum, and told us that they didn't think we should continue to have this recognition, mostly because of the lack of research by instructors and also the fact that there weren't very many advanced degrees among us up there. So they were concerned about the instruction staff.

Actually they did withdraw their recognition. It was quite a blow to us. We had had recognition by the New England College and Secondary School Board that everybody has. We got that all right and that continued. But it woke up the Academy to the fact that there were some deficiencies in the system apparently. There has been a lot of change in the faculty since that time. I guess we have as many Ph.D.s as anybody has now - percentage-wise. We have gotten back the recognition from the Engineers' Council for Professional Development, but only for the last four or five years I would say.

Q: They took their time in restoring that.

Adm. R.: Oh yes. I suppose they were reluctant to remove it from us, but having removed it they weren't very eager to give it back to us either. They observed for some time. I think they came to the Academy for over a period of ten years or more before they began to be serious about returning this thing to us.

It is a recognition that a relatively small number of engineering schools have. RPI has it I guess - I'm sure they have. Massachusetts Institute of Technology has it and I know there are a good many others, but it's relatively few.

During the time that I was at the Academy our classes increased. We had our first graduating class of approaching 200. We didn't make 200 but we had one class that had 190 in it. We had one bad difficulty while I was there. It was with the class that came in when I entered the Academy. When they finished their second class year, things were beginning to look better in Korea. A lot of these kids came in, I suppose, because they didn't want to be drafted. So a large number resigned at the end of their second class year and we had no hold on them of any kind.

We could say "We don't accept your resignation," but then they could go to their Congressman and appeal our not accepting the resignation. So they all got out and they had three years of government education and they got transcripts and they went into other schools as seniors and graduated. Of course, a good many of them wanted other things.

Surprisingly, I'd say three or four of those kids became ministers. They went into that kind of thing.

Q: They probably were CO's to begin with.

Adm. R.: I suppose. Of course, a lot of those kids would have been drafted and wouldn't have been able to do what they wanted to do. So they came and got educated.

Since then, there have been changes made so that after a certain period -- I guess it might be even after the first year -- if a person resigns and doesn't have a good reason for getting out, he can be held in an enlisted status for a certain period of time -- a couple years and maybe to finish the four years. So this is hanging over their heads now.

Q: It seems like a very sensible step to have taken.

Adm. R.: Yes. And another change that was made while I was there was: we required three years of service after graduation before they could resign. This wasn't economically a very good deal. Every year, of course, we had to figure out how much it cost to educate a cadet and the last time they / did it while I was there, it came out to be $40,000. So that's a lot of money.

That was a lot of money at that time and it's a lot of money now. You don't get it back in three years. For three years the fellow is really learning his way, he's just completing his education.

Q: It's almost an apprenticeship, isn't it?

Adm. R.: Yes. So this is changed and now it's five years which is better. Since that time, within the five years many of them go to PG school and they get a different look at the service and we don't have as many resigning now as we did before.

When I was a young officer nobody ever resigned. When I was commandant of cadets I had letters from General Electric and from some other big outfit that wanted to have representatives come and talk to our graduating class. We didn't let them do it but I know that they talked to them afterwards and they got quite a few of them eventually after the three years was up.

So I enjoyed very much my session as Commandant of Cadets and I was simply amazed at the amount of talent you find in a group of young people like that. Whatever you want to do you'll find somebody who has had a smattering of it or a desire for it and a talent for it and some of these kids when they put on shows, these kids would volunteer. They would turn up a very good performance.

We had a young man named Rooney who was in the class of '56 -- so I was only with him a couple of years -- but his father had been working in connection with the stage. He wasn't an actor.

I think he had had some small parts, but he was connected with management and direction and things like that. This kid must have listened to his father at home because he really could do marvelous things in getting together a minstrel show or some other kind of show and directing the thing.

We at that time improved the quality of the musical displays of the cadets. We got a fellow named Janz and he, as many others, had gone to school somewhere and had a degree in music and he came into the Coast Guard band, enlisted in the Coast Guard band. Many young men do this to serve a little time in there for experience. Then after their time is up they get out.

This fellow was a very talented man himself. He has a beautiful voice and he took on the glee clubs and the choirs. He formed a group called the Idlers who still perform down there. There are 16 of them in the group and they are a marvelous singing group. They performed in the White House and a good many places. They are excellent performers. He did a marvelous job with them. He stayed on after his time was up. He extended his enlistment, I think, for a year or something like that. Then he got out and he went back to school and got himself an advanced degree. Then he came back to the Academy and came in as a civilian. He's a civilian professor down there now and he is in charge of all cadet musical activities. He's a great guy; he's a marvelous fellow, and a good influence on cadets and turns out quality things. He can direct shows and all that. Other people get him to work with them when they put on shows too because he is so good at it.

There have been so many improvements, aside from the actual academic improvement and military education, that people don't think so much about but that have such an important effect on the morale and the education and overall well-being of these kids at the Academy and the final product.

Q: You're dealing with the total man and his development.

Adm. R.: Yes. It has improved a tremendous amount. At the time that I was Commandant of Cadets, the curriculum was so made up that everybody took the same thing. There was no choice at all. At one time they had had a choice of French and Spanish, but they finally dropped that so that there was no more Spanish and then finally they dropped the French. But everybody had to take the same thing. Everything. All of the math courses, all of the science courses, and everything, all the engineering courses and everybody graduated with exactly the same training. When I was Commandant of the Coast Guard, the Academic Advisory Committee met with the Commandant once a year. They came down early in my tenure down there and they made a report. They had met at the Academy first and then came down and made a report to me. It was a social thing, more or less.

We had a dinner for them each year and it was a good time as well as a report to the Commandant. After they made their report the fellow who was chairman, who was Dr. Arthur Adams (Beanie), said to me it there anything you would like us to do. I said, "I think we lose a lot of cadets because they don't have the talent for this curriculum. They come in there and these kids aren't all engineers. Some of them are probably better qualified in something else and not so well qualified in engineering, so we lose some of these kids. Their interest isn't in that." I said, "I think it would be a good idea if there was a split somewhere in the curriculum, maybe at the end of the second year, so that from there on one group is being developed in management and the others still engineering if you want to keep it that way."

So he jumped right in. Maybe they had been talking about it. He said he thought that was a good idea and all the others spoke up and talked about it. I didn't have any more to say about it but that I thought it would be a good idea and I would be in favor of making the change in the curriculum. They changed the curriculum within a year and they did it that way. They split it that way.

Now there are nine options. There is oceanography . . .

Q: This is after the first two years.

Adm. R.: Since then there has been continual change. The fellow I told you had just died -- Paul Foye. He became very active and he was present at that meeting. He became very active in this business. Now, maybe there are too many options, I don't know but anyway, it's working out well. And they are losing far fewer cadets. The attrition is down a great deal.

Q: Have they put the languages back in again?

Adm. R.: I can't answer the question. They probably have.

Q: Why did they drop Spanish and French?

Adm. R.: I don't know. It might have been because of the difficulty of getting instructors. At that time most of our instructors were officers. Admiral Spencer, who is retired and lives out there, tells the story about when he was a young officer. He went to the Academy and the Superintendent was an officer named Jacobs. He didn't know why he was being sent to the Academy. He knew he was going as an instructor but he didn't know what he was going to teach. So he got there and he went in to see Jacobs. They talked about the weather and things like that. So Jacbos said, "Mr. Spencer, you will teach French." Spencer said, "I don't know a single word of French." And the fellow said, "Mr. Spencer, you will teach French." And he did teach French.

Q: How horrible!

Adm. R.: I think that there was probably a lack of French and Spanish teaching people in the Coast Guard. Jimmy Hirshfield taught Spanish one time at the Academy. But he comes from San Antonio and his Spanish may be Mexican-Spanish but he speaks it fluently, so he was all right.

But then they finally got a Frenchman named Gaston Buron. He came into the Academy in the late '30s. He came in while I was in my first tour of duty at the Academy. He was a real Frenchman and he took on the job of teaching French.

Then there was a man named Colby who came along and he took on the Spanish job. Well, things went along -- these are both civilians -- and Colby left. They couldn't get a replacement for Colby or they didn't any way. So Gaston Buron got the job of teaching Spanish as well as French. He spoke Spanish all right, it turned out, and I guess he taught Spanish as well as he taught French.

He was famous for some of his sayings. He was very tough on the cadets. He had one case where a cadet was having trouble and he got him and raised cane with him and he gave him some extra things to do, you know, to improve the performance in French. Finally, the cadet came back to see him again and he said to Gaston, "Am I doing better now?" Gaston said, "Well, you do better but you still flunk." And that kid did flunk. That was one of the sayings around the Academy for quite a while. When anyone was having any trouble and was studying like hell, he'd say "I'm doing better but I still flunk."

Anyway, after a while for some reason, they dropped the Spanish -- when Colby left -- and Gaston got both. Then they dropped languages altogether. Gaston went into the History Department and he stayed on and retired from the Academy in about maybe ten years ago and went to work in schools in New London. He separated from the Academy. But they didn't get anybody else in immediately when that happened to teach the languages. Now I don't know whether they have them or not. I'm not sure. They may have them because they have a pretty wide variety of things in the curruculum now. I think they would have them, because there's need for it.

I want to say just another word about Dr. Williams. He was a great help to me at the Academy as a psychologist. He was one of these psychologists that is an interviewing psychologist, not a head-shrinker.

Q: Not with therapy.

Adm. R.: Yes, and he was a great help to me. He has had a very good influence on the Academy in his specialty and as Director of Admissions he has improved the system, I think. During his time we changed over. We had our own examination which was made up by the same people that make up the college boards up in Princeton -- anyway, they made an examination for us for the Coast Guard Academy. This was the way we got cadets. But now we have changed to the college boards, so we don't have our own examination any more. We use college boards now. He was influential in doing that. One of the reasons, of course, was the cost of making an examination was getting larger and larger and always was, I guess, pretty big.

The number of applicants to the Academy was almost 10,000 this year. Almost 10,000 applied and there were somewhere around 6,000 records actually arrived at the Academy for evaluation. The class was 350. It's such a small group that you don't need that many in order to get a good group.

Q: What an advantage you have in terms of selection.

Adm. R.: Oh, tremendous.

Q: You get the cream.

Adm. R.: And the fact that there are no appointments, anybody can take it. For the 10,000, I suppose most of the people who applied in this large number were unable to pass the physical. There were something like 2500 women who applied.

Q: What's the quota on women?

Adm. R.: They haven't set a quota but they say that they are going to take about 30. They haven't set a quota but this is what they are thinking about. They are going to eliminate them somehow because they don't want too big a dose at once. I think that's pretty smart. I'm glad they are not going to load up the class with them. There isn't much need for them either.

Q: What do you anticipate in the way of duty for the women officers in the Coast Guard? Will they serve in navigation aid stations and that sort of thing?

Adm. R.: Yes. There have been some few things written up on this. Of course, we have some reservist women now. Out in Seattle there was a picture in the paper one day of a girl in the Coast Guard out in Seattle in a boat, about a 40 or 50 foot patrol boat, and she's the skipper of the boat. She had a crew of about three people in there and she was the skipper of it. I don't know if this was a publicity stunt or what.

Q: Of course, the Coast Guard not being a part of the Navy in peacetime doesn't have the restrictions the Navy has on service in combat in vessels.

Adm. R.: I'm sure that we will follow that same thing. I don't think we are going to put people aboard ships, women aboard ships that are going to go to sea for a long time. I think they are going to be in administrative jobs. The enlisted ones, I suppose we'll have some of them, some welders and people like that, maybe. But among the officers, I don't think we are going to send very many to sea overnight. Maybe we will send them overnight but not for a prolonged period. I think it will be dangerous.

When I finished my tour of duty at the Academy I was reluctant to leave because I had enjoyed the assignment so much but I was assigned to what turned out to be equally interesting, I guess -- more hard work probably. I was assigned to the National War

College in 1954.

Q: Tell me how the Coast Guard makes its appointments to the National War College.

Adm. R.: The selection is made in Coast Guard Headquarters. I had not asked for assignment to the National War College and there is only one Coast Guard officer who goes to the National War College each year. So there isn't any system of raising people into the thing. I don't know how I was selected except probably whoever made the selection knew me and thought I might like to go. I wasn't asked.

Q: Does it imply a certain grooming process for higher office?

Adm. R.: It has turned out to be that way. It is very definitely an important thing in the Navy and also in the others, the Air Force and the Army. I talked to a man who is retired and lives here in Old Lyme the other day, a man named Henry Day. I didn't know it but I sat next to him at lunch one day and I found out from him that he had been in the State Department for 25 years before he retired, in the Foreign Service. So I said, "I probably know some people that you know because I went to the National War College." I named off a group of people and he did know a good many of them. He said, "This is a very prized assignment in the State Department. People want to get this because it is an indicator for advancement."

As far as the Coast Guard is concerned, most everybody who has gone has made flag rank.

Q: Does the Coast Guard also send its men to the Naval War College and the Army?

Adm. R.: Yes, we have representation in all those schools. We have more representation than we have in the National War College. We usually have a couple people on the faculty at the Naval War College. We have had people on the faculty in others. We also send people to the Industrial College.

Q: What about the Armed Forces Staff College down in Virginia?

Adm. R.: I'm not sure about that. But we probably do because I think we're involved in about all the schools now. We have gotten more involved in the Naval War College in recent years. I think we used to send two or three at the time I went to the National War College but I think we sent more now.

I found the National War College to be a very interesting thing and it was useful to me too, because later on when I became Commandant in my travels around the world I would run into these people who had been classmates of mine, all over the world. Tokyo and Taipai, all over the place. It's helpful to meet somebody you know who was part of the organization in that place.

Q: This is one of the things that so many men tell me who have been to the National War College. That they've met former students all over the world in positions of importance and where they could be useful to them.

Adm. R.: I read about them in the newspapers. One of the assistants to the head of the CIA recently was a guy who had been a classmate of mine in the National War College. Seom years ago something was going on down in Santo Domingo - a revolution, and there was a lot of shooting going on. The ambassador talked to the State Department while under his desk - talking over a telehpone. He was one of my classmates.

It was a busy time. This was another occasion when Jane didn't come with me. I lived at the National War College. So I was there all the time. I came home weekends, usually.

Q: And your home was where?

Adm. R.: New London. Jane had acquired the house that her family had lived in in New London. When I left the Academy we moved out of the quarters, of course, and she moved into that house down town. We didn't know where I would go at the end of the year at the National War College. So anyway, she stayed in New London with the kids and they went on with their schooling.

Q: Tell me about your life at the National War College.

Adm. R.: I lived at Fort McNair in the officers' quarters there.

The routine was every day a lecture. We started off in the morning with this lecture. Afterwards we would meet in groups. One group would meet with the lecturer and the others would meet separately, the idea being to talk about the subject of the lecture. This was always an interesting thing.

After that, we went to the rooms that were assigned to our committees. We were always assigned to a working committee which was working on a specific problem and would work on the material that we were getting together for a report on the problem. The discussions at these groups were often a little bit ahead of me because the people had been talking about them in their car pools, which I missed because I was living at Fort McNair. So the people that attend the National War College are pretty carefully selected and there are a lot of very articulate people among them and all of them are pretty intelligent people and they really can tear problems apart. Some of them have some pretty wild solutions.

We had a great deal of fun as well as producing some pretty good answers. In the year that I was there, several of the committee solutions that were presented to the faculty at the War College were then sent on to the Joint Chiefs of Staff and a good many of the things were incorporated in national policies and in national actions. Some of the material was used in the United Nations.

Each of us individually was required -- besides the committee problems we worked on -- the committee problems changed about every month. There would be a committee that would work together for a month on a specific problem. Then we would move to another committee and we'd have a different problem and different people. So we had one of these every month. In addition each one of us had an individual paper to write. There was a large selection of subjects. I chose as my subject "Soviet Uses of the United Nations."

In the course of this year while I was working on my paper, I visited United Nations three or four times and the whole class visited United Nations a couple of times. So we saw a bit of it and met with the people on the staff, particularly the military staff, but we did meet with the other people too. In the end we made a foreign cruise. One was to the Middle East and one was to South America and one was to Europe and one was to the Far East -- and I made the one to the Far East.

Q: Was this a matter of choice?

Adm. R.: It was a matter of choice within limits. A lot of people wanted to go to the Middle East at that time so there were a lot of applications for that. My application was for the Far East. I hadn't been to the Far East and a good many of these people had been in the Far East. They had been stationed out there and had had experience. So they weren't so interested. But my choice was the Far East and so that's what I got.

I really enjoyed and worked harder. I certainly read more. I went home from that place with a couple of books under my arm every night. There was a small golf course on Fort McNair, too, and

I hated to be missing so much of that. I did get a crack at it once in a while.

We met a lot of interesting people. The faculty was a fine group of people and a down to earth group of people, too. There was an Air Force officer who was the -- his name was Craig [Lt. General Howard Carig] -- was the head man when I was there.

Q: You mean he was the President of the College?

Adm. R.: The President of the College. The Navy man was the best public speaker I ever heard. Major General Byers was the Army man and the Navy was Rear Admiral Chester Wood. The State Department was Ambasaador Hickerson. Then, of course, there were other people on the staff.

While we're talking about those names, one of the people from the State Department who was there was named Howard Trivers. He was the fellow who reviewed my paper on the United Nations. He was the one who reviewed it and okayed it for me to go ahead and submit it. His son has gone to the Coast Guard Academy and graduated from the Coast Guard Academy and is now a Coast Guard officer. My son is about to become the commanding officer of the Electronics Engineering Center in Cape May and the executive officer down there is Trivers' son.

I think they carefully choose the people who go as students there but they must give exceptional care to the staff because every one of them was just as nice a fellow as you could ever meet, just as easy to get along with, all like an old shoe and all of them just as sharp as they could be. If you don't amount to much when you get in there, you'll come out with the idea: if I'm going to be like these guys, I better sharpen myself up and get to work. They really set a marvelous example to the people who are there. They are so ready and so adept at expressing themselves. It's really a tremendous experience just to associate with them for a while.

Q: Tell me about your brief tour in the Far East.

Adm. R.: We were gone about four weeks. I guess there were probably about 30 of us on this trip. The class is about 130 people. The Navy gives one of their vacancies to the Coast Guard - that's how we happened to have one. There wasn't at that time a vacancy for the Coast Guard. Maybe there is now. But anyway the Navy gave us one of their vancancies.

We went to Seattle and refueled and then went up to Anchorage. There was a large Air Force installation up there and a large Army installation and we visited those places and had a talk with the staffs up there and the commanding officers of those places talked to us about their problems. Those outfits were still under construction or expansion at the time we were there. There was a lot going on of building the places up.

We stayed overnight there and then we went on to Adak the next day and visited the naval installation there and refueled. From there we went on to Tokyo, from Tokyo to Taipai, and from Taipai to Hong Kong, from Hong Kong to Okinawa, and Okinawa to Bangkok, then to Saigon and then to Manila and then we stopped at one of the islands in the Pacific on the way back, principally for fuel. And then from Honolulu back to Washington.

Q: Is it my understanding that when you visited a foreign country you had a chance to talk with one of the leaders of government?

Adm. R.: Yes. There was a pre-arranged schedule of parties and lectures. We talked to the head of government, I guess every place we went -- Taipai, then in Hong Kong, of course, the British put on the show for us mainly, although our own Treasury Department people added quite a bit there in connection with the smuggling operations and the dope and all that kind of business. There were quite a few secret service people and other intelligence people over there, as well as quite a few open custom and immigration people. There were a lot of undercover intelligence people. They had some really interesting information.

In Bangkok we didn't meet the king, but we met the prime minister. The defense minister had a huge party for us at his home -- a couple hundred people, I guess, of all kinds of big rank. The College is well accepted throughout the world. Of course, a lot of these people will appear at the College later on as lecturers. If they happen to be in Washington, they get them over. So some of the people that we saw on this trip we had seen during the year. This was at the end of the year that we made our tour.

In each case the ambassador was involved in our visit, too. Saigon was an interesting place, there was a general who was there, head of the Military Assistance Group, named O'Daniel - General Pappy O'Daniel. He was very interesting and we didn't stay in Saigon long but we were there a whole day and we had lunch with his staff. It was very interesting to hear them talk about their experiences over there. They had quite a few people who were out in the field who were unarmed. They had to be unarmed. I don't know whether they all were, but he did say that when they went down in the Delta - this is in 1955, you know, only a year after the treaty - they couldn't go down there unless they were armed and prepared to resist some sort of an attack and often they went with part of the Vietnamese armed forces when they went in. But otherwise, they just couldn't go into the Delta area. He said, "It is full of Communists and they are all from North Vietnam."

Q: And as you say, the Geneva Convention had just been drawn up.

Adm. R.: Just set up a year - 1954 was the Geneva Convention and this was May of 1955. So that was a particularly interesting thing. Then as time went on it became more interesting to think back on it, you know. Did you even run across Pappy O'Daniel?

After we left our interesting but rather short visit in Saigon, our next stop was in the Philippines. We stayed out -- we landed at Sangley Point and stayed out there. In the course of our stay at Manila, which was for three or four days, we were entertained by the ambassador and we had an interview with the President of the Philippines at the time, Magsaysay. He said before we arrived, that he would not be able to spend more than ten or fifteen minutes with us, but he would be glad to see us. So we went in to see him and he was a very impressive fellow. The Filipinos are usually little people but he wasn't little. He was well over six feet tall and a very well developed man, a nice-looking man, too. He was interested in seeing us. He did nearly all of the talking.

He got into discussions about the Huks. There was with him a little fellow who was introduced as Colonel somebody and he was a standard-sized Filipino, a little fellow -- he came up a little above Magsaysay's belt, I would say. He didn't join in the conversation very much. But Magsaysay would begin talking about these adventures that he had had and he would get to a point where he was a little bit puzzled and he always turned to this little fellow and would say something to him and the fellow would answer him, and then Magsaysay would go on and talk.

This kept going on and Magsaysay finally said that this man was his companion and had been his companion for some time and that they had had many experiences in fighting the Huks and always together. He said, "Now I forget some of the things." He said, "He never forgets. He always remembers everything. So I'm delighted tohave him with me all the time." And he talked and talked and talked. He just went from one end of the Philippines to the other, discussing these things. Where he had said in the beginning, ten or fifteen minutes, at the end of an hour he was still talking and he didn't look as though he was ever going to stop. Everyone was listening to every word, he was a most interesting man. He expressed himself very well. He had an accent but his English was very good. We were all very much impressed with him. I don't know how long after that he was killed in that airplane accident. It wasn't too long after, maybe a year later or so. I think that he was quite a loss to the Philippines.

    The place where we met him was -- I think they call it a palace. It wasn't an elaborate place. It looked a good deal like a city hall in the United States inside. It was surrounded by people and there was a line-up of people. It was explained to us that he spent a good bit of his day meeting these individuals. He would talk to each one of them, as much as he had time for. He didn't select them either, he took them as they came. The people really had a strong feeling for him. I think he was a good leader of the Philippines and it was a shame -- although he did have some political troubles later on. He wasn't having them at that time, but he did have some later on, about the time he was killed.

Q: One would speculate as to whether his colonel companion was lost with him.

Adm. R.: That, of course, I don't know. Yes, it's an interesting thing. I don't know that this companion occupied a government position. He may have been an aide. I don't know what his job was, but he certainly gave us the impression that this guy was indispensable. I think any of us in my class who had thought much about our futures and was ambitious would hope that when we get to the highest position we occupy we would have an aide like that. And maybe most of us did later on.

From there on our visit -- the Coast Guard at that time had some Loran stations in the Philippines that we manned. We also, surprisingly, had an aids to navigation vessel that was stationed in the Philippines and was assigned at Sangley Point. It operated from there to service some buoys that were in the vicinity of our Loran stations, I think, or maybe these were -- I'm sure they were -- they werebuoys which were there for the convenience of our armed forces who were then in the Philippines. They operated some boats that went back and forth between these units and they needed aids to navigation so this aids to navigation vessel, which was a fairly good sized tender, something like 150-footer I think, did those. It made a trip a year to Okinawa. There were a couple of buoys up there that they went and serviced once a year.

Q: This leads me to ask you if the Philippine government maintained a program of aids to navigation since they had so many islands.

Adm. R.: Yes, they did and they, I think now, have an outfit they call the Coast Guard. They have sent people to the Coast Guard Academy, Filipino cadets who left and became officers in -- maybe the Philippine Navy, I'm not sure -- but anyway they became officers in the service of the Philippine government. There have been quite a number of them. They may have them right now. They have had them within the last few years, I know, because I have had some of them.

I had an opportunity to visit a couple of our Loran stations down there during this trip.

Q: Were Philippine personnel employed at the stations?

Adm. R.: No.

Q: It was entirely the U. S. Coast Guard.

Adm. R.: In each case our station was in an isolated location. It was away from other population. At Sangley Point we had aircraft stations there. These aircraft serviced our Loran stations. They, of course, were in the population center and they had Filipinos working with them in their stations.

Q: I would take it then that since the Loran stations were so isolated that you had to have the policy of frequent transfers.

Adm. R.: A year. As a matter of fact, my son at one point in his career had a station up on an island -- there's a group of islands north of Mindanao called the Batanes Islands. When I was Commandant I visited that station. He wasn't there, but he had been one of the -- I think he was the second commanding officer out there and had apparently become quite popular because when I visited the station, it was the first time a Commandant of the Coast Guard had visited the station and we came in and landed on a hill, at a fairly good angle -- we landed in a C-130. We taxied around and all the people from the town were gathered around. They had signs -- Welcome, Admiral Roland, and all that kind of business. The kids were out of school to meet us. When I got out of the airplane, there was a group of people and I was talking to them. One of them was an old lady and I talked to her particularly and she said to me, "Admiral Roland, we are very happy that you have come here, but we would rather have your son come." So he had become pretty popular there.

He told me the story -- they had outdoor dances in this little town and his crew would go to the dances. He said that he always danced with the mayor's wife and the mayor's wife came up about to here -- about his belt on him. He was six feet, four. So he joined in with them in their merry-making and so became pretty popular.

Anyway, I didn't visit that station but there were some

others on this National War College trip. But there were others that were closer to Manila and I did visit a couple of those so I had an opportunity to let them know that there were other people in the Coast Guard besides the one or two that were out there.

At these Loran stations there was one officer at each one. He had a crew of about ten or twelve people, mostly electronics technicians. At that time they were considered to be pretty sophisticated electronics gear. Now I think they are probably unattended. At least they are probably operated by the Filipinos now. This is the case in most cases.

At one time we had an awful lot of those Loran stations scattered all over. For instance, in Greenland we must have had a dozen of them. Now we operate only one in Greenland and that's up near Cape Atholl about eight or ten miles away.

Q: That's because of the improvement in the technique, is it?

Adm. R.: Also because of the training, the fact that there are now natives that have been trained and can do some of these things. But improvement in the equipment has a lot to do with it. There is much less maintenance in these things.

Q: And it's also not classified today as it was.

Adm. R.: That's right. The Norwegians have taken over the stations in Norway, too. The British are operating some and the French are operating some and the Spanish are operating some.

So I guess -- the Loran A stations, which were the first ones, are less sophisticated than our Loran C stations -- are operated by natives in most cases now. I think there are some of the Loran C stations now too. There's one on a little island just north of the main island of Japan that I visited while I was down there and when I did visit it, it was operated by the Coast Guard, but now the Japanese operate it. The Japanese also operate several of the other Loran A stations, too. It doesn't take long to train a Jap. Pretty soon they are better than you are.

When we finished our visit to the Philippines, we were really on our way home then. We had one fueling stop in the Pacific and one recreation stop in Hawaii. They really gave us an all-out briefing in Hawaii on the situation in the Pacific. Admiral Felt was one of the officers, I think, who was out there at that time. I don't know what he was at that time but I think he was there then.

Q: Then you came back to Washington and disbanded.

Adm. R.: We stopped at Clark Field on the way and then on to Washington.

Q: Had you received orders by that time?

Adm. R.: By that time I had my orders, yes. The orders were to go to Coast Guard Headquarters so there wasn't any move involved for me, but there was for my family. I became the Chief of the Program Analysis Division in Headquarters, one of the groups under the Chief of Staff. Our graduation at the War College -- our trip was in May and our graduation was early in June and then I immediately walked down town and got myself a little leave and went up and got my family and moved down.

A friend of mine, a naval officer named Whitey Whitehurst, had orders to leave Washington and go up to Boston as the Chief of Staff up there and I walked in and rented his house sight unseen, so that we would have a place, because places were pretty scarce then in Washington. It was on 44th Street, N.W. right near Georgetown University -- it was right at the edge of Foxhall Village.

So I went home and got my family. My son Eddie had graduated from high school and he wanted to go to the Coast Guard Academy. He hadn't been a very good student. So I suggested to him that he go to college for a year or else go to a prep school and he chose to go to Severn. So he moved down with us and shortly after, not long after, he moved over to Severn and spent a year there. Much to our surprise he was one of their good students because he hadn't been a good student before.

Q: Maybe he learned how to study.

Adm. R.: They did a good job on him. I think that his motivation might have been a little lacking before, but I think that it picked up and they did do a good job on him down there. He was always a good athlete but never would dig into it as I had done when I was an athlete, you know. When I was engaged in athletics it was my whole life. I didn't think of much else. But he would take part in things. He played football up in New London but he wasn't head over heels in it like I was. But when he went to Severn he learned to play lacrosse and he was on their team. He got to be pretty good and he loved the game. It was a good, rough game and he liked rough games, I guess. But his attitude changed a great deal at Severn. It was a good thing for him that he had gone there. He passed his Coast Guard examinations which came along at the end of the year and he went into the Academy somewhere in the lower half of his class and every marking term after that he improved his standing and he wound up in the top 20% of his class. He worked hard to get through the Academy and he deserved a lot of credit for it. I'm sorry that he didn't stick with it. He's the one who has resigned now.

Q: He's with the company in Long Island.

Adm. R.: Yes. But anyway, we moved into this place and I moved into the Coast Guard Headquarters. The fellow who had the job wasn't anxious to be relieved. He kept hanging on and I stayed with him. The Program Analysis job in Coast Guard Headquarters is a very interesting one, a good job that I was really anxious to get.

Q: Was the tour of duty ordinarily two years for an assignment like that?

Adm. R.: It would be about two years, yes. Generally two years. Finally after a couple of months, I did relieve this fellow and about that time I was made Deputy Chief of Staff. So that meant I moved out of that job, but I did have direct supervision of it. The other fellow who had been moved to some other place in Headquarters came back into the job. I think he might have pulled some strings somewhere to arrange this thing. All this happened from the middle of 1955 until the end of 1955.

Then in March of 1956 I was selected for promotion to flag. Then I continued as the Deputy Chief of Staff until the following June. I was in the position as Deputy Chief of Staff for the presentation of the budget. The Deputy Chief of Staff has a pretty important part in the preparation of the budget so that I had very good experience during that time in the preparation of the budget.

Q: Before you tell me about that will you tell me about -- describe Program Analysis and your involvement in that for that brief time.

Adm. R.: The Program Analysis Division has -- There are a number of details in connection with the Program Analysis business. There are a lot of studies that have to do with the acquisitions, the construction and so on, and the planning of new units and also in planning of new directions in which the Coast Guard should move. There is a lot of original planning in Program Analysis. But there are also a lot of details.

Q: What about the reverse side of this coin? Do you also recommend the decommissioning of units that are no longer useful?

Adm. R.: Oh yes. There are a lot of details of matters that bring on criticism and a lot of arguments. For instance, there was one branch of the Program Analysis Division that has to do with the setting up of complements for units, personnel allowances, and the changing of personnel allowances and so on. Of course, this fits in with the budget thing because in many cases you have to change personnel allowances to fit budgets. This is a matter that causes many cries from the field when you change allowances, particularly when you reduce allowances. So this is one of the activities of that Division that takes time and requires diplomacy.

But the main purpose, I think, is to determine originally the first plan on the budget, the actual numbers aren't put down in this division. There is a budget section under the Comptroller that actually puts the numbers down on sheets of paper to take over when you make the presentation. But what they put down is determined in the Program Analysis Division and by the Deputy Chief of Staff and others. Of course, the Commandant takes a big hand in this, too.

Q: This job is at the very core, then, of the operation.

Adm. R.: It's a very important place, a very important job. Under the Chief of Staff there is that one and there is another one, Administrative Management or something like that, anyway it has to do with management within the Coast Guard at various levels and sets up standards and regulations and things like that for management. That is also a very interesting one. Those two things under the Chief of Staff are very important things.

At one time before we became more modern, the Deputy Chief of Staff was also the Commanding Officer of Headquarters. That meant that he managed the military people who worked in Headquarters.

Q: Did he get involved in space requirements and things like that?

Adm. R.: Yes, he did. He was involved in that and space requirements at Headquarters because he was the Commanding Officer there. Then later on a separate fellow came on who was only that - who would only handle the personnel affairs of people in Headquarters and space, too. But this happened after I had left Headquarters. We didn't have a Commanding Officer there when I was Deputy Chief of Staff.

As Deputy Chief of Staff I still was pretty much involved in the workings of this Program Analysis Division.

Q: You were over them.

Adm. R.: Yes, they worked directly under me. So I was involved in that.

Q: Was there any feed-in from other departments and other services in the government as to possible new endeavors for the Coast Guard?

Adm. R.: Yes, continually.

Q: Give me some illustrations of that.

Adm. R.: Every district has a planning division within it which looks after its operation with its present facilities and also plans for improvements and expansions and other changes.

Q: What set of criteria governs this sort of thing? There is danger of empire building in a sense, but in the more practical way, what are the requirements that you consider when dealing with additional duties for the Coast Guard?

Adm. R.: I'm trying to think if there is anything that is written along these lines. If there is anything written along these lines, it would have come out under Commandant of Program Administration in Headquarters. Operation manuals contain a lot of such information. Operation manuals set forth limits on what you can do with what you have and, of course, your facility manuals set forth your physical facilities. I think that within these things people have a fairly clear field in which to work in the districts on this sort of thing. They have joint meetings with the naval facilities in the district, with all of the law enforcement facilities, and fish and wildlife and all these people are calling on the Coast Guard all the time for help. I think that they have a pretty free hand, not in taking on these jobs, but in recommending that they take them on. They have some limit of authority to cooperate with these people.

Q: But on a spot basis, I suppose?

Adm. R.: Yes. Fish and Wilflife, for instance, we did a lot of work with them. When I was stationed in Boston as the District Commander, we carried their people in our airplanes to observe the fishing fleets, to see just what was going on for their purposes, you see. A lot of our law enforcement is enforcement that is cooperative and other people have the main responsibility, like the Fish and Wildlife.

But, in customs, you know, we enforce custom laws. We do it for Customs. One of our big operations in New York now is, or was when there were more ships running, to carry the customs and immigration people out to these ships and meet them to put these people aboard. We maintained vessels just for that purpose that did hardly anything else.

There are many things like that. I think that as far as this planning for expansion and taking on new duties,--in spot cases you would have the authority to do that -- but to take them on as a permanent thing, you have to get approval from higher authority and have it written into your operations manual.

Q: Can you think of any specific request or suggestions that came to the Coast Guard when you were Assistant Deputy to take on new duties?

Adm. R.: I don't recall any of them right now. You see, that would have been in late '55 or early '56. I can't recall anything of any moment at that time. I know we had all sorts of plans submitted to us. I think annually you get suggestions to change plans from each one of the Districts.

There have always been suggestions about the weather stations, about discontinuing some, and setting up new ones. One new one was set up toward the end of the life of the weather station which operates only during the hurricane season and operates south of Long Island and off of New Jersey several hundred miles at sea, three or four hundred miles at sea.

Q: Investigating disturbances.

Adm. R.: Yes, and it operates only in the hurricane season and it is, I think, the only station that is still operating.

Q: Is it Coast Guard planes one reads about going into the vortex of a hurricane to test its velocity and all that?

Adm. R.: No, we don't do that. We don't have the proper kind of planes and we don't have the equipment in the planes for doing that sort of thing. I guess the Air Force does all of that now. I guess the Navy does some of that, too. But we don't do that.

Q: In case a request did come from some department that the Coast Guard take on a new kind of duty and it was newly considered in the Operations Analysis and the high echelons in the Coast Guard and the decision was made to do it, in your time there was it necessary to have concurrence on the part of the Secretary of the Treasury under whom you worked or was it a matter of information for the Secretary of the Treasury?

Adm. R.: There had to be concurrence by the Secretary. I can tell you about one. It didn't happen while I was Deputy Chief of Staff, but it had to do with oil pollution. We have always been an enforcement agency for the oil pollution laws. Our job was to detect oil pollution, take samples, analyze them, and fix the blame. This has become a very scientific thing now. It was pretty scientific then. Then after we had built up the case, we just handed the whole thing to the Army Engineers who had the responsibility for oil pollution. We were only an enforcement agency.

Well, in most cases the Army Engineers didn't go any further, they didn't institute suits. They got our records but I guess oil pollution wasn't an important thing to them. They probably had other things that were more important to them and took their time. But in most cases there wasn't much done about the cases that we reported and we reported hundreds of them. So we had recommendations to get the law changed so that we would be responsible for the whole thing.

Q: To carry it right through.

Adm. R.: To carry it right through, and this has been done. Now we do that. It was recommended from somewhere in the field. I don't know just where, but probably some place where they had a lot of cases like New York, where the captain of the port was probably using his forces to detect this thing and to take samples and to have them analyzed and to run down all the details and was getting no results. It would just happen again.

So that's a sample of one that was a pretty big deal as far as effort and cost is concerned. We did put a lot of effort into it.

Q: Your involvement in oil pollution at that time, was it meshed with your duties as Coast Guard for the security of ports and that sort of thing? Was it related to that?

Adm. R.: Yes, before we had our port security forces to the extent that we have them now, and we have had them for a number of years now - before the second World War - we had this enforcement duty and we continued to have it as we went along and built up our port security forces. They were a natural, of course, for the detection of these things and, of course, oil pollution is a matter of port security. So this became one of their pretty important activities. Mostly their primary duty was the detection of activities that might have to do with sabotage or some such thing as that, but there were a number of other things.

Q: Now, oil pollution -- sometimes the problem extends beyond any given port and is involved in the pollution of beaches along the ocean. Does this constitute a different problem for the Coast Guard? Say a tanker is disabled offshore, maybe a hundred miles offshore.

Adm. R.: The Coast Guard is involved in it to quite a large extent. There was a tanker, a small tanker, but a tanker that carried fuel up to the city of Norwich that hit a rock out in Long Island Sound and spilled a couple hundred thousand gallons of oil. We were deeply involved in the containment of this oil spill and in the building up of the case and in the suit that followed. We were the government agency that had primary responsibility for that. And we would have -- well, the TORREY CANYON thing would be a responsibility of the Coast Guard.

You see, we have built up a lot of experience now. We hadn't at the time I was on that committee, of course, in the containment of spills like that.

Q: The Santa Barbara episode - was the Coast Guard involved in that?

Adm. R.: Yes. And a good bit of this now is by contract. There are several companies along Long Island Sound and on the coast of New England that have contracts with the Coast Guard, with the Federal Government, for getting on the job and putting their equipment to work in containing these things. And they get paid, of course. The people who are found to be responsible, if the responsibility can be fixed, are required to pay the bill to these guys who do this. If the responsibility isn't fixed, then the Federal Government pays it. But if responsibility is fixed that is the case.

Q: You were talking about the contractors whom the Coast Guard has for taking care of oil slicks.

Adm. R.: This is an activity in which we are pretty deeply engaged now. When I was on active duty, the law was changed. While I was Commandant the law was changed so that we gained the responsibility at that time. But our building up of the system has taken place, mainly I suppose, since I retired. But it is an effective system now. I'm sure that in some cases, some pollution matters would be beyond our control.

But for the normal kinds of pollution, including the small tanker thing, we are better able to handle it now.

Q: I was about to ask would you be strained to the limit with some of these modern tankers, 300,000 and 500,000 tons in case they had a collision or something.

Adm. R.: I think that it would cause many headaches. I don't think that we would be able to immediately go out and know what to do even -- a thing like the TORREY CANYON, you mean.

Q: Yes.

Adm. R.: It would be a thing that we wouldn't be -- I'm sure that we have plans on what to do at the time but I'm sure that any two of those things would be entirely different. The currents would be different and other circumstances different, the spread of oil from the wreck is a thing that you can't pre-determine unless you know exactly where it's going to happen.

Q: Now, when oil pollution reaches the beach, does the Coast Guard activity extend to the beach and cleaning up the beach?

Adm. R.: We have engaged in it but this is the sort of thing the contractors are for. They have improved their equipment to a large extent; they are able to do a lot better now than they did just a few years ago. They are steadily improving their efforts.

Q: And what about this aspect of it: since the Coast Guard is humanitarian in nature, what about the spoiling of wildlife on the beach, the birds and that sort of thing, and what does the Coast Guard do about that, if anything?

Adm. R.: We have no direct responsibility in that case, of course. But we have gathered quite large numbers of fowl in a number of these cases and taken them into places where they could be treated. I think it is sort of a general responsibility, it isn't a specific one.

Q: That's very interesting.

Adm. R.: But this is one of the things about the Coast Guard that I always liked all through the time I served, that we were willing to do some things that weren't written down in the book, if they were in the humanitarian line. If they helped somebody in real trouble.

Q: In that area you simply have to be flexible. You can't write rules for some of these things that you can't anticipate.

Adm. R.: Yes. You have to do what you can and then find out how bad you might feel by doing it or whether you did something you shouldn't do. If you can get results, this I think is one of the important things. If you get results and then apologize for the things you've done wrong and get the rules changed so that if what you did was best then in the future there won't be any question about your doing it.

Q: I'm projecting myself just a bit into your job as Deputy - Assistant to the Deputy Chief of Staff and budget-making - it occurs to me that the Coast Guard should not have great difficulty with its appropriations from Congress in many cases because it is engaged in humanitarian endeavors. This appeals to the idealism of members of Congress. Is that a valid observation?

Adm. R.: This is true to some extent. We have a good relationship, or we had at least when I was actively involved, we had a good relationship with our legislative committee, the Merchant Marine Fisheries Committee. This is our legislative committee. And we had a very good relationship with our appropriations subcommittee. Most of the people who are on those committees are people who come from districts where we have facilities that are important to the district. I suppose that's arranged by the Congressmen themselves in getting themselves assigned to the committee. We have spared no effort to make this relationship better and it has really been very good.

There was a chairman of the Merchant Marine Fisheries Committee while I was Commandant, not during the whole time but during most of the time, who was Herbert Bonner, who came from North Carolina. He had been a Congressmen for a long, long time; he was very influential and, of course, associated the Carolinas with the Coast Guard. There are families that go back for a long, long time in those places down there.

Q: Port Elizabeth and places like that.

Adm. R.: Yes. There was another man who was a Democrat, so he was chairman while I was the Commandant. On the appropriations subcommittee there was a Republican named Gary, who was the senior Republican. He had been the chairman in the past and he came from Virginia. He was a very great admirer of the Coast Guard and a very great help to us. He was influential with all the people on this committee, even though he wasn't the chairman because of his politics.

We made some junkets with some of these people, too. I traveled - my determination when I became Commandant was to get out and see as many units in the Coast Guard as I could in the four years that I was going to be there. I saw an awful lot; I did a lot of traveling.

I think that Al Richmond did a lot of that too. He did quite a bit of traveling. Jimmy Hirshfield did a lot as Assistant Commandant. Frequently when they were making a trip, they would call the office of the counsel of the committee and tell him we were going to make this trip; we have room for this many people. So often they would - somebody would go along. They said that they did it, not because they wanted to make junkets, but they said, "We are handling your affairs, we should know about your units and so we want to go along." I have taken them as far as Port Clarence up in Alaska, which is only 30 or 40 miles south of the Arctic Circle, which has nobody within several hundred miles. They have traveled to many places where we have units and traveled long distances. Of course, they like to go to Honolulu.

Q: Let's go back, Sir, to the time when you were serving as Deputy Chief of Staff and involved immediately in budget preparations. This was a brief period of time before you achieved flag rank. Tell me about that.

Adm. R.: The system at that time, and I suppose still, is every year, every district sends in a plan for the following year including costs. These are the basis for our budget. They come in to the CPA and, of course, all of the offices in Headquarters do the same thing. These things form the basis of putting the budget together. We have people in Headquarters who are experienced in this thing and pretty good at weeding out the fat and the wishes. I don't know whether they used the term in this, but the first thing we send to the Treasury Department we call our "letter to Santa Claus." And probably that's what we get, the letter to Santa Claus from every district.

But there is a lot of good information in that and this is weeded out and put together and then when we get a thing put together then we talk to the budget people in the department first, who in the meantime have talked to the Bureau of the Budget -- we talk to the budget people in the department in which we operate which in my close knowledge was the Treasury Department and they set a limit on it.

Q: Based on the estimate you've already assembled?

Adm. R.: No, based on what they have been told by the Bureau of the Budget. They don't know anything at all what we are going to ask for. But they set up a limit for us before we -- as far as they know, before we even start to make plans. Of course, the plans are going on all the time.

Q: And how is this limit, as prescribed by the Bureau of Budget, determined?

Adm. R.: It's determined on a political basis, of course. It isn't determined on our actual needs. They are receptive. They listen to us and we sometimes do ask for more than they put in their limit and tell them that we feel that we have to do it. Of course, frequently they will say there isn't any more money. You've got to reduce. So then we go back and do it over again.

But sometimes we are forced into asking for more than the limit and there isn't any rule that says we can't ask for more except that they say this is all you can have.

They set a limit for the Treasury Department. The Treasury Department then sets limits for their bureaus and we get one of those limits. By that time, we have a plan all made by the time we get to that. So then we begin whittling.

Q: Is there usually some great discrepancy between your plan and the Treasury plan, or was there in those days when you were doing it?

Adm. R.: Not as big as you might think. We always want more than we are allowed to ask for. We always do. I guess everybody does, because no matter how good the job is that you are doing, I think that you can probably do it a little better if you had more facilities or better facilities and that means more money. You can always think of a way to use it in order to improve your performance. This is what we try to shoot for; it is to improve the performance. We always want to point out that we are going to do a better job next year than we did last year. We want to improve all the time. Usually this means more money. So if they didn't put a limit on us, it would indeed be a letter to Santa Claus we sent over to the Department of the Treasury.

There is, of course, constant intercourse between the budget department in the department and the budget department in the Coast Guard. There is constant communication. So I don't think we ever surprise them completely when we go to the Treasury Department. There is the same thing between the Treasury and the Bureau of the Budget, too. They know and they are building up their arguments, too. But if you surprise them, you're not going to get it. You've got to convince them before you get it. If you surprise them, you're not going to convince them on the spot, you can be sure of that. They are never for anything unless they understand it.

As far as the humanitarian angle, it is good and you can talk about a lifeboat station and they are usually in favor of improving the performance of lifeboat stations, by, say, putting a helicopter at the lifeboat station.

This is another thing that has been suggested and has been an improvement, is to put helicopters at lifeboat stations. We were talking before about suggestions that were made.

Q: In the Program Analysis.

Adm. R.: Yes. And this has been done in many cases. Helicopter platforms have been built at a number of lifeboat stations. As a matter of fact, one of them is one that they used to use out near Nixon's place, you know.

Q: San Clemente?

Adm. R.: Yes. That's where he landed on our platform out there. So these things -- they favor them and you probably get better consideration for something like that than you do by asking for new furniture for the Commandant's office or some such thing. But still if you ask for it, and it's brand new to them, they're not going to say "Yes, let's help more people." They don't say that. They want figures. They want figures on traffic and activity in the vicinity and all that. They want to know a good bit about how many people they're going to use there and next year how many people you're going to put there. They want to know what you're going to do in the future with it, too.

Q: You have to launch a kind of public relations campaign along with the figures.

Adm. R.: Oh, you do. I think this has been going on for a long time and the best results have been obtained when the public relations program has been the best. The public relations program has an awful lot to do with the success in budget matters, besides the feasibility of what you want to do, the feeling of the people that you're talking to has a lot to do with it.

Q: This is in a sense articulation, to articulate your needs to the practical planner.

Adm. R.: These people get in a lot on your plans, too, by serving on committees with you. One of the things that I think -- and it was a very important thing in the Coast Guard -- was the study of roles and missions. This is the thing that was completed shortly after I became Commandant. It was going on for some months before, but it was completed shortly after I became Commandant. The people serving on it -- there were people from the Navy Department and people from the Treasury Department and there was somebody from the Department of Commerce on there -- but there were about three guys from the Bureau of the Budget, all on this committee, studying roles and missions of the Coast Guard. So they were involved deeply in this. It involved a lot of money; $10 billion in ships over a period of twelve years, I think it was.

Q: Now these are the men that I'm told are the corps of experts in the Bureau of the Budget, experts in different fields.

Adm. R.: That's right. These are people who have been doing this sort of thing for some time.

Q: And acquiring a great deal of knowledge about the specific service.

Adm. R.: Yes. So lots of times you can go in and talk to people in the Bureau of the Budget and you can just talk yourself into a hole because pretty soon you find out they know more about it than you do. You have to look this guy over before you tell him everything.

INDEX

to VOLUME I

REMINISCENCES OF ADMIRAL EDWIN J. ROLAND USCG (Ret.)

ADAMS, Dr. Arthur (Beanie): Chairman of the Academic Advisory Committee for the Coast Guard Academy - changes made, p. 340-2.

AIDS TO NAVIGATION: In 1955 Coast Guard Maintained a tender in the Philippines, p. 358; visit to a Loran station, p. 360;

USCGS ALEXANDER HAMILTON: p. 10; p. 24, p. 26;

AZORES: U. S. planes based there help with convoys - WW II, p. 207-8;

BAKER, Irving: football coach, p. 38;

BALBO, General Italo: his mission from Italy to the Chicago World's Fair (1933), p. 62-3; Coast Guard sent to guard his planes in Lake Michigan, p. 62;

BILBAO, Spain: USCGC CAYUGA (1936) calls there in effort to evacuate refugees from Spanish Revolution, p. 93-4; p. 97;

BONNER, The Hon. Herbert (Member of Congress): Chairman of House Committee on Merchant Marine and Fisheries, p. 377;

BOWERS, The Hon. Claude G.: U. S. Ambassador to Spain, p. 92;

BUDGET MAKING: p. 366-7; preliminary budget making, p. 379-80; letter to Santa Claus, p. 379; p. 381; value of Public Relations Program to sell budget figures, p. 382-5;

BURON, Gaston: French instructor at the Coast Guard Academy, p. 343;

CAMPBELL Class: new Coast Guard ships of 327 feet (late 1930s), p. 115-6;

CANADIAN SHIPPING: USCGS MACKINAW renders assistance, p. 240-1; p. 268;

CANISIUS COLLEGE: Roland attended prep school and college in Buffalo, p. 2; team plays game with new Coast Guard football team, p. 30;

CAR FERRIES on the Great Lakes: p. 279;

USCGC CAYUGA: p. 56 ff; p. 89-100; added duties with communications as result of Spanish rescue mission, p. 101; see also entry under U. S. COAST GUARD ACADEMY - summer cruise, 1936;

CHEBOYGAN: difficulties with harbor and the turning basin, p. 235-6; race prejudice, p. 253-5; see also entries under USCGS MACKINAW.

U. S. COAST GUARD ACADEMY: Roland takes qualifying exat at suggestion of his congressman, p. 3-4; Roland arrives at the Academy (Sept. 1926), p. 5-6 ff; organization of first football team, p. 7-9; teaching staff, p. 9; teaching methods, p. 10-11; hazing p. 11-12; attrition, p. 13-14; athletics, p. 15-16, p. 28-30; discipline, liberty, etc. p. 16 ff courses of study, p. 18-23; accreditation, p. 20-21; summer cruises, p. 24; buildings and physical equipment, p. 31-32; survey site of the present Academy, p. 32-34; Roland assigned there(1934) to assist in athletic department and teach physics, p. 72-3; p. 76-7; Roland runs the Cadet Store, p. 73-73; grading system, p. 77-78; role of the superintendent, p. 78; role of faculty, p. 79; Roland's perspective on kind of education necessary when he returned to Academy in 1934, p. 80-82; increasing activity in Athletic Department, p. 82 ff; Roland comments on improved status of graduate as result of athletic program, p. 85-6; summer cruise (1936) on Cutter CAYUGA, p. 89-100; increased number of subjects forces summer study, p. 1937-8, p. 104-5; inauguration of four year course, p. 105-6; mission of the Coast Guard as formulated by Adm. Harry Hamlet, p. 107; Religious training at Academy, p. 86-8; Adm. Hamlet pushes for Chapel at the Academy - finally accomplished in 1952, p. 109; Roland indicates his desire for Academy duty, p. 305; returns to Academy (1950) as Commandant of Cadets, p. 308ff; how Academy differed from previous tour in 1938, p. 310-11; athletics, p. 311-312; the handling of demerits, p. 315-7; the honor system, p. 319-321; meetings with battalion officers, p. 325-7, p. 334; a cadet hostess in named, p. 328-9; a psychologist is added to the staff, p. 330; greater freedom for the cadets in drills, etc, p. 331-3; establishment of several boards: Academic, Athletic, Disciplinary, p. 334-5; problem with professional recognition as an engineering school, p. 335-6; a change is made in service obligations of a cadet before graduation and after, p. 336-8; a display of talent among the Cadets, p. 338-40; the changes made in curriculum under Dr. Arthur Adams, p. 340-1;

U.S. COAST GUARD ACADEMY - Summer cruises: 1936 in CAYUGA, p. 89 - 100; use of schooners in 1937-8; p. 102-3; the CHASE, p. 103;

U.S. COAST GUARD FOOTBALL TEAM: Roland assigned temporary duty with team(1929-31) while serving on the DD SHAW, p. 35 ff; President's Cup awarded yearly - reason for Coast Guard team, p. 36-38;

U. S. COAST GUARD HEADQUARTERS - ENLISTED PERSONNEL ASSIGNMENTS: Roland on duty there as Chief from May, 1942 to Oct. 1943 - nature of his duties, p. 134 ff; the work grows - SPARS come to help, p. 137-9; problems with space, p. 141-2; method of assignments, p. 142-3; problems with rapid growth of the Service, p. 144-6; task of assigning groups for specific training, p. 147-8; boat crews for transports, p. 148-149; replacements, p. 150-1; promotions in wartime, p. 151 ff; aviation billets, p. 157; personnel for beach patrol, p. 158; Guard duty personnel and dogs, p. 159; guards for cryolite mines in Greenland, p. 159-160;

U. S. COAST GUARD HEADQUARTERS - PROGRAM ANALYSIS: Roland becomes Director (1955-56) and in a few months thereafter Deputy Chief of Staff, p. 364 ff; some of functions of Program Analysis, p. 365-6; preliminary work with the Budget, p. 366-7; proposals for additional duties of the Coast Guard, p. 368-9; p. 382; ad hoc examples of additional functions, p. 369-70; an example of Coast Guard action dealing with oil pollution, p. 371-2; more on preliminary budget making, p. 379-82;

U. S. COAST GUARD INTELLIGENCE: activities in World War II, p. 163;

U. S. COAST GUARD LIABILITY IN DISTRESS CASES: p. 241-3;

U. S. COAST GUARD - NINTH DISTRICT: Roland (Apr. 1946) becomes Chief of Staff, p. 272 ff; Roland's duty on MACKINAW qualifies him for the job, p. 275; p. 282-3; question of Life Boat stations, p. 284-5; problem of supervising the annual regattas, p. 286-290;

U. S. COAST GUARD - POLICY: for dealing with liquor on board ships, p. 55-8;

U. S. COAST GUARD TEMPORARY RESERVES: A status given boat owners who turned over craft to Coast Guard for wartime use (WWII), p. 125-6; Roland distinguishes between a temporary reservist and a reservist, p. 127-8; their use in port security work, p. 129-130; p. 202-3;

U. S. COAST GUARD - TRADITIONAL SERVICES IN WARTIME: p. 156 ff;

CONGRESSIONAL COMMITTEES: Coast Guard relationships with legislative committees, p. 377-8; committee members accompany Coast Guard on trips to various stations, p. 378-9;

CONVOY ESCORTS - World War II: Roland commands Escort Division 45 of Task Force 60 (1943), p. 181-4; headquarters in Bermuda, p. 183-4; p. 185-6; Roland's first convoy, p. 185 ff; attack on convoy in Mediterranean by German planes, p. 188-190; p. 198; p. 200-201 rescue efforts while escorting convoys, p. 203-4; communications within the convoy, p. 206-7;

U. S. CUSTOM'S SERVICE: p. 54-5; p. 71;

ENGINEER'S COUNCIL OF PROFESSIONAL DEVELOPMENT: p. 335-6;

ERICKSON, Captain Frank A.: helicopter pilot with the USCGS MACKINAW for spring breaking of ice in the Lakes (1948), p. 276-8;

USCGS ESCANABA: 165 foot icebreaker - Roland assigned to her (1932) for duty in Great Lakes, p. 58 ff; a search and rescue mission (1932), p. 65-67; enforcement of safety regulations, p. 68-69; p. 71; Roland leaves her in 1934 for duty at Academy, p. 63; p. 72;

FRIGATE: World War II design, p. 170-1;

GREAT LAKES: (see entries under USCGS MACKINAW); foreign traffic in the lakes since opening of St. Lawrence Seaway, p. 265 ff; shipments of iron ore on the lakes, p. 217 ff; p. 247; details of loading, p. 269-270;

GREAT LAKES NAVAL TRAINING STATION: p. 290;

GREENLAND: cryolite mines guarded in WWII by special arrangement with U.S. Coast Guard, p. 159-161;

HALL, Rear Admiral Arthur: p. 330;

HAMLET, Admiral Harry: p. 87; his stated mission of the Coast Guard, p. 107; p. 108-9;

HEELING TANKS: use on ice breakers, p. 221-2;

HELICOPTERS: Coast Guard develops the helicopter in World War II, p. 169;

HIRSHFIELD, Vice Admiral James A.: p. 262-3; District Commander, 9th C.G. District, p. 271-2; scope of District activities, p. 272-3; p. 282; p. 342; p. 378;

ICEBREAKING on Great Lakes: p. 60-61;

KEY WEST, Florida: builds up rapidly as port with advent of neutrality patrol, p. 118;

KOREAN COAST GUARD: U. S. Coast Guard helps in its formation - becomes eventually the present South Korean Navy, p. 179;

KOSSLER, Captain Wm. J.: p. 9; his connection with helicopters and Adm. Waesche, p. 169;

LAKE CARRIER'S ASSOCIATION: close working relationship with the Coast Guard, p. 262-3; p. 276; rents the two car ferries on lake Michigan for ice breaking activities, p. 279-81;

LAKE ERIE: Shallow nature of the lake, p. 260.

LAWRENCE, Lt. Comdr. Al: becomes head (1935) of general studies department at Academy, p. 79; p. 82; p. 104;

LORAN - : Development in World War II; one version for operation from a truck, p. 175-6; modern versions, p. 177-8;

LORAN STATIONS: In Philippines and elsewhere - improvement in equipment, training, etc. p. 360-1;

USCGS MACKINAW - icebreaker: commissioned Dec. 20, 1944 for duty on Great Lakes, Roland as skipper, p. 209; her special characteristics p. 210-213; p. 219; ship trials, p. 213-15; personnel p. 215-6; her mission to keep iron ore shipment route open as long as possible in winter season, p. 217; her special ice-breaking ability, p. 218-9; p. 223-4; technique employed in clearing channels of ice, p. 225-6; the first job (Jan. 1945), p. 227-30; going through the locks, p. 230-1; p. 234; towing a Navy minesweeper through the ice, p. 244-6; demobilization (1945-6) as it effected the ship, p. 252-3; race prejudice encountered in Northern Michigan ports, p. 253-4; cadet cruises, p. 256-7; plans for nine ships of same design, p. 261; her remarkable condition after thirty years of service, p. 265; use of planes to aid operations of MACKINAW, p. 270-1; Roland as Chief of Staff comes back to her to direct openings in the spring season of 1948, p. 276; helicopter maintenance on board the MACKINAW, p. 278; p. 290-1;

MAGSAYSAY, The Hon. Ramon - President of the Philippines: National War College delegation with him in Manila, p. 356-7;

McELLIGOTT, Rear Admiral Raymond T.: p. 9; instructor at the Academy, p. 18;

MERCHANT MARINE HEARING UNITS: p. 164-7;

MERCHANT SHIP SAFETY: what Coast Guard requires on the Great Lakes, p. 239-240;

MERRIMAN, Johnny: comes to Academy (1929) as athletic coach, p. 15; p. 22; p. 28-29; p. 38; p. 82-5;

MORRILL, Comdr. Arthur G.: Head of training division in Personnel Office of Coast Guard Headquarters, WWII, p. 147;

NATIONAL WAR COLLEGE: Roland assigned to the college, (1954), p. 347-362; the special tour of the Far East, p. 353 ff;

USCGS NEMISIS: 165 foot patrol boat - Roland becomes skipper (1938), p. 109; mission was search and rescue - and control of smuggling, p. 109-110; the sponge fishing boats off Tarpon Springs, p. 110-111; p. 112-3; ship refitted in Jacksonville (1939) for anti-submarine warfare, p. 114; neutrality patrol, p. 114-5; her capabilities as a patrol ship, p. 115;

NEUTRALITY PATROL: p. 115-6; Coast Guard permitted to perform Search and Rescue operations after being taken over by Navy (1940) p. 117; Coast Guard ships operate out of Key West, p. 118; special training activities, p. 118-119;

NEW ORLEANS, La.: Headquarters 8th Coast Guard District; Roland reports (Jan. 1940) as communications officer, p. 121 ff; keeping track of ship movements in Gulf of Mexico, p. 122-123; Coast Guard takes in large number of small craft - offered by owners for wartime use, p. 124-5; p. 130 ff;

OIL POLLUTION: Change in law giving Coast Guard full responsibility in dealing with infringements, p. 371-2; oil pollution and its relationship to Port Security, p. 372-3; contracts now let with private firms, p. 374-5; side effects - humanitarian efforts, p. 375-6;

PERSONNEL MATTERS: the Wish Card, p. 304-5; spot placements, p. 306; Roland's son and his career as example of present day personnel policy, p. 306-7;

PINE, Vice Admiral James: executive officer at C. G. Academy (1934), p. 78;

PLEASURE CRAFT: wartime service, p. 124 ff; status of Temporary Reserve, p. 125; special contract covering use of these boats, p. 125-6;

PORT SECURITY: a task assigned Coast Guard in World War II, p. 129-130; p. 146;

PRESIDENT'S CUP: an annual award in Washington for service teams in football competition, p. 36 ff; competition died with advent of Great Depression, p. 37; p. 40-41;

PROMOTIONS IN WARTIME (WWII): p. 151 ff; the draft and C.G. Personnel, p. 153-4;

RICHMOND, Adm. A.C.: an ensign at the Academy (1926) p. 6; p. 378;

ROLAND, Adm. Edwin J., USCG: personal data, p. 1 ff; early education p. 2-3; he meets his future wife at the Academy, p. 34-35; his captaincy of Coast Guard football team, p. 36 ff; his accumulated experience with Coast Guard personnel, p. 39-40; his son Eddie prepares for the Academy, p. 363-4; his early selection to flag rank, p. 391-2;

ROLAND HALL: gymnasium at the Coast Guard Academy, p. 34;

RULES OF THE ROAD: differences in the Lakes from the ocean route, p. 236-8; p. 266.

RUM RUNNERS: p. 41 ff; role of U. S. Custom's Service, p. 53-4; on the St. Clair River, p. 71;

ST. AUGUSTINE, Florida: Coast Guard maintained an anti-submarine school there in World War II, p. 182-3;

ST. PIERRE and MIQUELON: French islands off coast of Newfoundland - base for Canadian rum runners (1930s), p. 44; p. 52-3;

SAKOUNET RIVER: p. 48; favorite spot for rum runners, p. 51;

USCGS SHAW - DD: Roland assigned as gunnery officer (1929); p. 35; p. 41; rum runner patrol, p. 41-4; the crew hides contraband liquor on board, p. 45-6; the case of the YVETTE JUNE, p. 47-50;

SPAIN: Coast Guard cutter takes refugees from north coast to safety from revolution (1936), p. 56 ff; p. 89-100; during rescue mission the cutter CAYUGA under operational orders of U.S. Navy, p. 98-100;

SPARS: use of SPARS in Personnel work at headquarters, p. 138-9;

STRATTON, Captain Dorothy: first head of SPARS, p. 139;

USCGC TANEY: Roland commanded her in 1949/50 - based on San Francisco, p. 291-2; her principal duties were weather patrol, p. 294 ff p. 303-4;

TARPON SPRINGS, Florida: sponge fishing port near St. Petersburg - location of much smuggling, p. 109-110; p. 113-4;

TRAVERSE CITY, Michigan: p. 270; p. 273;

USS VANCE (DE-387): flagship of Roland during convoy duty (1942-3), p. 199; Roland gets news of his transfer (1944), p. 200-201; p. 258; See also - entry under CONVOY ESCORTS.

VIETNAM Conflict: the Coast Guard contribution, p. 179-181; supervised loading and unloading of ammunition, p. 181;

WAESCHE, Adm. Russell R.: Commandant of Coast Guard, World War II, p. 117; p. 167; brings Lighthouse Service and Merchant Marine Inspection into the Coast Guard, p. 167-9;

WEATHER PATROLS - World War II: Coast Guard use of old freighters - disappearance of one under command of Capt. Chas. Toft, p. 173; p. 294-6; passengers rescued from downed trans-ocean planes on weather patrol routes, p. 297-8; need for them diminished as trans-ocean planes improved, speed increased, etc. p. 299-300; improved weather service with satellites, p. 301;

WENDLAND, Capt. James C.: instructor at Merchant Marine officers school in New London, p. 165-6;

WIND Class - Icebreakers: lease-lend to the Russians, p. 172-3; see also various entries under MACHINAW.

WISH CARDS: Their use in personnel assignments, p. 304-5;

WOMEN IN THE COAST GUARD: p. 345-6;

SS YVETTE JUNE: a Canadian rum runner - her story, p. 47-50;

www.ingramcontent.com/pod-product-compliance
Lightning Source LLC
Chambersburg PA
CBHW080621170426
43209CB00007B/1487